I Married A Mouse

Hazel Ward

UK Book Publishing.com

Typesetting and publishing by UK Book Publishing

www.ukbookpublishing.com

ISBN: 978-1-917329-48-4

Contents

Foreword

BY MICHAEL MOUSE

*C*arnforth Railway Station, Lancashire. Celia Johnson and Trevor Howard approach each other shyly and nervously, attempting fitfully to build a relationship. They accept their relationship is not going to continue – a Brief Encounter.

Stockport Railway Station, Cheshire. A train stops. I get off the train, expecting to meet my date. She is not there. I wander apprehensively towards the booking office, wondering if I have been stood up. I notice a woman in a green coat scampering up and down many station stairs, and I think, "she's not bad." She came back to the booking office where she saw me.

She sees me: "Michael?"

"Hazel?" I reply.

This is no Brief Encounter. A loving relationship ensues and has done so for nearly thirty years. This book is the proof. So many things about Hazel captivate me.

Her design creativity which has displayed itself in every place we have lived in.

Her love of motoring forged on the rally dirt-roads of the Australian outback.

Her dedication to her two children.

1

Her gastronomic genius: the way to a Mouse's heart is through his stomach.

Her overcoming personal problems.

We invite you to read a stunning personal odyssey.

Michael Ward (Mr Mouse)

8 November 2024

Preface

OR HOW THIS BOOK CAME ABOUT

I want to leave a legacy of my life, for my children and grandchildren to read about and for them to be proud of me. With some surprises, I hope.

Not without the wonderful help from my Editor Mouse! I could *not* have done this without his Editorship guidance and *total* dedication and diligence to pulling this book together.

I also wanted to share what I've done and where I've done it with people everywhere. I think, hope, many can gain from my experiences and travels and my outlook on life!

There's almost a "something for everyone" in this book. Young, older, invalids, housebound, anyone in hospital (!), anyone looking for a laugh - not difficult! And more besides. For hikers, huddled in a tent half way up a mountain or even in a "retreat!"

Aircraft/holiday reading. Chilling out by an infinity pool?! Or in a transit lounge. And with many holiday delays yet to come, don't those always rear their heads!?

It's *our true love story that is still going on*, and touch wood (my head comes to mind!) for many years yet, for Mr Mouse and me! Also proving love is everywhere.

This book shouldn't bore. It's "armchair travel" at its best, I hope. What I didn't include are the too many pictures, on my tiny camera, of my favourite tree - the Birch tree, of which Russia has millions. I really got carried away there! Even our shower curtain has birch trees as a reminder! Thousands of miles of train tracks and so many Russian homes, the size of an ordinary British garage!

Especially for those who for whatever reasons can't travel to these places, and my insight on them.

I also feel I have a lot of experiences that will help many others and that isn't just the cancer experience but driving as in cars and the rallying, (which I would urge anyone to do by joining a Car Club for the camaraderie and the increased comfortable feeling that only comes from time behind a wheel and that can only make our roads safer.) The different places I've traveled and experiences of life that I've had, and there's been a few!

And the pain of losing people is something that should resonate with many, and I wouldn't wish on anyone.

Plus living in three different continents has been interesting but came at a terrible cost that I would never recommend as it played its part in damaging aspects of my relationships with both my children. Hindsight is a wonderful thing.

Theo played his part here too, and did try to teach but he's not a natural teacher. He didn't have the warmth, and especially not towards my children. Enough said there.

Again, hindsight is a wonderful thing. One cannot undo damage but one can recognise that it was done, and to use that awful cliche, try and help them "move on." Too much living in the past.

Must try to live for today and make happier memories!

But I keep trying and I will never give up.

I've had many things to improve within myself, and hopefully "some" have been achieved.

I adore my son and daughter (and Aurora) and hope in time they come to realise I've only ever wanted "better" for them. It didn't always happen but the adoration I've had for them has never left, and never will.

I know they love me. They are my most precious.

You take it with you (from Ghost.)

I pray they carry my aching love for them within themselves.

Dedications and acknowledgements

To:

Daddy, Leslie Joseph Ward, scientist.

Mummy, Ruth Ward and later Ruth Roland, highly respected painter and sculptor.

My two darling late brothers, Russell Brian Ward (43 in 1989) and Cedric Robert Ward (33 in 1982) both adored and so missed. Gone far too soon.

My son Stuart Leslie Blain, respected freelance photographer and with wisdom beyond his years. So adored by me.

My daughter Lisa Esme Blain, a wonderful cook and Anthropology graduate, and Mother to my granddaughter Aurora. So much incalculable love. MLh**.

Neil Roland, "baby" brother, published author of Taken For A Ride, and a respected photographer with commissions at The New Royal Courts Of Justice, London and The Christie, Withington, Manchester amongst many others.

Jesse Rivera Weston, doing an admirable job as Daddy to Aurora, as in Aurora Borealis, as she is bright, vivid, gorgeous and so memorable.

Holly. Our Jack Russell for almost twenty years. Such a sweet temperament.

Jan Stark, my best friend in Sydney, Oz, who has known about the book for some time now and who has been very positive about it, and who has given me wonderful memories.

Liz (Pritchard) of Buxton, my best friend in England, and a wonderful person I can always turn to.

Nat, a new neighbour who has become a very good close friend. Always good for advice, tech savvy, a brew and a laugh.

Yanky Fachler, himself a published author who initially kindly agreed to proofread a few chapters and give his feedback, labelling my style "quirky."

I'll happily take that and run with it! Has also been replying to all queries re content. A font of information!

Ruth Linton who also read three chapters and gave her feedback.

Tecnikk, computer business in Macclesfield, where Darrell and Leo are always on hand, willing to help someone not tech savvy, going that extra mile.

Ruth Lunn, my editor at UK Book Publishing for always having helpful advice.

Jay Thompson, my desginer, who has been in regular communication with me, "holding my hand" and dealing with my 'quirky' ways of getting a point across. Or deleting it for that matter. Lovely variations of my book cover (drawn by Mr Mouse) but not losing my 'essence'. What more can a techno peasant wish for! Thank you Jay for your infinite patience and pleasantness all through. You and Ruth should be made Honorary Mice!

BASH, of Cafe Mustard, Chestergate, Macclesfield who will happily display this book. Highly appreciated. They do deeelicious food consistently!

Jordan Sutton of Ryman in Macclesfield, who helped me send the photos to the publisher and who helped enormously by being much more tech savvy than I (not difficult!) with my cell/mobile, and did it all pleasantly and with *patience.*

Barry Spillane, bookbinder, very good friend of the family, who gave valuable and hugely appreciated insight into my adult children's psyche after their parents' break up.

Richard (Whatmore) handyman, Macclesfield, who helped turn Mr and Mrs Mouse's Mousehole into Mouse Cottage.

And, last but not least, my own editor supremo, Mr Michael Mouse, without whose editorial skills this would have stayed in the embryonic stages. This book has come together purely through his efforts at navigating my little quirky writing style. Also very handy - not adverse to being asked a question at 3am!

And a gentle husband, and loving and squeaking Mouse for nearly thirty years. And I have his permission to say so!

Chapter 1

LETCHWORTH - "WHERE THE SUN NEVER SETS"

"**M**astermind" is a British quiz programme that was and is very popular and has the distinction of being the only quiz that I know of not to give money as prizes. It comprises the contestant answering questions for two minutes on a specialist subject of his/her choice and, at one time, two minutes of general knowledge questions (now two-and-a-half minutes.) It was the prestige of being on it, and it had another "trademark" if you will, of attracting all walks of life from a barman to a street sweeper to a lawyer or a teacher. And anyone else in between, including both sexes. I never dreamt it would be used as the start of a book I would write!

It put my childhood town on the map when someone offered the specialist subject "How to get to anywhere in Great Britain by motorway, provided it started and finished in Letchworth…" It didn't get accepted. Hopefully, this book will put Letchworth back on the map…

My family consisted of Daddy (Leslie), Mummy (Ruth), Russell, Cedric and me.

I never get tired of seeing that lovely town's name in print. My late Mother Ruth (Ward after marriage to Lesley Joseph and after widowhood and subsequent second marriage Roland) used to wax lyrical about it whilst my stepfather Theo used to tease her with, "ah, where the sun never sets." It was, and still is, a special place and unique in its own right. As the first Garden City, Letchworth was the clichéd better, gentler time, with happy memories of my first family - now all gone.

I have a "baby" brother Neil, born of my Mother and stepfather. I never got on with him, my stepfather that is, almost never having any eye contact bar maybe twenty times in 40 years, and that's being generous! I think partly because I looked like Daddy too much, and that was a daily thing Theo could well do without and there I was as a constant reminder that he was husband number two not number one. But Neil and I have a very strong wonderful relationship and long may that continue. He's always been there for me.

Living in Letchworth at a time when you could all play with neighbours' children in the street or the woods - mostly without fear of the bogeyman. Although we all had decent-sized gardens and usually played in those. Much freer times. Simpler times. And a lovely town to boot. There was an allotment behind our home and it was wild and overgrown. That was where the supposed "bogeyman" lived! I have visited it a few times and it has now been built on.

It was a time slower than now, when my brothers and "Daddy" were still alive. When I first said "Daddy" to my daughter Lisa she really baulked at that terminology, seeing it as a sort of childishness. She and her brother Stuart call their father "Dad" as most children do nowadays. I only *had* "Daddy" till eight, so didn't decide it was too childish: I was still a child. I have since discovered (as of 2023) that it apparently becomes "Dad" at around 13-14.

We had a huge climbing tree in the back garden and two main branches going off in different directions like any tree. These branches had a gap of around 3 1/2 feet – which not many seven-year-olds could stretch to - without a safety net. I could barely make the stretch and if I'd slipped – a long drop. A height of about 40 feet. Enough to possibly kill me if landing badly. Luckily, I always judged it well and never fell. The tree has gone now, which is also sad as another generation won't get the same pleasure from it. My Mother had occasionally seen me do this daring feat, with her heart in her mouth. I could get onto next door's garage roof which had a little wall all around the top that I used to duck down beneath and hide when called for lunch. Hide-and-seek was too much fun even if I was on my own at these times. I don't know where my brothers were at these times. I have no-one to check with and Neil hadn't been made!

Then there was starting a fire under my brother Russell's bed! And it worked! Though I cannot remember which neighbour was conned into doing this with me. All I remember is we DID manage to start it, and then dangerously left it ALIGHT, and went downstairs. Sheer bloody luck the house didn't burn down! I have absolutely no idea how I started it!

We had a tortoise, Mr Mummery, after the teacher who "tortoise!" He was lovely, and once when my other brother Cedric held him up he peed all over the morning room rug; a milk-coloured liquid! He was probably frightened being held up, but we stroked his head and all seemed well.

I have just realised in some very small way we were like the Durrell family. I decided one day I wanted my own pet dog, and I presume Daddy and Mummy didn't agree (I didn't know then that Daddy had had a dog when young.) Daddy had a vegetable garden, and Mummy was a good cook. According to her, Daddy had shown her how to cook and how to "be logical!" I've always been surprised at that. I've never thought one could be "taught" logic. You either have it or you don't.

Back to getting my own pet - or trying to! I had thought it out and dug a deep square hole at the back of Daddy's veg garden (about 2' square) and cleverly covered it with bracken so as to fool the dog I wanted as a pet. Unfortunately, it also fooled Daddy as he didn't see it and promptly trapped Daddy when he fell into it ripping his Wellington Boots. I laugh every time I think of it, but was lucky he didn't break his leg! I was never scolded for this. I am still laughing whilst reading this again - in December 2023 and late June 2024.

Mummy's favourite vegetable was the runner beans, long, slightly bent and fairly flat. I adored them. And watercress, the slightly peppery kind. Very good for the blood I read recently and this is what probably helped her live to 90 plus three months. I only wish I could have acquired the taste for the peppery watercress. I hate it. Chomping on cress almost daily - now there's a nutritional hint!

Cedric had a bedroom with wallpaper going over the ceiling too. Very appropriate when the pattern is clouds. Russell had the biggest bedroom. He was the eldest of us children, so it was the natural order, and I followed suit with my children. I had a smaller sized room right next to Mummy and Daddy.

Mummy had her favourite flower, then, on the wallpaper, big cornflower blue roses on a white background on all four walls, but it was a big bedroom and could handle that. Magical, and the memory always takes me back to another happier time.

Letchworth memories for me are: family, the actual houses, and the whole place. The main street had awnings over each shop, very handy in bad weather, and they gave it a cosier atmosphere. Wouldn't go amiss in other towns everywhere, eg, England and Canada. They are in some towns…and they have them Down Under, too.

The Internet hadn't been invented and as we had only recently got tv there was much less connection to the rest of the world and thus possibly a safer place. A tweet was from a real bird near one's kitchen window!

Yes, there were probably still paedophiles then as there are now, but people kept their children a lot closer, literally, and back gardens to play in where they could all be seen. Less chance of the "bogeyman" coming to take them in the first place.

Enough typing for now. I've gone cross-eyed!

By my way of thinking food back then was not so adulterated as it is now and is so much more varied and with all those additives, colourings and the like it HAS to lead to mental impairedness on a grander scale?

Daddy graduated from UMIST (University of Manchester Institute of Science and Technology) and was assistant chief engineer with English Electric, and a scientist who, as Mummy used to say, "helped put guidance into the first missile!" She told me this proudly every time we talked about him but many years later added that she supposed it wouldn't be looked upon so well by certain quarters as missiles did cause deaths. That said, Daddy had been "part of the war effort to bring about an end to the suffering" and trying to bring it to a shuddering halt was the whole idea of missiles. This is why he hadn't been called up.

Daddy must have been a sort of pacifist. As Mother was always telling me as I grew up. He was a gentle man, and he adored her. He never smacked us, but I remember knowing right from wrong (though I discount the fire under the bed here!!!!!) so they both did "us three proud." She loved to tell me how "he taught me logic!" I never thought one could be taught logic! I know, I stated this slightly earlier. He succeeded with her, but she did have a good mind, so much so that when she was in her very late eighties my "baby" brother Neil got a tape out and she just talked about growing up in the late 1920s and early 1930s and beyond. I didn't even know until Neil later typed out what she'd spoken about, that she had wanted to read medicine, but they had been too poor to afford the financial burden of medical school. I think it was definitely a case of "meant to be" as there's only one Ruth Ward – painter/sculptor/ interior designer, while later she signed her pictures Ruth Roland. And with exhibitions in Manchester, London and Lodz (pronounced Wooj) in Poland - and private homes all over the world.

There is no better epitaph than what Lowry the painter said about her later: "she brought to the modern world what he had brought to the industrial towns." He sat for his own sculpture, by Mummy, many years ago. Just his head. It was even put on public display in the Lowry Hotel in Salford, on its own plinth at the top of great stairs till someone decided they wanted it for their own private collection and got someone to walk off - with just the head! Amazingly, it *was not attached* by chain to the plinth and someone "took it for cleaning!" The plinth was attached but not the head! It has yet to turn up.

I dearly hope the family of those related to the person who has this in their private collection realises how it came about and finally returns it to the Lowry Hotel with belated apologies on behalf of the real culprit. An apology to Mother's family wouldn't go astray either!

I'm already discovering the hard fact that I should have only written long hand on one side of the page and not both! It is SO hard to read my own notes! Crap! Such a mistake! If I'd tried reading them all sooner I would have realised this earlier – logical...Maybe I can implore Michael Mouse to read them out! He tells me every other day he loves me – good way to find out if he can put his money where his mouth is! Although as a freelance writer I don't think it's going to happen anytime soon but I am an optimist!

One thing I have learnt is that things happen when they're supposed to happen and I appreciate this word processing/whatever, now that I can utilise it. As you can see, I am an unashamed techno-peasant and Michael feels that too to some extent: even though he can work around a Mac computer we're still out-and-out peasants and not ashamed to admit it!

While Mother's favourite from Daddy's vegetable patch was green runner beans, her other favourite I have just remembered was watercress, with its peppery flavour. Funny, I hate this but found out just how healthy it is for anyone. It is bursting with so much goodness and I remember her at any given lunchtime just happily chomping on a handful. She got the same pleasure from that as others today would get from a hot dog. The only difference being hers was giving her good nutrition and theirs would be wrecking it! And the difference there again is that many with a hot dog are not even aware just how bad they are. Actually, correction, nowadays people must surely realise they are crap! But we all love them, and even we have them, Mr Mouse and I, when we do go to the cinema.

I remember Daddy's vegetable garden with long rows of tall sticks and string to bind them, to tie the growing vegetables to as they grew tall. It was a large area but we were lucky and had a large back garden. There was also my swing which my brothers pushed me on. Loving sweet gentle brothers whom I adore. I'm very lucky in that respect and am well aware of that. Throughout my life I've heard of brothers giving their sisters a hard time. Never mine. Daddy and Mummy - you did such a good job.

Children played outside more, or at least we did, and were healthier for it. I remember having five friends around and when we got hungry I promptly went to the fruit bowl and handed out a banana to each one going through Mother's bunch in one swoop. I only have pleasant memories of that time.

We didn't have cell phones back then but then we didn't really need them either. People just rang a landline and if you weren't in there would be no answer! We didn't need expensive toys. Simple, clean, cheap fun that didn't need a brand name and didn't have children clamouring for the latest new toy to be bought. Companies have a lot to answer for. Friends didn't have what hadn't been invented yet. All very "Enid Blytonish." Children now as young as ten have their own mobiles/cell phones. At ten they shouldn't be far away from home in the first place, or maybe I would like to think of this time as making a comeback. I was of these times. I had a doll with a plastic moulded hairstyle! Not even real hair, but she was pretty in the face, walked and moved her head and I was thrilled with her. Probably in some landfill now, probably not totally biodegraded, I'll bet.

At home in our next place, 36 Framingham Road Sale, I was electrocuted once, luckily only briefly, when I accidentally touched the gold pins in the plug in my bedroom. Cedric was in earshot and must have heard me shudder or moan or whatever I did, because he rushed in, scooped me up and took me to my bed and stayed with me till I stopped shaking. I still love him so much, and always will. So much love there.

I was a regular tomboy and absolutely loved climbing the huge tree we had in our back garden. Although from the mention of my doll you'd maybe not think so! I also thoroughly enjoyed, and always have, having two older brothers who were always there for me, and I just instinctively knew that. There was never any pigtail pulling. Not that I had pigtails, but if I had, they wouldn't have. I think we were just encouraged to be there for each other, always, and I don't remember anything different to that. I'm very lucky in that respect. I meet men or women who have siblings that they don't get along with. I always feel sadness for such relationships that weren't encouraged enough to bloom that way.

I remember the winter of 1961 into 1962 because in those days we had real snow. By real I mean snowflakes the size of a man's splayed-out hand and these flakes came floating gently down so achingly beautiful. I was very naughty one night. I had gone to bed but came down, and opened the front door to these snowflakes all just gently falling down in the silent night. Absolutely wonderful and a memory I treasure. Mummy and Daddy would be horrified to know that I did this and of course I never thought to enlighten them the next day!

We also had a "yacht!" It sounds grand and it *was* a decent size – 40' long - though Daddy bought it second-hand and worked on it every weekend. The weekends became known as "going down to the boat" which was moored at either Lowestoft or Great Yarmouth. A lovely boat which slept six and has given me even more memories.

Cedric slept in the bow. Poor thing faced the toilet! Russell slept opposite him but both faced one of the two hatches above allowing them also to look up at the stars. I slept in a deep "drawer(!)" right at the steps to go up and out. It really was a drawer, just deeper and wider than normal and perfect for a little girl!

Russell was right at the front at the bow and we had the hatch there and he could look straight up and watch all the stars. Cedric was further away but could still see stars. The main galley had seating which turned into the base for the double bed for Mummy and Daddy. She cooked wonderful meals on a tiny stove that was rimmed around its edge with a metal rod to stop anything sliding when in choppy seas.

Skipper Gordon joined us somewhere along the line. I don't know how he came into the picture, but it was he that showed Daddy the ropes and he who accompanied us all to Belgium, through the biggest gale. Ginger haired and ginger bearded. Funny, Daddy had a blonde/ginger moustache, and Russell and Cedric had darker auburn beards and moustaches somewhat later and so have both my husbands. I've always loved and trusted (most!) beards and that will never change. Warm, loving people — and to me — sexy many times! A moustache enhances a face — definitely. I despair over young people who find fault with it when they've never really given it a chance. They can be very becoming.

We would drive down to either Lowestoft or Great Yarmouth for a weekend of messing about on the boat and it is a time full of memories. Good and the not-so-good. And it was from one of these that we set sail to Ostend, Belgium, in *very* high waves. I was lassoed to the railings by a special coated wire (nice to know I was considered so precious!), but then Daddy *had* pranged the car on the way home from hospital after finding out he had a daughter. He'd been delighted to have two sons but I was very "welcomed aboard!"

I remember when we sailed to Ostend, with fondness, although there were dead fish floating in the harbour. Nothing intrinsically bad about that - just a memory really. A better memory is at the promenade where they had special bikes — like three-wheelers but with small seats at the front for two and a baby one behind in the middle. Actually, a little like the Mini Moke! Mummy and Daddy allowed Russell and Cedric to hire one of these and me being the baby, well, littlest, sat behind them in the middle able to see everything. Such a simple but very HAPPY memory! I wonder if those bikes are even still there. Or even the promenade?! I remember this like it was yesterday!

I remember one weekend when we were out on the high seas and a storm blew up. Mother made a beef or lamb mince and presumably accompaniments for lunch. Then the storm came up and so did everyone's lunch – except, I'm very proud to say, not mine!

I watched everyone throw up overboard, all of whom were careful to make sure the wind was in the right direction! And I followed it with, "there goes four good dinners!" I've always had a cast-iron stomach. Long may that continue!

Back to Letchworth, or rather Great Yarmouth/ Lowestoft, it varied. We had a dinghy with the boat. There is a picture somewhere of me rowing Daddy a few feet. My end of the boat is somewhat out of the water because of the slight weight difference between me and Daddy(!) but it is a memory and a lovely one at that. In writing this I'm realising just how many wonderful images there are in one's life.

The house was gorgeous too (33 Broadwater Avenue) and I have seen it quite a few times since leaving Letchworth. At one point I seriously played with the idea of buying that house if it ever came on the market and bring my own children up where I had had such happy memories. That never happened of course but "we" did get a part of that house and I don't mean my Mouse and me. I mean brother Neil when he later brought the original front door back! He has had it put in on the side of his house. I had harboured hopes of having it but then logically reasoned we both shared the same Mother and he had the same right to it, so I never brought it up.

Things often don't go to plan and my life was no exception and I found that out in early 1962 in February.

Daddy and Mummy, as I've said before and as I was brought up to call them in those days, had had a lovely day out and had gone to the "pictures" in the evening. They came back happy and relaxed and later went to bed.

Mummy was awoken to hear Daddy talking in his sleep, but also slurring his words (this isn't the first time she had told me this story but when I was around she shared much with me. It wasn't the kind of thing to share with one's new husband.) At first she thought he was drunk but that didn't make sense and they obviously hadn't had drinks the night before. Mother wasn't a drinker and, from what I can gather, neither was Daddy.

She realised something was seriously amiss and woke up properly and realised things were worse than she thought. She called our GP. He came over, took one look at Daddy and rang Hitchin Hospital, the same hospital I had been born in. Mummy accompanied him to the hospital and told me she sat around waiting for a while. According to her the doctor came and spoke to her and asked if she could wait to which she told me she said, "oh no, I've got three children at home."

"I can't leave them," she said later to me. "I was so stupid, I didn't realise I think he was telling me that Daddy wasn't going to make it but I didn't understand that at the time. It wasn't specifically pointed out and I had three children on their own at home..."

Mummy continued to tell me that she was told to ring in at around 8am to find out how he was, but she was rung instead (which is so wrong anyway as one should ALWAYS give bad news in person in case of a bad reaction) at 7am to be told that he had died.

He was 46 years old. February 11th 1962.

Mummy told me she lay in bed for six weeks from the shock of losing him. Well, that's probably a slight exaggeration now that I come to think of it, as she did have the three of us to look after, but I think she did take to their bed many times. She did tell me that same day Russell just immediately took over getting the fire ready every day for the lovely open (Baxi) fireplace we had in the lounge.

It had been such a lovely home and now everything changed, and not for the better, well, not for the most part. Mother wanted us to be in a Jewish community and felt this was the time to have more family around. So she sold that lovely house, home, that has always held such happy memories and moved us all up to Manchester.

Chapter 2

MANCHESTER: FROM TSOURIS
(SORROW) TO SOURIS (MOUSE)

Manchester for many years was not a happy place for me. Living daily with a stepfather where there was no eye contact made being in the same room very uncomfortable. And nothing I said was "right." He found fault constantly or was asking questions that just had me freeze up. Uncomfortable every day was the name of the game. There were no real happy memories from that time.

We never had conversations in the normal way people do. He would ask the questions, invariably putting me on the spot, and mocking when I came out with my "oh I forgot." He'd repeat it back to me. After that I'd be left tongue tied and wanting to leave his presence but unable to do so. A horrible feeling. This was almost daily, or it was to be ignored as though I didn't exist, which in his eyes, he'd have probably preferred.

We moved up to Manchester in 1963 so that Mother could be around her two brothers and back within a larger Jewish community. Mother found 36 Framingham Road, a decent-sized five-bedroomed house, and set about making it home-like. Being the designer she was, I distinctly remember her getting tiles: blues, greens and turquoises, with burnt orange. And these were no ordinary tiles but each one a mini-abstract with a raised surface and she had them put around the fire surround, choosing which ones looked better next to each other. The end result was phenomenal. She was very ahead of her time design-wise although I would adore to see some similar tiles. I wonder if the house still has them?!

And burnished orange full-length curtains separating the lounge from the dining room. A pale blue kitchen door makes me suddenly realise all her favourite colours coming together. No different to what I would do - or anyone else - but it's interesting realising now what was going on design-wise. It's only taken me more than 40 years!

For the first time at around 11 years I was allowed to choose my own bedroom wallpaper and I really went to town! I saw this glorious shiny wallpaper covered all over in brilliant Birds of Paradise with vivid green plumes and orange beak. Absolutely stunning, and ever since the Bird of Paradise takes me back to Mother and her allowing me whatever I wanted there. It's no wonder that bird was called such! Sigh. I was terribly lucky to have been "given exceptional parents," plagiarising Neil's eulogy to Mother years later in 2011, but this time including *my* Daddy in it.

LED ZEPPELIN! OR: I RAN AWAY FROM HOME!

I ran away from home when I was about 16. I remember most of it very clearly, and took some clothes in a small bag. I remember leaving the front door pulled-to so it didn't slam and so that I wasn't heard. I'd just had enough and was oblivious to the pain I was about to put Mummy through.

I was hitch-hiking down and found my way to the start of the motorway (I have no idea how I got there.) I think I had three cars altogether but can only remember two. The second one had kinky leanings. He had several photos of himself holding his own "member!" He pulled over and gave me them to look through. Each one was a different angle of the same penis, and not very exciting at that. He said he'd pay me 20 pounds if I took a photo of it again. I simply said no to this, which I'm sure surprised him especially with the temptation of money at my tender age of nearly 17. I just felt I was better off saying no, and with that he pulled over just after a roundabout near the next section of motorway and said I could get out there. I didn't need asking twice!

My next driver was the manager of the then group Led Zeppelin! He was very sweet and shocked at my last car journey and did what I suppose many well intentioned people might do and actually delivered me to Russell's ground floor apartment in London – it must have been at Ladbroke Grove because his last place was a basement apartment and this one was a few steps up to the front door. I thanked this manager profusely and he stayed to see that Russell was in, and I waved again. I would SO love to thank him in person or his family if he's passed on.

ISRAEL, 1973

I decided I wanted to go and stay on a kibbutz. My sweet eldest brother Russell had previously surprised me by buying me a second-hand record player! Probably to make my time happier at 165 (Brooklands Rd, Sale) but I was not aware of the reasoning behind the gift). When I started to save for this trip I sold the record player with much regret, but I still remember it well. Boxy, grey and it came from Russell.

I am suddenly remembering the time I was in Israel BEFORE the Yom Kippur War. It's remembered by journalists of a certain age as the Yom Kippur War because both Egypt and Syria attacked on the eve of Yom Kippur (Holiest Day of the year when Jews atone for their sins of the previous year (1973.) Very clever timing really when people are preparing to pray and are certainly not thinking of War. Israel now has much better relations with Egypt and Jordan and long may that continue.

I remember my old boyfriend from that time, too. Ephraim. He was gorgeous. And in the army. His family lived at Rosh Pina and I visited them there briefly. A very small place then. Less even than a village. It must be huge now…I haven't been back since.

On the kibbutz I was assigned two different tasks which made for very different days: apple picking and chickens! Apple picking for three days and I couldn't look an apple in the face for four years! Not a whole one anyway. Apple puree yes, apple pie yes, but not the actual fruit.

Then came chickens. In a big barn - huge, and thousands of chickens. They were going to market, I presume. I had to go up to each one (there were several of us doing this and it's quite fun!) grab their feet between your thumb and forefingers and in the process you lift them up, upside down. Then we'd carry them out swinging, and onto the back of a truck, and off they went. They righted themselves by the way!

The smell was overpowering - ammonia from their poo, yet within minutes one completely forgot about it. It was fun and short lived and then, over! Another lovely and unexpected memory! I still love chicken - and to pre-empt Michael, oh Mouse of mine who didn't even exist for me yet, I love them both ways - alive and in a barn or on a plate!

It is romantic being in love in wartime. You never know how long you might have together. I'm referring to Ephraim again. No, that does not mean automatically what you think! We did not jump into bed together! Or even slowly for that matter! I was a good girl and I stayed that way. Ephraim and I went down to Tel Aviv and visited Jenny. Friend of the family and so bright. She studied PPE at Oxford but was already a linguist like Michael is but even more so! She spoke six languages! Fluent in Polish (where she was originally from), English, French, Arabic, and Hebrew and later on I found out she started learning Italian!

At one point I stayed with my late cousin Edward. Back then he had an apartment near Hadassah Hospital in Jerusalem. When the first air-raid siren went up I was in the most inopportune place - the bath! You never saw anyone get out of a bath so quickly!

I loved Jerusalem! It IS another world! And the old market, very small shops, built into solid rock. Like a double sized Tardis, except they aren't any bigger inside!

In Israel, when they know they're going to war they send out coded messages via the tv so every single soldier knows when he is being called up.

Later that first day I made my way to the home of our family's close friends the Fachlers, pronounced with a guttural sound as though (to quote Michael teaching his

Greek classes) you are a camel clearing your throat! The Fachlers knew us back in Letchworth. Remember the start of this book, where I was raised? A wonderful place and England's FIRST Garden City! I am proud of that. The Fachlers were/are very orthodox but we'd grown up with them in Letchworth and we loved each other. That has never changed.

That day, when war came to Israel, everyone pulled together. As it should be in any country. Israel, for those who don't realise it, is approximately the size of an elongated Wales, half of which is the Negev desert! Thus a *very* small country.

Some people bring their children up on hate. Not a way to grow up. And some would like to say, as Tevye (the late Topol) did in Fiddler on the Roof, in response to the comment "an eye for an eye and a tooth for a tooth" "Yes, then we'll all be toothless and blind!" Says it all really.

Getting back to the Yom Kippur war. I went over to the Fachlers' apartment and I wasn't the only one. Several of us went outside armed with bags of sweets for the various soldiers who arrived – IN TANKS - on their way to the Jordanian border having been called up in turn via that coded tv message. It now has a Peace Treaty with Israel and long may that continue. As Hawkeye once said on tv's M*A*S*H "War Is Ugly."

Many soldiers gave me pieces of paper with their names on them and their parents' home phone number and I would take these back inside and there'd be a mass phoning session to inform the parents what their sons or daughters didn't have time for. Yes, females too played their part in keeping Israel safe.

Chapter 3

I MOVE TO THE LAND DOWN-UNDER

I went to Oz as a new bride in 1975. I met my first husband, Gerry Blain, in Lewis's, Manchester. He had come over to visit his father Sidney, who now lived in Manchester, after marrying his second wife Shirley.

Gerry had gone to Australia as a TEN POUND POM! He'd loved the journey: a six-and-a-half week super lovely cruise and he docked in Sydney. The ship was the Ellenis.

Out of six men who had met at The Leather Bottle pub (now gone) in Edgware, only two actually went through with their plans and physically arrived in Sydney. Gerry doesn't know what happened to the other one except he didn't last the distance and sometime later returned home.

Gerry had gone out leaving his parents and one brother, Barry, behind. His mother Esme passed away four-and-a-months after he got to Oz. At the time of her death, the Australian telecoms service was on strike so no calls were getting through. Gerry only found out that his mum had passed away a week later and that his maternal grandma had also passed away probably from the shock.

Gerry had not been able to return for his mother's funeral. When he was able to return, that's when we met. Gerry was in Lewis's basement level where he'd been relegated to "demonstrating" household products. In this case it was the shammy leather! I saw this rather handsome, black curly haired fellow with a little black moustache. And I liked what I saw, and apparently so did he!

I got chatting to him in between his "spiels" and got invited for a coffee. That led to another date and another etc. He proposed about a month later and we married ten weeks and four days later although it wasn't plain sailing; Gerry's step-mother Shirley decided I was too young on the cusp of 22.

He was going back to Sydney and my Mother was having kittens. She got Theo to tell Gerry all my bad points (like leaving the top off the toothpaste) in a bid to put him off me. It didn't work.

While writing, all this was contrary to the remark by one of my Mother's friends (I shall never discover their identity) who remarked *wrongly* that our wedding had been a shot-gun marriage. Not so! And I was upset that that thought had even been countenanced, and they obviously did not know me at all. We had six-and-a-half years before we "started" Stuart, and followed him up three-and-a-half years later with Lisa.

Stuart was born in 1982 and he was *gorgeous* and I am a completely biased Mother but considering every time we went to the supermarket we were accosted by little old ladies who told me how sweet he was. I know I'm right! What could have been half an hour in the supermarket regularly turned into an hour and the rest. Well, I *did* like little old ladies telling me how gorgeous he was (and still is in a more grown-up way.) I still get compliments about both and how lovely they are. They both engage well with people. Stuart had blonde-brown hair courtesy of my ginger-haired father. It's darker now but still luxurious.

I'm remembering that back in Sydney I lived very differently from Letchworth and Manchester. Sydney doesn't have distinct seasons. At least not in my view. Summer was long, hot and, much of the time, muggy. I hate muggy. I can't function in humid weather and if I was living there now I'd have to be at least getting sea breezes to write anything.

One other factor was the Aussie accent. Gerry had joined the Mini Car Club of NSW (New South Wales) and we went to our first meeting. Afterwards, people were talking to Gerry and I would hear someone say something and I would then have to ask Gerry, "What did he say?" There were so many "what did he says?" It took about six months for my ear to accustom itself and understand what was being said. After that I wondered how I could ever have not understood it!

Before Stuart arrived, I worked for one or two companies including Grace Brothers store in Sydney. For those who remember the British comedy Are You Being Served, I was working for the real one! One difficult incident occurred when two individuals with whom I was getting on well discovered I was Jewish and then refused to speak to me. Mercifully, I did not have to deal with them again.

Gerry worked hard to become an accountant and was successful. Indeed, he did it the hard way, at night school for four years. He was one of the few that graduated; there was a huge "drop-out" rate. Gerry had actually told me that another guy on the course had quit half way through and his girlfriend said it was up to him what he chose to do. When Gerry himself started flagging, half way through, I said to him well you've done half of it, you may as well finish it, and have something to show for it. If you leave now you've not only wasted two years but cannot offer the Diploma up as something achieved.

And he did! He later got work with John Singleton Advertising and if he had abandoned his course he would never have been offered it.

THE CAR ACCIDENT THAT AT LEAST CHANGED MY LIFE TO A DEGREE

Going back in time again, to when Lisa was about 18 months old, Gerry and I went out to a car club party by car. Returning, and I was driving, I had stopped at a set of traffic lights. The uninsured car behind us didn't stop and plowed right into us, the driver later trying to claim I had stopped on green. It wouldn't have mattered if he had been right, which he wasn't, as he shouldn't have been that close in the first place. The law was already on my side. He shoved us *so* hard we were shunted from one side of the traffic lights to the other! We didn't realise that till we got out of the car, very stiffly and awkwardly. When we got shunted we discovered just how far we'd been pushed. Completely across the whole of the intersection – a huge "shove" of about 50 feet!

Our upright seats became skewed and complete recliners! IF Lisa had been in the child seat behind my seat her legs would have been broken or worse. It was late and we saw our GP the next day as is the best thing to do. My left calf had had the seat adjuster's small black handle get shoved *SO* hard into it and as a result went completely black.

And whiplash, which has weakened my neck and has been with me ever since.

To get compensation we had to see psychiatrists and we did – for five long years, and the sum was paltry (all because of a guy who likely shouldn't have been driving in the first place.)

AUSTRALIAN BUNNY BUSINESS!

At some point we, Gerry and I, decided to make a little dosh - and it was very little but it was fun whilst it lasted. Breeding rabbits! Mustard was very good at breeding with Pickles. She was the "wife." Like a typical rabbit - good at sex! She was brown and Mustard was white. It's all he was good at but he was soft and sweet! We set them up in the spare downstairs bedroom that led directly into a screened off area in the garden. Absolutely ideal for them. Their cages were set up, left open during the day and closed at night.

During the evenings, we would be watching tv and suddenly Mustard and Pickles would come along from the far bedroom, through the hall and into the lounge and onto the rug in front of us. Pickles, more often than not pregnant, would stretch out on the rug and I would gently stroke her bulging stomach. It was quite fascinating as you could see the outline of all her babies. And I was very gentle and she constantly allowed me to stroke her. We had a wonderful relationship.

When it came time to give birth she was very clever. I got up that morning to find she'd been into our bathroom which is between our room and where their cages are. She must have smelt the pure white toilet rolls prior as I've never encountered any bunny in the bathroom before!

There was an 85% unraveled toilet roll stretching from this bathroom (and the roll was at the far end under the window - a distance of about 7 feet) out of the door, round the corner, into the other room and into the cage!!!! And the cage was full of this perfect lining for this "bunny home!" I thought it extremely enterprising and I still get blown away thinking about it. We often think the smaller the brain size must mean less clever but I think that is obviously very wrong and this idea had been ingenuous. Luckily there are no coloured toilet rolls made any more for environment's sake so she "knew" instinctively it was all alright.

One baby didn't make it. In the animal world a Mother can tell if a baby is sickly and Pickles discarded this one for the sake of the others. I was able to very carefully check them after I'd had the bright idea of rubbing my hands - thoroughly – with the hay beforehand, and then held one of the babies. They are so tiny and pink, and with eyes closed and two tiny buds for ears, very like a raw miniature saveloy, only cuter! Kitty litter was provided and they did their pee in that. Just as well.

Once Pickles had finished nursing and the babies were strong enough, we would be sitting in the lounge of an evening and all the family of six would come round from their "home" along the hall and into the lounge: they would suddenly appear en masse and come and join us in the lounge and onto the rug in the middle. It was so sweet.

RIP all of you. You gave much pleasure and that special relationship I had with you, Pickles, will never be forgotten.

MY VISIT TO NEW ZEALAND AND ANOTHER EXHILARATING SPORT!

Gerry and I were now (1994) separated. Our marriage lasted 19 years and I have no regrets. I have two beautiful children who are lovely on the inside as well as the outside and I would never have had them if I hadn't met Gerry, so utterly no regrets.

However, I hadn't returned to the UK yet, and decided to give myself four days away. Darwin came to mind as I had always wanted to see it, especially since Cyclone Tracy. In Darwin all the homes were built on stilts to give them more stability. The cyclones then go around and under and don't take the houses with them so much. Cyclone Tracy reduced that and then some, and after discovering it was nearly always hot there, I changed direction and found that I could do white-water rafting AND whale-watching in New Zealand!

White-water rafting is another natural high. We were taken to a building to be kitted out in a wet suit. Very aptly named and once one starts - nowhere to strip off for a pee... Gerry once termed our USA holiday as a "toilet tour of Europe." Well, it sounded better than a toilet tour of America! Course, if I had pee'd in the raft no one would have been the wiser! I was asked if I'd like to sit at the front, the very wettest place as the raft goes head first into the swirling waters and yes, drenched at every turn, but very exhilarating! I wish I'd said yes, but I had visions of falling out and never being found! I ended up sitting at the back and still having a very good time. The raft would be somewhat sticking out of the water giving a rather good "overview." We'd all gone down Grade 5 which is the hardest, I was very proud to discover.

All this time we were doing this there was a photographer taking shots all the way through and we all got copies. Fantastic, and those pictures were! They hang on the wall here now. Something else to share with grandchildren.

Next came whale-watching - on a large schooner. I joined a large group - 29 Japanese tourists and me, all with our clicking cameras, to see a most wonderful display of this huge whale, who may have suddenly realised he was on show and dived, and in the process his (or her?) huge whale-tail/fin(?) suddenly pointing upwards towards the sky - a phenomenal sight I will never forget as long as I live! It was over too soon but I am SO glad I partook of it. That's what memories are made of.

Before I finished my time in New Zealand I went into Christchurch and saw "THE WIZARD!" He will have died by now, so I'm really glad I was one of the many that have experienced him. He wore a long caftan in vibrant, shiny, silky stripes and a big black pointed hat. His caftan not unlike Joseph's Coat of Many Colours! And he stood near another New Zealand oddity that will have rusted away possibly by now...the front end of a VW Beetle, and another front end of the same. Put front against front! I've got a picture somewhere of both Beetle and Wizard!

You still get memories even after just four days!

I'm seeing a parallel between Mummy (Russell always used to refer to her as Mother, and I've started to, vacillating between both names!) taking us three back up north to Manchester to be with family and me leaving Sydney with both kids in tow, back to my family. One move through death, one move through divorce.

Chapter 4

CEDRIC

I am standing at the sink at our first apartment together in Sydney, with little Stuart at about ten months of age sitting in his highchair. The phone rings and my then husband Gerry answers it and I hear him say: "How's your Mother?" Then he comes back into the kitchen and I turn around from the sink but leant against it to hear what he has to say.

"Cedric has been walking the Andes Mountains and he has had a heart attack."

At 33!!!

I looked at Gerry and said, "Well, yes, what hospital is he in?" Gerry just shook his head, and I SCREAMED. I felt instantly sickened.

Gerry immediately said, "You're frightening Stuart," who was grinning his adorable beaming face at me with two little teeth SO cutely at the bottom. I stopped and gave Stuart a very weak and false smile. That has also been one of the hardest things I have ever done. A simple smile. I have that same picture of Stuart in our hall now. Utterly adorable, and with no idea what I was suddenly forced to face.

And to add to that pain was the fact that I never made it back for his funeral. Later this same day I phoned Mother but couldn't ask her for the ticket home. Just hoped she'd offer. She suggested I come after the funeral when we'd have time together. I think she didn't want to have to cope with me wailing through her own grief. Once the funeral was over, we just dealt with our pain in different continents.

That trip never materialised and I never asked. Without any visitors, and with any friends (in the Mini Car Club) we had, all ringing Gerry *only*, and sending their condolences through him, I saw even less of people. Nobody wanted to visit me and actually share my pain. A very lonely time. TG I had Stuart to look after and cuddle. Many don't know what to say, so they stay away, yay, that helps, not! They couldn't even come and be with me and say nothing!

Cedric, older than me by four years and younger than Russell by three years, had been on a year's sabbatical to the Andes. He planned to walk the Andes range, not the whole of it obviously (extensive even by his standards!) but he had been a travel writer with the Sunday Times (UK) Magazine Supplement and they liked what he wrote.

He'd gone to Lake Titicaca, and described a mountain nearby with snow on it as, "looking like a botched wedding cake!" He wrote most descriptively. He visited Machu Picchu and to La Paz where he took a hotel room.

He had then gone down to the local railway station and joined a queue to get tickets down to the Brazilian rainforest. Writing on a card whilst he stood in the queue that he planned to send, he wrote to Mother, "I feel like I'm dying." He returned to his room at the hotel and did.

That was where the chambermaid found him, apparently in the bathroom. Amongst his possessions was a telegram (we still had them in those days) I had sent him but pretending to come from Stuart, his nephew: "Love you, Miss you, Aching to see you, Love Stuart Leslie Blain." It was one of the last things he read as he referred to it in one of his last letters to Mother and a separate letter to Russell. He kept in touch with us all, feeling the loneliness of being in South America and feeling it acutely. Cedric had written how he thought it was brilliant purporting to be from Stuart.

Cedric and I had been so close. He even visited me and Gerry on our wedding night, March 2nd 1975, at the Post House, Northenden, Manchester…and gave me a lovely surprise turning up as he did. I had excitedly booked a hamburger and chips from Room Service. Just excited to use room service! Cedric had a couple of bites and then reckoned he should be off. He'd only been with us about ten minutes. I had a cuddle at the door and kissed him on the cheek.

Then he was gone. Never to be seen again by me. It's the stuff that soap operas are made of, only this was too real, my brother, and he really did go, FOREVER. I'm weeping again, and my eyes are moist, 42 years later. I was very lucky. I had adorable brothers.

Treasure your siblings whilst you CAN.

On October 18th 1982, Mother awoke at 3am with the top of her head burning hot. Theo had always looked after her and this was no different. He went and got a flannel and saturated it with cold water and brought it back for her head. It dried out almost instantly. He did the same again. And again, till her head went back to normal.

Three days later the police visited. They had had a call from Interpol. Cedric had died at 3 am – exactly when

Mother's head had been overheating. She viewed things differently about certain things with the Afterlife after this.

When Interpol contacted the local police they sent two constables around. Never an easy task but oh, I wouldn't wish this job on anyone. They knocked on Mother's door and Theo answered. Did he have a son Robert Cedric. Getting the names back to front, apparently that can happen quite often. Theo called Mother down but knew the outcome. You don't usually get two cops coming to the front door unless it's bad news.

Cedric was to be returned home – as "cargo." That was one of the hardest things to wrap my head around. It's taken many years to be able to talk about it without dissolving into floods of tears. I'm in floods merely proofreading this, yet again.

You don't ever "get over" the death of someone very close, be it a brother, sister, or possibly a parent. Some may add cousins to that mix, or even a good friend. You DO learn to live with it – in time, but you must give yourself time to grieve. And that time is different for every single person. Anyone who does not comprehend that has never lost someone very close. It depends on the strength of the relationship. The pain can be all-consuming.

When Cedric died my ex Gerry had a female work colleague who, after hearing about my brother's death, said three days later, "Shouldn't she be getting over it now?!" That "moron" had never lost anyone, except an Uncle who "nearly" died, so had no real concept. I'd like to think she's the only idiot who thought like that, but I guess there will be others.

I did briefly contemplate suicide to join him, but equally realised that as I hadn't been with him in recent years because of living in Oz and that to choose to live with him suddenly "in the next world" was very much a knee jerk reaction and not the way to go. It's very much a one-way street and once there there's no way back. Quite a sobering thought. Not forgetting that I had a very new son that I adored and the idea of someone else bringing him up was – to quote Michael Mouse – "a non-starter." No one could adore Stuart Leslie Blain as much as me.

One place that Cedric had worked was as a teacher at the now closed Lord Mountbatten High School in – Hemel Hempstead - where he'd been taken on as a biology teacher. And not knowing anything about biology he looked it up the night before and taught it to his 14- and 15-year-old pupils the next day! That couldn't happen nowadays. He was very popular and when they had a concert at the school they suggested he dressed up as Adam Ant as there was a likeness to him, though Cedric was taller. I never saw any of this till much later when I visited the school as I was in Oz in the 1980s, but Cedric was very popular. I think one of Adam Ant's lines was "stand and deliver!"

When he left to go on the year sabbatical they all expected him back. It didn't happen that way and they were all massively shocked when they got the news. In memory of one of their favourite teachers they planted daffodils in the school grounds to come up every year. In the nearby park, the Gade Bridge Park, they planted a new baby oak tree. One day Neil visited the park and found out from a tramp who approached him, not knowing who he was, and who told him that the newly planted oak tree had died…(the same day Cedric had died) - and oaks live hundreds of years!

I want to visit it one day.

Cedric had indeed become a teacher at Lord Mountbatten High School in Hemel Hempstead. He'd only become a teacher because his wife Barbara hadn't wanted to leave her London friends, even though Cedric had become a Geologist. His wishes weren't taken into account at all!

His teaching of 15- and 16-year-olds biology was achieved by reading it up the night before, which was impressive when one realises one wouldn't be able to do that nowadays because one couldn't get the post in the first place unless one had a real background and degree in the subject. Things are definitely too PC now.

Cedric was doing his sabbatical "climatically" and would be in Sydney later to meet his new nephew, Stuart. He walked the Andes for three months and wrote wonderful and descriptive letters back to Mother. He talked not only about seeing the monumentally famed Machu Picchu but was also fascinated by the Lost City of The Incas. He visited Lake Titicaca and met the colourful locals who chewed the leaves of the coca plant that gave them a natural "high." Many people who visit the Andes experience altitude sickness – and apparently water and dark chocolate are the answers. I've no problem with the second one! The first one is not all it's cracked up to be, well, not for me. I wish I loved water!

Cedric would be in Sydney later to meet his new nephew, Stuart. As he said to me in one letter, he hadn't intended on Oz in the first place, but suddenly a brand-new nephew changed all that! It would have been the same with Lisa.

HAVIVA

Just a wonderful woman. Our GP in Sydney initiated a meeting with me going round to Haviva's home in Bondi. This should also get a mention as she was a wonderful soul whom I have never forgotten and who in 1982 listened as I sat and talked to and wept in her kitchen after hearing of Cedric's death.

The shock of his death on my body was immense. My periods used to be regular as clockwork, right at the beginning of the month. On hearing of Cedric's death they went completely haywire and took FIVE *full* YEARS to straighten out and get back to normal. I can't believe it's now 42 years since he's gone. I date it from Stuart's birth of the same year, 1982.

Have good relationships with your brothers or sisters. You never know how long it will be before they get taken. The pain is immeasurable and I wouldn't wish it on my worst enemy.

Cedric had initially decided to read Geography and Geology at Exeter University, as I said earlier. He was fascinated by fossils and collected quite unique pieces and was able to show Mother their delicate structure and markings. At Neil's home are two such fossils that are coral pink in colour and almost completely round with a slightly flattened base and a hole at the top. And hollow. Little markings of dots, a bit like an airport runway of lights making for a pretty pattern. There were other pieces too, more actual rocks or stones with the imprint of insects from thousands of years ago. Quite fascinating. He collected other pieces too, like an original 1940's telephone. Those tall things that they had in 1940 movies in the USA. And a gas mask from World War 2!

Cedric – so adored – and gone too soon. Isn't that often the case? Sweet, loving, caring and genuine. What more can a sister ask for?

Chapter 5

CAR RALLYING OR
CONQUERING THE OUTBACK

Thanks to Gerry, I got into car rallying big time and loved it as one of the most natural "high" givers of all time. I ADORE being behind the wheel of a car but, I must stress, a MANUAL car. I do not count an automatic as a car. Yes, they'll get you around but if you need to react quickly you can do a better job if you have more control in a car and that car is a manual. I am sure there are people who disagree (I now have an automatic out of necessity.)

Well, I cut my teeth in the Mini Car Club of New South Wales and a nicer bunch you couldn't find. I'm talking the people and couples that were there when I first arrived and for the next few years going back to 1975. My G-d that's fifty years ago! Another lifetime!

The President then was Tony French who died in 2023 RIP and his equally lovely wife Carol. Such lovely people and such fond memories (there was a luncheon in Michael's and my honour in 2002 which was, as I said to Tony when he asked how the luncheon had gone…magical. That summed it up for me.) That was 22 years ago at the time of writing! Incredible. Another time, another continent and… another husband!

And the rallying in outback Australia was the second biggest bonus ever. And the people I met in the car club – to use a Canadian expression – were AWESOME! Or as the Canadians say "R-some." Not to mention my best (Australian/British) friend Jan.

Jan and I met at the first meeting of the Mini Car Club of NSW, along with her now ex Gary. They had a Mini Moke, none of which I've seen in yonks. It looked a fun car but had the teeniest boot - a tin box welded to the back seat with a lock. The size of a medium-size tool kit. We'd go down to Bondi beach in both of our cars and have a ball. With surf life savers constantly on guard. Jan now lives in the Blue Mountains, west of Sydney. Up near the Three Sisters, a wonderful look out point for tourists. Just visit it!

Speed has an adrenalin function all of its own and car rallying fulfils that so well! Car rallying is much more fun than merely racing around a circuit - my opinion, but driving through a forest at night knowing the track has been off limits to all locals and is cut off at certain points making it relatively safer, is just brilliant! One sees the odd wombat or badger and squirrels dart here and there but mostly it's just masses of trees, dirt tracks and the odd field that one has to jump out of the rally car, quickly open the gate to said field and close the gate properly afterwards and jump back into the rally car. All this is against the clock - but it also makes for a wonderful and quick...pee-break! And late at night in a forest, when one's bum is not in view!!! In a part day-time car rally one could also see koalas, depending where the rally was held. And they are - just koalas. They are not related to the bear family and do not have that word after the first one! A koala is a koala!

There are a couple of stories that make up my

involvement in car rallying. The best natural "high" one can get. As background, we all drove with the windows open so the dust did come in but never had a chance to settle.

One incident that we heard about (thank G-d it wasn't us!) is where a team of two seasoned rally enthusiasts came to a field which had a few cows in it. Now that's not usually a problem but this rally driver managed to get too close to the cow on the navigator's side; as a result, the cow's behind was pushed and his rear end raised...and the navigator's window was open as they usually are for all the dust to be blown away......This cow had other ideas and must have wondered what was happening. He/she SHAT herself through said open window right onto the navigator's lap! That was one rally that that twosome was not likely to EVER forget! The poor cow probably didn't enjoy it either!

The other incident happened to us, thankfully a lot less smelly! The forest I cannot remember but our car, our Datsun 1600, had been slightly modified although still within accepted guidelines. Datsuns were fairly popular in our rally driving era. Gerry had had special lights put on the front of the car, in addition to lights already there. You almost can't have too many lights on a rally car. These were attached to the bumper bar very securely; they had to be for what the car would go through, and allow us to travel through, at speed. I called these our Dolly Partons for good reason. They led the way! BIG, round and masses of black tape securing them in place - until one big rally with a "river of mud."

(I only noticed recently that in Toronto bumper bars seemed to have been discontinued from the design of any car made nowadays. I hadn't noticed till mid-late 2022 but that was in big part to my not then driving daily anymore.)

Something I did miss, especially in Canada where they "drive on the wrong side!" Apparently, it doesn't take long to get used to that! "Don't you believe it," says Mr Mouse; well, he IS the exception to any rule!)

Anyway, back to this wonderful rally, they're all wonderful and always memorable in one way or another. It does make one very comfortable behind a wheel and that can only be good. It makes one more confident. This rally had a large section that included a very muddied river crossing - or whatever it was "supposed" to be. We were all told, as we arrived at it, to take it carefully, keep well to the right and try and bypass the thick mud.

Explicit instructions that we tried valiantly to comply with: drive down and go to the right side and try to stick to that side and you may avoid most of the mud.

Ho, ho, ho. We drove to the right, and s - l - i - d back immediately to our left and right into the middle of the stream of mud. And *that* was where we stayed whilst trying to figure how to extricate ourselves. I should mention that by now it wasn't dark any more. We were fast running out of time (for the uninitiated all rallies are timed) and a very early sunrise was due soon (TG!)

The organisers had a four-wheel-drive on the other side ready for such lamentable occasions as these, and by now we were knackered. They get to be very comfortable behind the wheel and that can *only* lead to safer drivers. So here we were in the middle of G-d only knows which forest, and us going nowhere and for some reasons our lights were on the blink. The only good point - if it can be classed as such - is that it was starting to dawn and that we had just about run out of time, and could just about manage without the lights.

It's at this point one almost doesn't care.

Tired, and without quite our usual exhilaration, we allowed the car to be tied very strongly to the rear bumper of the four-wheel-drive vehicle, and the driver got in and revved up and started to pull…NOTHING. So he pulled again…NOTHING. So he pulled AGAIN and the wiring AND THE DOLLY PARTONS AND THE BUMPER, ripped from their moorings, flew up in the air and landed with a "plop" in the mud!

Two huge "boobs" attached to wires on a now useless detached bumper-bar adorned the river of mud…and we were exactly where we'd been when we slid into place. We hadn't moved one INCH! *Then* we were pulled out via the rear bumper bar. Luckily that was still intact: otherwise we'd still be there now!

The sun is really climbing, albeit slowly now, and we are so "out of time" it's not funny. Classed as an NF (non-finisher!), nothing proud about that, but another story to tell. With the sun coming up, we were dusty and tired - but still exhilarated from our rally. It's a wonderful sport and so good for one's children to get involved in because in time they get their chance to be behind a wheel and when it's at a motorcross or similar they get the chance to practise driving in a very safe environment that the only things they should be knocking over would be witches' hats.

They get to be very comfortable behind the wheel and that can ONLY lead to safer drivers.

Somewhere in Sydney(!) We had a day out with the Car Club and were taking turns in going round a rough circuit. Gerry on his own this time and he caught the front end of our Datsun 1600, which somersaulted twice and I shut my eyes tight in real fear of losing him. Tony French (President for all our time there) reassured me. I was screaming with my eyes shut in horror! "Hazel, open your eyes, he's ok, he's out of the car!"

The same couldn't be said of the car. Dented quite a bit as she'd clipped the side of the raised earth at the edge of the circuit and had flipped twice mid-air! Luckily she landed right way up. Out popped our windscreen so it was a very draughty drive home!

Yes, I was very relieved.

THE RALLY CREW PLAY THEIR PART, TOO

My ex, Gerry, went through "several car bodies" literally, when they got pranged enough times. Car Bodies are the car shells, just the outer body and one then puts the Halda, Paddy Hopkirk seats (wonderfully like armchairs one could go to sleep in!) and complete harnesses back inside, not forgetting the Odometer.

Rallying Down Under was a wonderful time and Stuart enjoyed this too, being made a part of the Rally Crew who looked after our car. A Datsun 1600, as many of them were in those days and they had to be looked after.

Gerry wanted the rally crew to be matching and organised lovely red matching canvas overalls and Stuart got his own, slightly smaller version and he was thrilled. Pictures in our albums show him in his rally gear next to the car and crew. He kept the "Dolly Parton" lights clean and checked them thoroughly before every rally.

I DRIVE IN THE WORLD
RALLY CHAMPIONSHIP!

My involvement in the World Rally Car Championship was in 1981 in the CASTROL GTX RALLY, down in Canberra, Australia. I was driving with Terry Boardman, an Aussie Vietnam veteran. Wow, it is now 43 years later that I write this and again a whole other lifetime! In fact, it was also another country and another continent. So much has passed since that weekend but I remember the rally as if it was yesterday.

Rallying is a natural "high." It doesn't get more exhilarating than trying to drive as fast as one can, allowing for wheel spin in the dark and with powerful headlights in some night rallies. These were not the ones that were Gerry's and mine, the Dolly Partons, but, unusual for a car rally, they were Terry Boardman's lights on his VW Golf.

People may well say parachuting gives a natural high. Well, I've never tried that and that's how I like it. I'm getting vertigo simply thinking about it!

When Gerry and I had rallied we sat in very comfortable Paddy Hopkirk seats. The latter came with quadruple harness and a roll-cage. My G-d, talk about virtually an armchair! One really "fits" into one of those and I always felt so safe in those!

This rally had a particular part that all competitors were allowed to do two dry runs, which I took to be a good thing - till I saw it! The MINESHAFT - so aptly named as when one arrived at the top of it, it looked like a completely vertical drop. When we had gone down it, yours truly peeked through slatted fingers and Terry had the initial pleasure of it. He was not even Terry-fied. Sorry, I couldn't resist it.

When we'd gone down the first dry run with this Madam's eyes fractionally open, I kid you not, I looked back up and realised this had been very steep but steep was the operative word and "not quite" as sheer as it felt! Otherwise, I guess the car would have somersaulted over! The second time I allowed myself to look and it was more exciting. Still that urgh(!) feeling. Urgh is courtesy of my Michael Mouse! Indeed, this book would never have come to fruition without Michael, my editor and proof-reader and yet doesn't lose my "essence."

One thing in this rally that was a wonderful addition for me was that Terry had included an intercom attached to our crash helmets (that Gerry and I never had) and a very sensitive one at that. I softly asked Terry if he could hear me and a voice boomed back yes. What we weren't ready for was at the first checkpoint when some official said something to Terry and he replied - in a normal voice - straight into the intercom that was at mouth level obviously! Boy was that loud and he put his hand over the offending equipment thereafter, softening it hugely for me. A lovely guy.

We didn't do particularly well but we actually finished (31st!!!) and had a lot of fun - and after all, that's what it's all about.

Then there was another rally, at Port MacQuarie. This included a breakfast with everyone at 3am - including the legendary ARI VATANEN!

I can't wait to tell my granddaughter Aurora when she's old enough to "get" it!

Chapter 6

THE BERLIN WALL COMES DOWN, AND DEVASTATION

The year 1989 is seared into my brain. I witnessed two distinct events for me. The Berlin Wall did indeed come down but for me, that same year, there was an early morning when my world fell apart for the second time. Something I again wouldn't wish on my worst enemy. Stuart was seven, Lisa was four and it was November 2nd. The phone rang. This time it is my baby brother Neil. Not exactly a baby any more but I enjoy referring to him as that - he was 23 at the time, some baby!

Gerry answered the phone and I heard him talking: "How's your mother?" So I knew it was our side of the family.

It is 7.30am and I'm still in bed, about to get up.

It couldn't have been worse.

Gerry came back into our bedroom and sat down on my side of it. By this time the children had heard the phone ring and as it was too early for most phone calls, so had come down to see what was what.

There was no nice way to say it, so he didn't. "That was Neil. Russell has had leukaemia for the last two years and he died half an hour ago!"

Ahhhhhhhhh, I WAILED!

"MY Russell?" I asked stupidly, suddenly feeling I was in a very bad B grade movie and that was the pathetic kind of comment that was written into an appalling script. IF it came out badly, maybe I was just in a bad dream? I can remember it like it was yesterday. Sickening is what comes to mind.

This was so horribly real. Gerry spent the next couple of hours trying to book a flight out for me. He'd rung the advertising agency that he worked at first, John Singleton Advertising, to say he'd be late in/or not in, I really can't remember which. My brain was scrambled. He covered me well, by booking two flights on two different airlines. Neil, I found out later, had told Theo (his father and my stepfather) as well as the Rabbi, that no way was the burial to go ahead without me. Sweet and caring as always. He's always been there for me.

As was Russell's wish, and in accordance with what he wrote in his last letter to me, handwritten from his hospital bed, was that he hadn't wanted me "impossibly frustrated by our separation" and had made the decision not to inform me and had asked Mother and Neil to do the same. He stated as much when I eventually got to read his final letter to me, written in Hammersmith Hospital where he volunteered to be a guinea pig for anything they wanted to try out.

Russell was so sweet and NOW the tears have come again. Not much starts me flowing, but writing about it brings the floods, again. The letters on this keyboard are blurred now.

Memories.

You start remembering all the happy times, and in-between, reality hits and you start welling up. Again and again and again. Then it comes in bouts. Then you think you've done all the crying you can but one little thing might trigger it and off you go again.

That is Life. And the memories keep coming.

RUSSELL AND THE ROCK CONCERT!

Russell taking me to a rock concert!!! (I'm reading all my handwritten notes which are a bit of a pain because sometimes I can't read my own writing! It's not that it's that bad but hand-written notes are never as easy as the printed form.)

Russell approached Mother one day to get permission to take me to a rock concert! I have no idea where it was; somewhere in England is all I remember. The only thing I recall is lots of wind, music, mud and people. Being taken there was the thrill and will stay with me for ever! I was so chuffed at Russell wanting to do this with me. Late 2019 was 30 years, and I lit another yahrzeit (memorial) light in memory. Thirty years! Another lifetime.

We drove up to the concert in the car that Russell had now inherited, Daddy's Zodiac. One long front seat as they were made then. Russell surprised me half-way-up. Was I hungry? Yes, I suppose I was. Well, on the back seat was a tin with 24 homemade (by Russell that is!) chocolate cupcakes…and a sprinkling of "weed" in each one!!! He didn't tell me at first.

See if anything changes, was Russell's comment to me as I happily munched on one! Are the trees seeming brighter coloured, or any colour seemingly sharper!? Eh, no! I think something got "lost in translation" but it was a sweet bonding time! It makes me laugh now to think of this time, and my first dalliance with "W e e d!" This is done as in the voice when remembering.......Flowerpot Men!!! Bill and Ben and Weeeeed! Those born prior to 1965 will appreciate this more, especially those born in England!

When we got to the windy concert grounds there were masses of people and tents and music. Russell and I sat on the ground and he stretched his long legs out and turned inwards. Then motioned me to do the same – while he lit up some weed! No, I never did tell Mother. I don't think she'd have been surprised, but I do think she'd have had something to say about "influence over me" (wrongly!) It never did affect me. I never did drugs, and didn't particularly like the idea of being out of control. And the idea of someone else doing the right thing and making sure I got home safely doesn't bear thinking about. I don't want to rely on someone else like that. Or getting paralytic in a gutter, how revolting is that?!

We are so lucky, mostly, when we get brothers or sisters. I loved the fact that I had brothers only and I was the only sister. That made me feel very lucky and special and they were two very special brothers. Still are, even though they're in the next world, wherever that is.

One day both Russell and Cedric came to pick me up from school and boy was I the envy of everyone! Six-foot tall, lean and handsome! Many teenagers, especially the females, all looking at both of them, and thinking how hot they were, or "good looking" as we used to say. And they were MINE! The pride I felt in going to the front gate and walking off with them knew no bounds! I can remember it like it was yesterday! It would have been so good going into middle age and elderly years with them both. Mother must have said, "go and meet her at the gates. It will thrill her" and she was so spot on!

That said, I do have Neil, and we have a very good relationship. I'm very appreciative of that. So many brothers and sisters don't get on, especially as adults, and that's such a waste! You just don't know how long you have them for, and when they've gone - they've gone.

RUSSELL MEMORIES

Russell had initially read Physics at Manchester University and enjoyed reading Physics books in the same way I love to read about nutrition - and what passes for nutrition nowadays! He'd been doing this for maybe a couple of years. I remember when he announced to the family that he wasn't going to read Physics anymore and he was switching to Architecture. That's a seven-year course but he did most of it – something like six-and-a-half years and was going through exams when one of the examinees picked a query - on - a screw - on - a - hinge of the chairs he had designed to sink back into the floor creating a dance floor as another use for the room. A wonderful design that in Russell's eyes was being "nitpicked" at. It so disillusioned him that he stopped his finals and only resumed them a couple of years before he died.

He left Neil a most beautiful last letter in which he said he had been prompted to resume his studies because of Neil coming into his life late on and he wanted his baby brother (a twenty-year gap) to be proud of him. It was a very moving letter and these sentences don't really do it justice. I did, however, have my copy framed...

Over the years he has done drawings. All excellent and all done to scale. One was of the old Ford Zodiac that was Daddy's car before Russell inherited it. And that long front seat the way they used to be made. Once Russell got out of the car on the passenger side too quickly and burnt a hole in his jeans!

I remember him with me once walking through Letchworth on the way home from wherever and he must have suddenly realised we were late, because he started to run. Now, he was 6' 1" and I was seven at the time, so somewhat shorter but suddenly I find myself "flying" through the air with my feet barely touching the ground and this has been an abiding happy memory for me, albeit small.

When I had run away from home, as mentioned earlier, I had been dropped off at Russell's Ladbroke Grove home. It had his stamp all over it. Painted white throughout and a very modern bathroom. A decent size lounge and a simple kitchen where he made us dinner. I remember the meal! He baked chicken in the microwave along with jacketed spuds - I wasn't "anti-microwave" then! Although we have got one again now - after many years without...if you can't beat them...

WAS HE...?

Back in Sydney, Australia, I had started to wonder about Russell, having never seen him with a girlfriend. That said, I told myself, I've spent years away from England, so to not have seen him with any girlfriend wasn't really a surprise. However, it niggled at me till after about two years of on and off thinking (with life and car rallying going on in-between!) I suddenly and finally thought "maybe he's gay!?"

So, I decided to ring Neil and broach the subject. It went like this: "Hi, Neil, I want to ask you a question." He replied "YES" but it was a "yes" that answered the question I hadn't actually asked, but that he knew had finally come!

Yes, Russell was indeed gay. It didn't change how I felt about him, I only wished he or the family had told me earlier, but whatever their reasons, it didn't matter, and I had worked it out myself. He also wasn't overtly gay. Nothing to me that had indicated such. I adored him whatever his leanings.

He was also a photographer and there IS a picture, someone else took of him, half way up a mountain, rock climbing but he didn't do things by half. Oh no, he had one hand controlling the rope and the other holding a camera and using it!

Electric shock treatment was suggested by both Mother and Theo and completely rejected by Russell. I'm glad, because we ARE whatever we ARE because of our DNA. One cannot "undo gay!" Or anything else for that matter. It's ridiculous that these thoughts were even broached initially.

I had even met his partner James years earlier but not realised, but that didn't matter either. I'd love to meet James again. Apparently, he's been living in Amsterdam. He was 6' too.

I was possibly considered too young to talk about this at the start when he first realised himself, and later he possibly figured it wasn't on my radar and to leave it that way. It has never changed my love for him.

Russell surprised me one year, when I was relatively young by building me my own dolls house (or perhaps I shouldn't be surprised by a budding architect.) We possibly have pictures of it somewhere. And he bought a tiny red vinyl sofa to go in it and a few other pieces. Luckily it's in my memory. For a mature architecture student anything is possible!

One special picture I have is of Russell making paper pirate hats out of a newspaper sitting at a garden table in Mother's back garden.

So many images from a life, and this from my own life that had barely any adult time with two wonderful brothers!

Never to be forgotten.

Chapter 7

THE CHESHIRE CAT MEETS HER MOUSE
OR
1995 - A NEW CHAPTER IN MY LIFE...

Within three weeks of arriving back in England (for me that is, the children having been born in Sydney) I bought myself a copy of the JC (Jewish Chronicle.) It was not my normal choice. I preferred the JT (Jewish Telegraph) but it was a thicker paper and I knew I'd get more to read. Also, I wanted to see if there was anyone from my past living in London that I recognised. I have a very good memory for faces. I'm referring here to things under births, marriages and deaths. I realised all the people whom I had known had grown up, married and might not even be living in England any more. That was one disadvantage to moving to the other side of the world. That and not having Mother close. Or, as I said before, Neil.

Getting back to buying my copy of the JC. THAT changed my life forever...I read much of the paper but also found the "lonely hearts page." For amusement and curiosity I read most of that – and found one very interesting advert:

"Walking in a Winter Wonderland and through summery hills and dales. That's this 41-year-old N/O (non-orthodox), N/S (non-smoking) guy. Let's walk, let's talk."

My two favourite seasons are Winter and Autumn. Both for the glorious displays that are put on. In fact, we eventually (2014) returned from my trip of a lifetime – Russia, Siberia, Mongolia, and China – in January and February(!) A trip my ex and I had talked about, *my* Trip of a Lifetime that he later took his new wife on! (he *has* since said it wasn't planned that way.) Moscow and the Kremlin in snow – reminiscent for me of my favourite movie of all time, Dr Zhivago.

I sat on that newspaper ad for three weeks till I'd almost forgotten it and then decided to reply to it. As we had come over with very little, I did not have any decent writing paper so no Basildon Bond. All I had was a miserable reporter's notepad with a spiral top to rip off. I decided to add an air of mystery and wrote something like, "Dear Winter Wonderland, your words are lovely as they are my favourite seasons. It would be nice to meet. I hope you're not put off by the fact that I am not in London but Manchester. I have only recently arrived from abroad." That was also deliberate so as to pique interest and not give out ALL the information. I also signed it only with my telephone number and no name so he had much to find out!"

Meanwhile, sometime in those next few weeks I had a date – if one can call it that - with another Michael. Don't ask me how we met - I have NO idea! This first "riveting" date (not) had us taking a walk through Brantwood Park, Cheadle.

USUALLY on a date, especially the first one, one walks WITH the person they are with. NOT this Michael! He marched ahead around the park with me trying in vain to keep up! Some date! If he was trying to put me off, he was succeeding!

We went back to my home for coffee. Still polite enough to invite someone back although by rights I should have dumped him at the gates of the park! We were having a coffee and running out of conversation when my Mother put in an appearance to give him the "once over!" She sat and talked to him whilst I sat and said nothing. He was a chartered surveyor, and we had nothing in common and no spark of attraction whatsoever.

THEN the phone rang and I went to answer it.

"Winter Wonderland" said a voice at the other end.

"Are you trying to be funny?" I said to this voice that I'd never heard from before and I had *completely forgotten* about the ad! Every time I read that line "Are you trying to be funny," I laugh. It was like getting a dirty phone call!

I then proceeded to have the most enjoyable conversation for the next half hour, sitting on the stairs in the hallway, with a voice that was very good at mimicking others. In that half hour I got Patrick Moore. He asked where I'd returned from and immediately wrongly guessed "Israel?" I let him wait a moment and then said "Sydney." Michael later told me he was pleasantly surprised that I wasn't from North West London. He felt many females from north London were "hard-nosed, materialistic bitches that were foul-tempered and somewhat neurotic and that they wanted a six-bedroomed house in Radlett and a four-wheel-drive!!!" (not necessarily all of them, I hasten to add). I couldn't have been more different.

Michael is a linguist and a writer and journalist but wasn't going to "stretch to all this" and didn't want the kind of woman who aspired to that either. The fact that I had returned to outside London was a plus although according to him, and I think he's correct, many men also don't want to go "far from the ghetto" and had that "within ten miles radius" mentality. It doesn't help with dating!

Too soon Mother had run out of conversation and came past me perched on a stair with the "other" Michael trailing behind her. I said goodbye to both. I later got it in the neck from Mother for not having put "telephone" Michael into a shorter call and come back to the sunroom. No way! At the end of that call we had arranged for Michael to come up a week-and-a-half away, on a Friday. I booked him into the Village Hotel in Cheadle.

Ten days later I went to meet Michael's train (this is early December 1995.)

I was up and down the stairs at Stockport Station trying to establish whether his train had already arrived. He later told me he'd seen this figure in a long green coat running up and down like something from a pinball machine and thought she looked nice, never thinking she was THE one. Suddenly that figure was standing next to him:

"Michael?"

"Hazel?"

Rather nice - he'd already seen this figure in a green coat and liked what he saw! This figure in a green coat had seen this tall figure with a small suitcase and a beard and a moustache - two huge plusses in my book!

We found a taxi and started for the Village Hotel. I already thought "not bad." Tall dark and handsome, with a beard and moustache. RIGHT UP my alley as far as looks are concerned. NOT a bad beginning! Apparently, he thought similarly. Going well!

We got him booked into the Village and left his little bag in the room and made our way down to the bar. We found a small round table and sat opposite each other, suddenly slightly tongue-tied but there was a "frisson" a spark! There were smiles and then Michael said those magic, special words "there's a definite chemistry," and we could both feel it (that feeling has never left us.) We have now been married 27-years this past February 16th, 2024. We feel very fortunate.

We had a meal that night at the Village in their restaurant and later sat back in the bar in another area where we had another drink. I've never acquired the taste for alcohol (apart from three liqueurs), courtesy of my Mother. And I don't like wine or beer. I used to be a very inexpensive date!

As we sat just chatting and finding out about each other he mentioned he'd been an assistant guide on a tour of China. The highlight for Michael was travelling on the Hong Kong Metro and getting out at Admiralty Station. There was a display for the 1993 Hong Kong to Beijing Rally. Two drivers gave him their autographs: the late and much missed Colin MacRae, and Finnish legend Ari Vatanen.

When Michael mentioned Ari Vatanen my ears pricked up even more. Michael was surprised but also very pleasantly taken aback. I had done rallying and more back in Oz and had met Ari Vataten at a VERY early morning breakfast after the Southern Cross Rally (3am is early even in my book!) and we had sat opposite each other at a large table. It was lovely having something in common so early on.

Michael loves to collect autographs and has Sir Jackie Stewart's and Ayrton Senna's amongst several but a new girlfriend who adored being behind a steering wheel was something new for him. And I must admit I enjoyed this new found "notoriety" that he got with me. I took out my driver's licence to show him because I had it inside my CAMS "coat" - Confederation Of Australian Motor Sport. Something I am extremely proud of and that sent my stock up to a whole new level and I hope it is still there. The ego likes to be stroked now and then.

I was on about how Michael and I started to go out every other weekend when he came up to stay. Needless to add – he stayed in a guest house.

Our first date was to Quarry Bank Mill, out in the middle of nowhere. Well, not completely but almost: if you're without transportation it's a pain. We had a lovely time at Quarry Bank Mill and saw how they lived 200 years ago – child labour and all that. By the time we came out at 4pm (this being early December) it was pitch black and no street lights. We decided to walk in what we knew was the right direction. And we walked and walked and walked. Around four miles, or at least that's what it felt like, but I held Michael's big warm "paw" of a hand and felt utterly safe. There was no way he would ever attack anyone. He was a gentle giant then. As he said to me early on, "I'm a gentleman, and a gentle man" and that's very spot on. I likened him to a big cuddly teddy-bear and his Lewis's jumpers reflected that.

When we started going out, he said my grin was like that of the Cheshire Cat from Alice in Wonderland. He actually meant it as a compliment although writing this here makes it sound anything but! And while we were dating he would buy cards and post them to me to keep me happy in between us seeing each other. I started doing the same. It was rather nice looking for cards that were appropriate for that time, the "wooing" time. Michael would depict himself as a mouse and "tried" drawing himself accordingly. Badly!

Before the end of the year I was invited down for his New Year's Eve party he was holding but I was the only one who couldn't make it. I couldn't get a babysitter and I just knew it wasn't going to happen. I didn't feel too bad. I accepted the situation, and I did feel it would be a case of "absence makes the heart grow fonder" and I was spot on!

On New Year's Day Michael rang me to wish me Happy New Year and then said, "I love you --- I." I said: "what did you say?!," but I had heard it, of course and it was lovely and we went "onto a new level." I'd just wanted to hear it for a second time - crafty!

It was quite funny in a peculiar way when we first "had sex." I prefer the old-fashioned Barbara Cartland words (probably) that we made love. That said, I remember sitting on the side of my Queen bed in Cheadle and thinking "how do I play this?"

Obviously (before the deed) one cannot play the coy virgin at 41, especially with two children in the same home! They are proof one isn't a virgin anymore! So how did one "play hard to get" or indeed – DID one play hard to get? I've never been one to jump into bed with a boyfriend and I didn't use sex as a yardstick.

It was funny when we did, finally, "do it." We were in my bed and suddenly there's a knock on the door and my son Stuart pops his head around the door wondering what we were up to, or maybe knowing exactly! Michael Mouse has just reminded me that Stuart also put the light on! I can't remember what he said. Neither does Michael.

Luckily Michael was never put off by little interludes like this although, to be fair, they didn't come in very often at all and were just understanding. I was simply trying to set a good example and not climb into bed with anyone I fancied. That said, back in Manchester in 1995 it was very hard to find *any* males that fitted my criteria, were the same religion, and that seemed relatively "normal" and available, AND – they had to fancy little old me.

There were not many real social functions going on and the two I went to before Michael's phone call came on that fateful afternoon were abysmal with people hanging around waiting for someone to strike up a conversation with them. All pretty painful. I met a few that had been in the same position twenty-five years earlier and they hadn't aged! That was the good part. I felt as though I was in a time warp, and not a pleasant one. I hope the situation has changed for those still on that merry-go-round.

When I was 18 I started a thing in Manchester called "People To People" for 18+ and they all used our home as a meeting/socialising place. It was wonderful for a good long while. I'd like to think some men or women met their future spouse at my place.

Michael nearly blew it very early on in our relationship at a Turkish restaurant in Cheadle (Cheshire) just before Christmas. He had booked a table - so we were given a tiny table for two – in between two long tables so we could barely hear each other speak. Then he made the biggest gaffe that really had me wondering what I was doing there.

69

In a deepish voice that luckily no one else actually heard over the other two parties flanking us he says: "I like my women WIV' A BI' OF MEAT ON!" and the accompanying hand gesture to show someone sizing up TWO large BOSOMS! All I could think of was O-M-G! This "relationship" had better improve on that or this is not going to go anywhere at all! I must have had THE most appalled facial expression on because things DID go from strength to strength. My son Stuart says you can read me like a book. I CAN be tactful, and often am, but if I don't attempt to disguise it, it's very easy.

Hereonin we went out when Michael came up which was every two weeks for months. I'm guessing we went out for half of the time, say eight or nine months before I had had enough of that "routine" and wanted to increase it. Also figuring, rightly, that once he changed it to weekly he could hardly change back...now you know, My Mouse!

Early on, say one month in, my brother Neil invited us over for the classic British afternoon tea with him making all the goodies (he's a very good cook, and innovative.) Michael and I and my children went over and had a lovely time. This was on a Sunday afternoon. Afterwards, Michael had to get the train back down to London and Neil and his partner Sara and both my children and I were invited over to Mother's for dinner.

After dinner Theo (stepfather) said we were all going to watch an episode of Mastermind upstairs in their bedroom. It never occurred to me that the programme wasn't being shown on TV at the time...

We all seat ourselves. Mother and Theo sat on the bed up against their pillows, Neil and Sara plopped themselves on the floor near the door and Stuart and Lisa sat on the floor near my feet. I just parked myself at the end of the bed.

Four contestants walk in and sit at the seats provided. I watch them walk in, looking at each one, man, man, woman, MICHAEL! At that point the children crane their neck around to see my reaction and I watch the rest of the programme unfold whilst trying to take in the fact that Michael – and his specialist subject Formula 1 - is on TV and this time I'm the one in awe. As Stuart and Lisa kept twisting back to see my ongoing reaction I didn't get to really "enjoy" it.

Being under the spotlight would be sheer hell for me, and I'd immediately go blank. Not something I would relish at all, and wouldn't do it "for quids." I'm shuddering just thinking about it. Being under the spotlight – needless to say I didn't take it all in.

We are better matched than I think some people initially thought. We both love reading. Although I haven't read all the classics I have read Farley Mowat who died in 2014 aged 92, a great Canadian writer whom I discovered years ago. Kedrick Smith's The Russians is excellent. And one of these days I will finish(!) Richard Dawkins' The Blind Watchmaker. And my favourite books were, and still are true stories of WW2, like Richard Pape's Boldness is my Friend and Reach for the Sky by Paul Brickhill, the true story of MY hero, legless pilot Douglas Bader. Also, one of the best – Carve Her Name With Pride, the true story of Violette Szabo.

Our apartment had around 900 books. We've culled them over the last two years. We had to. And I left something like 300 books in Sydney, but I brought over mine on nutrition, all 33 of them.

I found out that evening of Mastermind that Michael had been on the programme in 1991 and had done well but was pipped to the post by ONE point by the lady whose specialist subject was Frank Lloyd Wright! I was still in awe. Still am. Michael is a linguist. Studying Modern and Ancient Greek at Birmingham University. He taught Greek privately to mostly young people back in Toronto who slipped through the proverbial net, and had not been brought up speaking Greek by their usually Greek speaking parents because they were too busy wanting their children to speak English - though being brought up bilingual would have been so much easier as children.

Michael has been complimented by so many people. Usually, middle-aged Greeks or older ones who are not always grammatically correct. Once he was asked in a taxi, "where do you come from?" He answered London. The taxi-driver said, "But, where are you from (that is, where in Greece)?" "From England." Look of surprise from the driver. High praise indeed.

Michael's cards to me every week depicted himself as a Mouse. A very sweet Mouse but often badly drawn - but that only added to the charm. He was going out with someone whose grin he likened to that of a cat, so technically, we were two different species going out.

On one occasion Michael and I went to Donington Park Circuit for the day and took the children with us. It was really a "Michael" venue with old racing cars that were now antique. And we were almost the only ones there that day, save for two men. It was rather echoey too and we went around more or less together. Then Stuart said something very tactless. I *cannot* remember what or to whom, but I thought I had to reprimand him and said what was supposed to be, "You have the tact of a peanut." Yes, I said – in a loud voice – in that same echoey place - "you have the tact of a penis!" And we all burst out laughing and couldn't get out quick enough!

A FERRY-TAILED ROMANCE!

Kind of obvious, but he won two tickets to go to Bilbao, Spain. It became a no-brainer to use that saying somewhere and I already have the title of the book, and I ain't changing that! Naturally Michael asked me to accompany him and naturally I said yes, thank you! Bilbao was quite nice, even with bad weather, but it was lovely being together.

Coming back was more eventful as we hit a Force 9 gale! Up and down the ship went making it hard for anyone, everyone mostly, except me (yey!) to eat. Remember the crossing to Ostend with Daddy at the beginning? Well, my stomach is still made of cast iron!

Anyway, here in the cabin was where Michael chose to propose. "Oh, Hazel, let's get married," Michael said. I burst into tears and said, "I'll try and be a good wife." (And so you have been, Mrs Mouse.) He likes to pretend he's not sure whether I said "yes" or "yeh" – as in upchuck. No!

Then there was an announcement made that the weather had slowed the ship and we'd all be late back and therefore to use the three public phones to ring business/home/loved ones etc to explain the delay. We queued up with masses of others to first ring my (now late) mother-in-law Doris to tell her we had got engaged, only for her to say in a typical negative way, "I don't know how it's going to work (she meant with me at that point in Manchester and Michael based in London.)" Not really insurmountable odds, just negativity coming from a woman who wanted something else for her son – and herself. Then we rang my Mother who was very happy for us and said, "for the first time, I'm speechless!"

So, we married in 1997, my Mouse and I, and that same year we went to see a Mr Bean movie, "Mr Bean Goes To America." Going as an Art Expert(!!!) Mr Bean was to be accommodated by the American Art Executive and his wife in their modern, plush apartment. Mr Mouse, my kids and I saw the film in South Harrow. Mr Mouse burst out laughing at one point (the car sequence with the biker putting his middle finger up at Mr Bean and Mr Bean raising middle fingers of both hands.) Mr Mouse is cackling away, and has started cackling away again now as we proof read this! And he had set the cinema off doing the same!

Many who did see this film will remember Rowan Atkinson getting a huge (rubber) turkey not only stuck over his head, but afterwards trying to fit it into an ordinary large microwave! It wasn't going to fit and he nearly wrecked it, the microwave, that is, and the whole bloody kitchen!

When the wife returns home later she discovered the kitchen in a bad (!) state and Mr Bean rather forlorn and apologetic.

She then privately said to her husband: "WHERE DID YOU GET HIM, PLANET ZOG"! ! ! ?

To which I turned to look at Michael and said: "THAT'S WHERE YOU'RE FROM - PLANET ZOG!"

Which gives one an idea of what I often have to deal with often, but luckily not DAILY, actually I'm not even sure about that!!

We make Mouse faces at each other often. We also think up all the mouse related words, like: mouse-guided, Mouse Tse-Tung, mousachino cherries, mousetache, the Count of Mouste Cristo, under mouse-arrest, and many more. Michael Mouse help me out here! (Michael here: Sir Stirling Mouse, Zorba The Squeak, mousturbation(!), Mouserati, a Mouse-boat on the Thames.) See the appendix below.

We were in Safeway supermarket several years ago in St Albans where we lived for six years and I got separated from my Mr Mouse so I went to the information desk and said to Mark, who worked there at the time and who knew me by sight, can you put over on the tannoy, "could Mr Michael Mouse please come to information!" And he did! Michael said there were several smiles when "Mr Mouse" came over the loud squeaker, but he came up with a sweet expression on his face. Said his whiskers were twitching and gave me a Mouse face. Always the romantic, well, much of the time. So sweet.

Across a street he will (try to) hide behind a lamppost, put his Mouse face on and see how long it takes me to notice it. One young girl in a car noted the above with great amusement. Makes us squeak with pleasure!

Every anniversary, or birthday, or whatever, Michael tries to find a Mouse theme. We're very mouse-orientated (kinda obvious now, I guess). I have a Family-of-Mice group of hooks joined together and yet to be fixed on the wall for anything to be hung from it. Keys, apron and the like. They are on the wall now. It only took 22 years!

When we go shopping, and possibly split up for the odd different item, I'll find him lurking behind anything that will help temporarily conceal him, whether it be a book stand, or some display, waiting, slightly visible and ready – with a mouse face. And to some degree holding his breath, but it is not easy to keep the mouse face and breathe comfortably. So he makes his sweet, endearing choice – and puffs up. Mr Mouse at the ready! Squeak! It makes me laugh just remembering many times!

At appropriate times I've asked, "are you a man or a mouse?"

"Squeak!"

I ask again, "Are you a man or a mouse?"

"OK, pass the cheese" (courtesy of Abbott and Costello.)

At any time in a supermarket my Mouse will come up to me forlorn, with a crestfallen face: "Mr Mouse humbly begs Mrs Mouse's forgiveness but this plonker can't reach x as this plonker mouse is arthritic and the said item is too low - or too high."

He KNOWS it works on me, MOST times. It would soften most hearts. When I get short-tempered (and it's more this way around than the other) he plays this one out, and does it well, for the most part. And in between often tells me that he loves Mrs Mouse. What could be better?

MR MOUSE AND HIS BEARD

Michael grew his moustache in February 1974. He then decided to grow a beard in 1986 on the Island of Crete and got 16 days of growth in before coming home to Mama and Papa seeing it!

EVERY single time we went to see his late mother Doris (born Deborah, but preferred Doris, which Michael never understood) would say, "oh, you've still got the beard" in the vain hope it would one day be shaved off (and under my breath I'd say "yes and it's staying!")

NOT happening on MY watch! I love beards and moustaches. They have a cozy warmth that has ALWAYS attracted me. Daddy had a moustache, and later on so did both Russell and Cedric and I TOTALLY associate it with gentleness, love, warmth, humour and goodness. Yes, I am sure there are individuals out there with both who are shit-heads, but MY feelings towards men with beards, moustaches, goatees and the like will never change.

Michael had an interesting "experience" that highlighted this attitude in the male-dominated world of London finance and the whole of the London core…a friend recommended him for an interview – with the CBI. The Confederation of British Industry obviously had people working there who had fixed ideas and narrow minds. Michael went for his interview and said later to his friend who'd suggested him: "it was a fairly short interview and didn't seem to go very well." When his friend later spoke to this woman who had interviewed him, she retorted, "you didn't tell me he HAD A BEARD!" O.M.G!

Next we'll be back to "his eyes were too close together" or some other such nonsense.

I really can't stand this kind of crap.

Michael (my Mouse!) is an expert on politics and history and should have been snapped up by any university to lecture in history, politics or certain languages. He's a font of knowledge. A mine of information if you will, and I should know. He's not referred to as the Prof for nothing. No, he doesn't have a PhD but from his own vast library

- in his own mind - he produces SO much and it's ALL fascinatingly put over. His lecture is one that people enjoy the most and he makes it interesting…He loves what he regales. He is a raconteur with all the facts! And I'm his PR agent for 10%!

CONTINUOUS LOVE

This romance of ours doesn't have an ending as such as we are still together and very happily so. I was going to add we wouldn't be together anymore if one of us died, but I'm wrong there though. We will continue into the next life, whatever that consists of, because we were "meant to be," and I can't think of anything nicer than being with Michael, here and beyond, plus my long-gone family.

Every day is romantic with us, not every minute, but a lot. And it's not forced. It's very lovely - and so is my Mouse! It's a lovely way to be.

One has to have a fair bit in common. Opposites do attract but if they like doing different things it's not ultimately going to help them stay together.

I remember an early first date with Michael, driving somewhere (no, Michael doesn't know where, either!) and Michael was driving (!!!) and I suddenly came out with, "you know, I couldn't stand Morecambe and Wise" and Michael said, "neither could I!" That was followed up with, "and I can't stand Mike and Bernie Winters" and Michael had the same response, so we were really getting somewhere even with our dislikes! Michael has just remembered and reminded me just now of the line that Eric Morecambe had said in reply to a question in an interview, "who would you be if you weren't funny?" The reply came, "Mike and Bernie Winters!" Loved that.

The more aspects you like about someone the longer you'll last. Yes, that of course is the answer but it's amazing how much people don't have in common with their boyfriends. That's made me realise in turn that dating sites might not be too bad! No, I know I haven't done that, but I did look in the lonely-hearts page of the JC London and see Michael's ad and actually replied to it three weeks later!

I remember very clearly (because we have all the letters that came from the first ad that my Mouse put in.) One explained how she talked too much and added, "try and stop me" which must be an off-putter if ever I heard one! Then another made the odd comment for Michael to contact her and, "we'll start the arrangements" which I thought was a very odd way of putting it. Another had so many outdoor hobbies that I was surprised she'd even found the time to reply to his ad!

Most of them described how they looked and what attractive features they had! All the things I couldn't promote of myself. One said she had long hair that many had admired and another gave her measurements! To me it would seem very cocky and while it's lovely getting a compliment I could not write that to anyone. This is long before texting and cell/mobiles were invented. Now I've been reliably informed by my techno-crap peasant Mouse(!) that mobiles had started ten years earlier, around 1985, but we didn't all have them then. Certainly not. I am now attached by an umbilical cord to mine!

Most of them indeed described how they looked and that they were considered pretty. What this did do for me was make me realise that to leave it all a mystery was the better way to go. I started with telling him that I had loved his choice of words and that Autumn and Winter were my favourite seasons. Then I added that I had only very recently returned to the country and added that I hoped he didn't mind that I wasn't living in London. All of this piqued his interest enough to ring me on the fateful day when I had the other Michael having coffee in my kitchen and my Mother trying to keep the conversation going - whilst the other Michael rang me and kept me amused brilliantly with mimicking well known people's voices! Patrick Moore I never get tired of hearing!

It's wonderful to laugh with and AT each other. Michael is strong enough within himself to accept being laughed AT and will always admit, especially to me, that he can often be a "plonker!" It's very endearing!

Finally, my Mother once said to me when I was complaining about something he had said or done: "Does he love you?" "Yes." "Does he tell you?" "Yes." "Does he beat you?" "No." "Well then…"

Chapter 8

ST ALBANS - THE ROMAN CITY FOR TWO MICE!

W e were living in St Albans, Hertfordshire. We were initially attracted by its Roman history.

Cedric had previously lived there, on Heath Farm Lane. A very short street. It had had many trees on the plot of land opposite it, though I suspect by now it's been built on. Cedric felled 400 elm trees on that plot in a relatively short time with the result he got tenosynovitis. I don't think it ever really left him.

However, before we moved to St Albans, we lived in Michael's one-bedroom flat in Redhill, and when we got both children (Stuart and Lisa) into Francis Bacon School, St Albans, we started a school run...using the M25! *and* we got them to school on time daily!

Mind you, getting up at 6am with Michael adding irritatingly to Stuart "it'll build character." I know Stuart added "F character!" And would nod off in the back of the car whilst he could. We were also praised for this (arriving on time, NOT the F word!) by the Head at the time, Mr Marshall, who noted that other parents couldn't always get their children to school on time and they lived in St Albans and close to the school!

It might have been Lisa being unwell one day that I stayed at home with her and Michael got a (rare!) chance to drive the car and he drove Stuart to school. Well, he DOES drive like an old woman! And I don't! My Mother once said to Michael, "she drives on two wheels", to which Michael replied, "as many as that!"

Back to Michael driving Stuart to school on the M25.

At one point a Belgian lorry driver, driving, as it happened, alongside our old Volvo in the next lane, clipped our car and in the process sent it spinning round several times and they ended up in the fast lane, suddenly stationary and facing the wrong way - and here was our old Volvo facing a very posh Jaguar! Each driver looked at each other with a sense of resignation.

When the police arrived, it was a case of the officer looking at Stuart and then Michael before saying: "I take it, Sir, that YOU are the driver of this vehicle?"

Michael wearily assured him it was so. He'd looked at Stuart, who was 15 and nearly 6' and the thought that these two had switched places had obviously crossed his mind. The funny thing is I know Stuart can drive, and very well. He also named his car after his favourite actress, Julianne Moore!

WE COULD HAVE BEEN THE RODNEY AND DEL BOY OF ST ALBANS!

We had a market stall back in 1999. Selling spices like sumac that many hadn't heard of, although by now, a few will have. It is a dark red powder with a lemony flavour and is wonderful sprinkled on hum-mouse!

We also sold blue-and-white china that I chose myself at a warehouse near Heathrow. We had fun doing it but getting up so early on Saturday mornings took its toll and rainy/Winter snowy days were the worst (I prefer looking out on snow from indoors!)

A POLITICAL MOUSE

It didn't occur to me to add this chapter to this book but I realised last night that I've been more interested in politics since I met Michael – and that's now 29 years!

When I arrived back in England after living in Sydney, Australia (the REAL Sydney!) for 20 years I was not in the political loop. Having fibromyalgia plays a little with the memory so I can use this as the perfect excuse to find British politics baffling! When William Hague entered the picture, it was slightly better because by then, Spring, I had decided I quite liked William Hague because he was all for keeping the pound and our sovereignty and he kept bashing that home. Of course, he was getting his points across to the parents of the people who have now finally "seen the light" and voted for BREXIT (or most have anyway, as over one million more people voted for BREXIT than didn't!) Nigel Farage at this point had been voted into the European Parliament and had not yet become leader of UKIP.

Through meeting my "new" husband (he's my number two, I'm his number one and last!) I became "involved" in politics! No gasps of horror, please. And, no this book barely touches politics as I recount only ONE foray into it: when I went into a cubicle in St Albans.

In a local election in about 1999, in a St Albans polling booth, two women manning the room are witnesses and were *amazed* at the following:

We go in and pick up the appropriate papers, with the names and the boxes next to the names. Michael walks into a secluded booth and does his bit and I follow suit, into another tiny booth. Except this time the choice was between Tony Blair and William Hague, since I had returned from living in Sydney, after 20 years. I hadn't followed Australian politics nor British politics and I certainly didn't have a CLUE as to who William Hague was at that time. I DID know who Blair was but if one watches the news, any twit can pick *that* up!

The women manning that polling booth had probably never heard these words EVER BEFORE: "Michael, which one of these do I vote for????" A GASP from these women said it all! At THIS point I did not know much about Blair at all, except the negativity from Michael. I now understand much more and would now *never* contemplate putting my cross against his name.

To say I hadn't been politically minded is a deep understatement. One should have the ability to be able to be the butt of a story, particularly a true one, and I am no exception.

Actually, I was *very* pleased when I heard that Tony Blair was going to be visiting a school in the St Albans area (it shall remain nameless; NB this is the first time I have used "shall.") I heard there going to be a demonstration outside the grounds. I still feel very strongly that propaganda/brainwashing children in a school that allows him unfettered access to children is extremely wrong.

If he says something is going to be the case, SOME are going to believe him. NOT a place teachers should allow the children to be accessible from. Politics should not be in the playground nor until further education or university. At school let it just be "normal" lessons and grammar to start with.

The woman I accidentally found myself standing next to, for this protest had come armed with two fresh eggs! A waste of good eggs, really. As I used to be shooter in the netball team, I was full of glee, and asked if I could have one, and when three cars with tinted windows came into view and up the drive I figured, logically, that for safety reasons he would be flanked front and back and therefore be in the middle and I was right.

That was where I aimed my fresh egg. Now I think of it, it should have been an off egg! I aimed well, I am a natural there, and landed it splat in the centre of the windscreen. One piddling amount of pleasure! Shame it didn't go onto his actual face or suit! It is just as well as I might have been presented with his dry-cleaning bill!

LISA'S TRAVELS

Lisa used to "swan off" into London, whether I "allowed" her or not. I worried to some extent but used to get a call about 11pm to say would I come and pick her up and she *knew* that I would. She also *knew* that as I loved driving and that Michael would, as he called it, "ride shotgun." I should have given them pocket money because then I'd have had a bargaining chip!

Then there was the time when Lisa rang from Alex's, a friend's place (to ask for the same "taxi" service!) She had told her friends the flowery language that Michael always uses (giving the definite impression of being born in the wrong era.)

The classic came when Michael and I were picking up Lisa and some of her friends outside a tube station. Lisa was leaning into the passenger window and said: "I feel like a prostitute!"

Another time, outside another home Lisa asked Michael, in order to drop him in it: "Who was Sir Isaac Newton?" Michael replied "He was the CHAP who identified gravity," and they all cracked up. Anything to get him to use his own vocabulary and he never twigged! He's the only one I've ever met who still says "I SHALL do whatever it is!" How old is "shall?!"

Lisa also made her mark on the field of hair styles. She and Michael had gone to Camden Market so that she could find something Bohemian. She certainly found something off-beat – a dark-red hair dye.

They both returned to the flat in Redhill. I don't know where I was but Lisa popped into the shower, attempting to apply the dye. It didn't work – it turned her shoulders dark red! And the bath looked like a murder scene! Lisa and Michael contacted our Redhill neighbour, Winnie, a former nurse. Her contribution was to burst out laughing.

LISA AND I GET OUR EARS PIERCED - OUCH!

I was once walking through part of London with Michael and saw this "woman" standing leaning against a lamppost.

She might have been a hooker. I really don't know and she looked rather common – but she'd had her ears pierced. And at that moment I was ready to have mine done. Lisa had asked me to have hers done and I'd said no up till that point. She was too young, but at this juncture I reckoned we were both ready, and we did have it done although Lisa doesn't handle needles well and promptly landed on the floor! It *was* like having a stapler through the ears! I've kept my holes opened as I never intend going through *that* again!

(My Mouse romantically keeps tabs. He has just reminded me we've been married 27 and-a-half years today, Friday 16th August, 1924!)

Lisa has a wonderful sense of fashion and is always smartly turned out. Well, except for one occasion… There was "a" funeral and that was a different matter. Lisa had dressed for Grandma's funeral in…leggings, low-cut top, faux fur scarf and a long coat. She had to hold this in front as it turned out to be a very warm September day and she hadn't bargained for that - nor for the fact that her derriere was shown clothed in leggings! Not something you want to parade in front of Rabbis, or any clergy! Why she chose this ensemble I will never understand!

My stepfather, Theo, at Neil's home, later stated "she looked like a prostitute," *thinking* I'd take umbrage. I shocked Theo by saying, "I couldn't agree more." Theo added, "how come you didn't say anything beforehand?!"

I replied, as though I was speaking to Lisa: "Oh, and by the way, Lisa, don't dress like a prostitute to your Grandmother's funeral. Yes, I was really going to think of that one in advance!"

Theo had no comeback.

I MARRIED A MOUSE

ASIAN COMMUNICATIONS - A
MOUSE AT THE HELM

Michael had applied for the post of editor at Asian Communications, based at Sutton, South-West London. The MD David Shortland rang up to speak to Michael, who was not in at that precise moment. He'd wanted to pencil in a time for the interview. I took my chance and intervened and added that most interviews Michael had ever gone to were always, in my view, too short, of about 20 minutes duration.

I added that there was a lot more to Michael but that it never got discovered. David Shortland said he'd take that on board, and thanked me. They later interviewed Michael for an hour-and-a-half and offered him the job!

It was a journey of 35 miles that he did daily, taking one-and-a-half hours each way. Eventually the rent on those offices became too great and Asian Communications moved out (I will never understand why companies prefer to lose a company for the sake of chasing a higher rent. Is it always worth it?)

STUART'S TWENTY-FIRST
MADE MORE MEMORABLE

We organised a dinner at a restaurant down a lovely alleyway in St Albans that has likely gone now, but being a listed area will still be wonderfully quaint there. It was very near the ancient clock tower. We invited Rebecca M (where are you now?) Lee, Amey Montgomery, Lisa, Neil, Sara, Mr Mouse and myself and several others. Stuart had asked me more than once "do you think Dad will come" and I said, "oh, it's a long way for him", trying to put him off – but of course he was coming but I wanted a real surprise and made sure Stuart was seated in the middle of the long table, with his back to the door!

Gerry entered the restaurant and declared: "It's a long way to come for dinner!" 20,000 km – it worked. Stuart was delighted!

A TEMPORARY BUDDING THESPIAN

On one occasion Stuart had popped back home to pick up his wig to play Igor in his local school's play (Francis Bacon School, now some Academy). I said to him, "you're nice."

Stuart to me, "no, I'm not, I'm shitty."

I replied, "all teenagers are shitty."

Stuart said, "No, they haven't all got Miss Bxxxx."

I said, "I wish I could speak to her for you."

Stuart replied with, "I'm 18 years old – if I can't start covering for myself now…."

And I dated it Wednesday 3.50pm, February 2nd 2000.

He's so wise and sensible, and caring, and genuine. I must admit my ex and I made two lovely children when we got together.

I have many such pieces of paper, and this is the only way to make sure these wonderful little snippets aren't lost forever.

Stuart is very like his Uncle Cedric and gives me huge pleasure in reminding me what Cedric was like. Don't get me wrong. Stuart has masses of good qualities of his own –

and much later (September 2023) seeing him on video with his niece brought that all home.

It's just nice to see that genes do continue in that way. Richard Dawkins' book "The Blind Watchman" tells of this in greater and fascinating detail. One of these days, maybe when I'm on an aeroplane, I'll get to finish it!

COMING UP – A REAL MEMORY...

A mild pleasant Bank Holiday in Spring 2000. Mr Mouse and I had been on the archetypal Bank Holiday, visiting a steam railway centre. The steam loco went twenty minutes down the line and stopped. There was no station so we couldn't get off. We then went back down the line for another twenty minutes but everything was OK because we had a cup of tea at the end! No, that is not the memory I'm referring to, yet.

We decided to visit Michael's mother Doris but she was around the corner visiting a friend. This was in Canons Park (part of the outskirts of London to the uninitiated!)

We sat in her lounge after making a coffee and decided to watch the TV...Fawlty Towers was on and it was the episode featuring the Irish builders whom Sybil found "shoddy, cutting corners and totally incompetent!"

Mr Mouse and I were watching this episode intently, and Sybil was berating Basil for even hiring them! And we looked at each other at that same moment and I said: "Do you know what this reminds me of?"

"Yes," said my Mouse, and in unison we said "US!"

It was another bonding moment.

We lived in St Albans for six years.

Chapter 9

TWO MICE IN CHINA - OUR
TRIP OF A LIFETIME

In 2002 Michael Mouse had gone to a conference in Birmingham (UK rather than Alabama!) that he nearly didn't go to. This was because it was in a run-down area of Birmingham and he almost forgot the address. We had been to Birmingham before, in the car - with me driving, naturally. We *do* want to get anywhere and back the same day! And my Mouse is a slow driver...

I digress (don't I often?)

It IS frustrating when he stays in the slow lane and takes FOREVER to drive anywhere. The best bit (NOT!) is on the motorway in the left (slowest) lane when he claims he cannot come out because the cars on his right (in the middle faster lane) are *"overtaking him"* and thus he cannot come out!!!!!!! Nuts or what? When G-d was handing out logic, Michael was hiding behind a very large tree! I state to him, "FGS! They're in the next lane because they're going FASTER, NOT because they're overtaking you!" Do you see what I have to deal with!?

And I never thought to ask for it, logic, that is! Well, when you're putting in your "order for a new husband" you don't necessarily think of everything. Logic THEN was not part of Michael Mouse's DNA. It is *only marginally* better now…It's only taken 27 years! Of course, I still love him: it just makes life "more interesting" if one cannot put too fine a point on it.

Anyway, back to that conference on telecommunications in China. A raffle and a woman who picked out a ticket: "It's the editor of Asian Communications!" Michael Ward!

A round of applause followed. The prize was a trip to China for five days, staying three days in Shanghai and two in Beijing, including at Shanghai's top JC Mandarin! A five-star hotel and we two little mice stayed on the 25th floor with panoramic views over the whole city! Magnificent! Did Mr Mouse have difficulty keeping the car on the road back home after the prize was announced!

We left Stuart in charge of Lisa which still pleases me when I think about it. He has a VERY good head on his shoulder and is one of the most trustworthy people I know. His integrity is second to none. He's one of these people who do not really surprise me when I hear accolades about them. It was Stuart's idea: "I'm twenty and I can look after her." And he did, and very well, too.

"Anyhoo!" (a Stuartism) Back to China!

I managed to convince my Mouse that St Albans to Beijing to Sydney was a "hop, skip and a jump" when in fact St Albans to Beijing was ten hours and Beijing to Sydney was eleven hours – some hop!

AUSTRALIA

It was 33 hours door to door from St Albans to Sydney, via transit in Beijing. We'd booked a hotel in Kings Cross,

Sydney. It wasn't quite the notorious place it used to be and suited us for its central locale.

I was meeting my best friend Jan S whom I'd first met on my initial evening meeting at the Mini Car Club of New South Wales (we held monthly meetings) back in 1975! Again, another lifetime ago. Jan and I would become best friends.

We were also meeting Terry Boardman (he had been driver to my navigator) in his Golf (a rarity in rally scenes, in my opinion) in the 1981 Castrol GTX International Rally, held outside Canberra, ACT.

It was so good to see both of them. Terry is also a Vietnam Vet, all 6' (2"?) of him. It was lovely to show my Mouse the city I had lived in for 20 years.

(he mimics the Aussie accent very well, but then he does do many accents very well, as I found out the first time we met - on that first phone call.)

So much had changed in suburban Sydney. Bondi Junction had condos galore and many were very nice but I'm so glad I wasn't living close whilst these were being built! Same can be said for all the new construction going up in Downtown Toronto as I type this. High rise condos at just about every intersection of the downtown core.

Sydney has Pitt St as its main street and a Harbour with views of the Sydney Harbour Bridge and of the Sydney Opera House, a magnificent structure built by Danish architect Jorn Utzon. Last night's news (October 19th '24) showed the picture of King Charles and Queen Camilla on one of the concave "shells" of the Opera House, and they looked magnificent too!

A luncheon in our honour by the Mini Car Club's President, (the sweet, late) Tony French with help from Kerryn Owers and Jan. Kerryn is a teacher, and was very impressed by Michael Mouse's speech. His speech covered Jack Brabham but for my Mouse the personification of Australian Motor Sport was a sports car driver called Frank Gardner. Frank Gardner commented and my Mouse is regaling it "there was a race in 1960. There were the great drivers: the Stirling Mosses, the Jimmy Clarks, the Alan Staceys. And out of the shit and mist came Jack Brabham to win the race." Tony, at this juncture said 'yes, that's Frank'! All regaled by Michael Mouse in an excellent Aussie accent with Kerryn claiming afterwards "he's done his homework, hasn't he?"

And Haviva drove us around to show us Bondi Junction's new areas. She was the one whom I sat in the kitchen of, in 1982 and wept over Cedric's loss.

We have a bond.

Sydney, a beautiful city. Visit it!

MAO ZEDONG HERE WE COME

The 25th floor of the JC Mandarin – OMG – the views of that city were phenomenal. What was interesting in China was that hugely poor areas butted right up against posh neighbourhoods, but that didn't stop us exploring and finding a tiny café nearby. Ordering with no English but with charades being the name of the game and done with curved fingers on the top of our heads to signify a cow. Actually, a bull but let's not get into semantics! We made our point(s) – no puns intended - and the lady brought out a carrot as a guide and we had Chinese beef and carrots and vegetables and it was - deeelicious!

Interestingly, I've just realised somewhat late in the day that I didn't think to ask them to make sure they had no MSG. I'm allergic to that - severely - and after an evening meal with that in it, I will wake up the next morning around 5am with the mother of all headaches that NOTHING will touch. On reflection, a simple place like that would not likely use it and use their own imagination and be tastier and better for it. I have, in the past, gone through three or four Ibuprofens, and three hours later the same again, and again, with nothing touching this POUNDING, and in the meantime lying on the bed with plumped up pillows, unable to read or watch tv or do anything constructive. Just hold my head while it pounds away. Or to be more accurate – one long continuous pound with no let-up in sight. I really wouldn't wish this on anyone.

When I made the connection, I also found out that MSG is an "excito-toxin" that NO-ONE, including the Chinese, should use because, although it is a food enhancer, it literally "excites your brain cells to death!" Who needs that?! Which also means the Chinese shouldn't use it in any of their foods and *if they're good at cooking it isn't needed*! Our favourite place in Toronto never used it…

I've been into plenty of good Chinese restaurants where they do not feel the need to enhance their food with MSG. They already mix whichever oils and garlic and ginger and whatever else they use. One day people WILL be up in arms when they realise they could have asked for it to be omitted and if enough people did that regularly we'd actually achieve protecting all our brains, and still having delicious foods, with innovative chefs.

Annatto is another one I have found I'm allergic to and even Michael has finally learnt to read labels. Annatto is used as a food colouring. Because it's found in nature it's deemed "good." What would be much better is the use of TURmeric (and please don't pronounce it as a tumour.) Read it properly as it has health-giving properties.

I also found out about Annatto the hard way (incidentally, it is the dyed orangey/deep yellow in some cheddar cheeses and is usually grated and then sprinkled on to some amazing dish like cauliflower cheese.) Again, instead of Annatto "they" could use paprika. It is good for us, deep red and, as far as I'm aware, doesn't have major side-effects.

But back to China.

We did what other tourists do and we visited the Shanghai Bund (pronounced with an "uh" sound). Part of this included the Antique Market. Big mistake because I love old pieces (that's why I married Michael!) The difference here was that all sellers were exhibiting their wares on a blanket on the floor like a mass of picnickers! We showed ONE man our interest in ONE item and, after looking down at it, I looked up and suddenly we were surrounded by about 12 sellers all proffering an old (supposedly) item, each seller up for haggling! It was quite the sight to behold!

Of course, we're clever (we think) and get the right price on two lovely items or at least what we're willing to pay – *that couldn't have been more inappropriate for a flight back home later.* What amounted to a super paperweight of a turtle with a duck on his back and another smaller animal on the duck's back making quite the sight. And weighing a small ton. Not the cleverest thing to buy! We were nuts. Two idiotic mice who should have known better.

And Michael wasn't much better (and neither was I.) He chose two battle-axes. Literally. He's just muttered under his breath something that I'm sure went "and I'm married to one right now." Where either of these are now is anyone's guess…Future trips and I will only buy scarves or a fabric bag or a small tablecloth. Lightweight will be the name of the game. We really should have known better.

Hannah was our guide and our driver was a man who didn't speak a word of English but we insisted on sharing a meal with him and that was an experience in itself! On beautiful white tablecloths we ordered, with Hannah's help, "sizzling bullfrog" and watched as our driver put a tiny but complete fish into his mouth (about 3" long and 1" wide) and proceeded to suck off the little flesh that was there: twa, twa, twa (that's the sound of spitting out quickly!) before promptly spitting the bones - not onto a side plate as we were expecting but onto the pristine white tablecloth, making a neat pyramid in the process. Unbelievable!

Looking back on that trip makes me realise just how much the Chinese make a meal out of nothing. Obviously here in Toronto and around the world one gets more meat and plenty of vegetables put together beautifully, and in such an appetising way. The same goes for meals in China and, for that matter, it also applies to Japan. Read "Japanese Women Don't Get Old Or Fat" by Naomi Moriyami. This book is wonderful to read, as are the recipes but what comes across in spades is the ingredients and amounts that go to feed a family.

They're such piddling amounts. Nothing like the mounds that go into a western meal. And there lies the rub - it's no wonder there is so much disease in the west when we put so much garbage western food into our own "systems." Not, I hasten to add, is Japanese or Chinese or any other Asian dish food garbage. I mean all the processed rubbish we buy in our supermarkets, masquerading as food. And I ADORE raw fish especially if it's wild (when we can afford it.)

I have learnt so much through my nutritional books that I've bought for interest/pleasure reading but have finally got my own mini library.

Anyway, once again back to China (!) and being with my Mouse.

Michael gets looked at everywhere we go. He's a mini-celebrity in that respect. It's his beard and moustache that are the "stars." Apparently Chinese don't/can't grow much facial hair. There was a rare exception to this that we met in Shanghai. A beggar in a back street one night. Yes, we felt safe before you wonder. This dark-haired man (they mostly dye their hair which I think is sad as I like silver/grey as it's rather becoming and a dye-job looks exactly like that – a dye-job, and usually badly obvious.) Anyhow…

He had a dark moustache – Fu Manchu style – AWESOME; the sides of it went down on both sides of his mouth about a foot! He could have been picked up and placed in a Charlie Chan movie and fitted right in! A memorable evening.

I went shopping as well and found a store with traditional Chinese dresses and looked for one with Lisa's name on it. And I found it, and she wore it at her Oxford Brookes

University Graduation Day. Red satin, full length, subtly patterned, traditional mandarin collar, sleeveless, and slit at the thigh. Absolutely Fabulous to use that comedy's title.

And a couple of years ago Lisa went out for the evening here in Toronto and had put her hair up and this red dress on and heels and a coat over her arm. I watched out of our window as she emerged. Now the entrance is at the side and we overlooked the main Church Street at that time and I watched her navigate across the street to grab a taxi.

A guy going across the lights on his bike twisted around and stayed that way for several seconds – his bike going south but his head facing north! And a car going the other way also suddenly was not watching the road properly. It was wonderful to watch! I've always said (although it must be noted here Lisa has an exceedingly good mind – not for nothing did she read Anthropology with Sociology) that if Cindy Crawford made a movie and had a younger sister in it (no, I have no idea whether Cindy C has a sister or not, but poetic licence could create one for a movie) then Lisa is tailor-made.

Back to China. We visited the Garden of the Humble Administrator which is also truly a sight. And we weren't even there when the delicate pink blossom was out in all its magnificence, creating a vision of loveliness with a true delicacy. Whilst in this wonderful garden we came across a lake – there are many bridges and near one of them was a woman in a little boat selling lotus pods to eat! We bought two. It is an acquired taste - we didn't acquire it! I did however take a photograph of a lotus-pod-seller which ended up gracing Mother's wall – and earning praise from those seeing it.

Whilst in Beijing we visited Mao Tse Dong's resting place/open coffin and laid the bunch of plastic flowers we had just bought specifically for this… and they then get gathered up after several bunches are laid, to be sold again and go round again!

When we first got to Beijing and were taken to our hotel just off Tiananmen Square, I thought I'd have a shower and then relax for a short while before going out again. I did this by switching on Chinese TV and who appears on the screen dubbed into Chinese and just proving one cannot fully get away, necessarily – Tony Bloody Blair!!! Yes, in case you're wondering – we're not fans…

Included in this Trip Of A Lifetime was going on an overnight train to Hohhot, the capital of Inner Mongolia. This will stay with me forever. It is just SO DIFFERENT!

My son Stuart used to tease me about using this word but it sums it up. There IS a magical quality being on the Grasslands of Inner Mongolia and I have taken photos and had them blown up slightly and they now hang along our stairs. One of them has three horses in it together with the *vastness* around them and it really speaks to me.

At one point we stayed for an hour or so with a family in their yurt and had some cheese. *This was no normal cheese*! Well, the colour was, and that's where the similarity ended. This was a piece of something that wouldn't look out of place in a Dr Who episode. Long, hard, knobbly and creamy yellow. About 3" long and half an inch wide. And one doesn't eat it in the normal way, either. One sucks it till it eventually breaks down. All very bizarre.

It's exciting to recall all these details and just how much these experiences enriched our lives. And they did.

We were given the Bridal Suite in this tiny village of yurts in the middle of nowhere, open plains. A magnificent and solid concrete "bed", permanently 'in situ', piled up with thin different coloured mattresses to attempt to alleviate what would otherwise be a Stone Aged bed. Wouldn't have looked out of place with the Flintstones! And the cold that night….!

We loosened our clothing but slept with them on, plus our coats plus blankets galore. That might give you some idea. Going to the loo in the middle of the night is not much fun. The blackened electric fittings in the bathroom left something to be desired. Not the place to have dodgy wiring!

Earlier that night we had been entertained by 300 men of the Army of Inner Mongolia and they were phenomenal. One lovely guy took off his peaked black hat and presented it to Michael. A lovely, sweet gesture. We still have it. I was offered a full length (well, on me it was!) army green coat with double brass buttons that I really appreciated. I had become very cold. In the middle of nowhere and late at night, with mountains not far away, it was f-f-freezing but I would not have missed this experience for the world. We both reminisce over this.

And the concert was about to begin!

Various people sang songs in Mongolian, and then the surprise of the night…Michael was asked if he'd like to sing anything! As he is a natural born raconteur and tutor and has done public speaking at political forums he didn't baulk at this at all and positively embraced it. This is fine for those who welcome it. I'M one of the faint-hearted who could not squeak, even as a Mouse singing, at least not in front of people. In the shower? OK.

Michael was introduced by the master of ceremonies as Yinguo (Yingwa) which is Chinese for Englishman, and Yinguo was going to sing for us. Michael sang The Lincolnshire Poacher and Land of Hope and Glory. Whilst he sang, I did go on stage behind him and took some shots, but it was dark and I didn't do very well, but Michael was in his element. Not that any Mongolian soldiers had a clue what he was singing about but it was very well received and a bloody good evening all round.

During this entertainment, we were presented with a bundle of grass, which we gratefully accepted. That doesn't sound like much. It wasn't a bunch of grass as we know it. This was a long bunch of well, more like wheat. As various people got up to sing, one singer passed the bundle onto another. At one point, someone rather important wanted to address his military Mongolian audience. Who should appear on the stage with his bundle of grassland wheat but Mr Mouse who scurried towards the rostrum just like a mouse (!) to present the speaker with the bundle. Much laughter all round!

Whilst here we got talking to different soldiers, like the one who lent me his coat. Suddenly I couldn't see my Mouse anymore. I started to wander around and found a large tent with a big circular table in it and people sitting all around it. Michael was standing up near the entrance but talking to them all, en masse. He'd been already offered – now it was my turn – to be offered fire-water in what looked like and was one of those little stiff foil ashtray-like dishes.

Now, I'm a teetotaler. There are three liquors that I like: Advocaat (made with eggs and lemonade added), Kahlúa and Bailey's Cream. This firewater was NONE of the above, but "I took it like a man" and took a sip, having just had a brilliant idea a split second before…Immediately I grimaced, which everyone loved - even if I hated that firewater (medicine would have been preferable!) I followed that with pulling Michael's beard towards me and planting one on his mouth in an attempt to get rid of the taste and inject some humour at the same time. He also yelped when I pulled his beard towards me and they loved that too!

It worked on every level and the people liked it and laughed. One could tell drinking was not me! Needless to say, I wasn't offered any more, TG!

We left the next day and travelled the countryside and discovered a pig farm! I captured this too on film, now also hanging on our stairs. I don't know if it was just the pleasant warm day or the fact that the buildings, as crumbling as they were, were already a soft pale mustard colour but it was all rather lovely and a feeling I'd stepped into a slightly mustardy sepia-toned picture. And the pigs go very well in it!

On the way back to Hohhot we come across a novel way of separating the chaff from the wheat. The farmer spreads it across the country road and every time a vehicle drives along it drives over the wheat separating it more and more. Bread starting life very differently!

Whilst in China we visited a biscuit stall in a market. I can't remember how that came about but their biscuits are quite "different." And rather bland. There's that word again that Stuart remarked on. Their biscuits are basically no more than flour, water and sugar, not quite the glue that we used to make as paste for our scrap albums but close!

We also visited our guide Hannah's boyfriend's home. Boy, that's an education in itself! A wonderful one and SO very "different" from ANYTHING in the West.

We had driven through the city of Hohhot with our driver and Hannah. She asked us if we'd like to visit her boyfriend's parents' home and naturally we said yes. What a wonderful education it might be - and it was, on every level!

We drove down this very dusty street with houses that only have their outer wall showing and basically it's like a line of walls along the street. There's no "kerb appeal" per se. We arrived at the abode and turned in. The driveway was an entrance between two walls leading us directly into a courtyard. Not dissimilar to how some pubs are set up in England where the coach used to drive into the courtyard (Fishpool St, St Albans comes to mind and with the Red Lion Hotel having the same coach entrance from yesteryear.)

We drove into this ancient courtyard where the house, actually a bungalow, is situated at the back in the middle, in its most basic form. This is no British bungalow. There are three rooms from left to right. It's quite simply not a bungalow in any western form whatsoever.

On the left was the second bedroom, very large with the ubiquitous stone bed (same as in the yurts) built in the centre and against the back wall. There was the parents' bedroom on the right - an equally large room, and in between are two small rooms, and I mean small. The front is the sitting room if you will but all it has is a small square table and two or three chairs and no sofa. This was just the "first room" one came to. It was only about 8' square. The room behind it would be laughingly referred to as a kitchen. It sounds mean but many people in China have similarly tiny kitchens like this one and I've seen the same size in Istanbul and they make brilliant meals out of them! Quite amazing! I suppose if one is creative and never had a western kitchen one can still "produce" because one only knows what one is used to. If kitchens were supplied in England like these there would be an outcry. After THIS kitchen anything is an improvement!

This kitchen was about the size of one-and-a-half ordinary British bathrooms and I'm being generous! And a narrow high-up shelf, about four feet off the floor, for implements, and two gas/electric rings. Talk about basic student accommodation! Actually, it would make all western students very appreciative of what they DO have!

Chapter 10

MICE ON THE MOVE

B uxton lies in Derbyshire, UK. It is the "Bath of the North" and really is a very lovely town. And it is where Mr and Mrs Mouse went to live for four years so that I could be closer to the only brother I had left, him living in South Manchester – and out of the expensive South.

"Mice on the move" is indeed a very appropriate title when we looked into relocating big time. Funnily enough Michael and I had a very early date in Buxton too, seated on the slopes of the Town Hall Grounds very close to where we would buy our second house, but we didn't know that yet!

Early in 2003 Mr Mouse was made redundant - and was no longer editor of Asian Communications. Time to start freelancing.

We loved the countryside of Derbyshire. We met the absolutely lovely and charming Liz and Derrick from the guest house. And there was - and is - a tattoo.

My tattoo is twenty years old as of 2024! It was performed on a rare day in Buxton – boiling hot (with the tattoo gleaming raw in the sun!) A cute little mouse sunbathing with the speech bubble removed because "he" was dreaming of cheese and they don't eat cheese, courtesy of daughter Lisa who used to have the odd rat. Also, less "needling!" Pun intended.

My Mother had her own views on tattoos. When we were first visiting again, a little while after it had been done and luckily after it had settled as it had looked rather red and unhappy initially, gleaming bright, raw red in the sunshine! I was in Mother's downstairs cloakroom and about to close the door to the cloakroom when she suddenly appeared at the doorway of the actual washroom and as she was long-sighted said something on the lines of "tattoos look so cheap and common" and in the same moment slapped both her arms where many people have had their tattoos done. On the high part of both arms. She followed this up with "it is a transfer, isn't it?" almost beseechingly, and praying she was right. She wasn't, but I looked at her and said "yes, Mother" in a withering way. She wanted to hear it was a transfer. So I said yes, and that was it. I think she just blocked it out of her mind, and to make it easier from thereonin I wore either capped T-shirts or even cardigans, and nothing sleeveless so it would all be forgotten. She never mentioned it again and neither did I. Part of me wished I'd introduced her to this sweet little male mouse. I don't know why he's male. There's no real reason why he should be, any more than boats or ships are "she" but every night (almost) when we go to bed Michael kisses my mouse 11 times, in the Summer when he has access. I like odd numbers and 11 is a favourite. We joke about which part he's kissing in the dark. Whether it's the mouse's belly-button or missing him altogether! It's a lovely end to the day, whichever way it's done.

I've since toyed with the idea of having a little lizard on one of my feet as though "he" (there we go again with assumptions!) is climbing up my foot but three things put me off that: one) is that a foot is bonier and thus apparently much more painful, two) my feet are not attractive any more as they're swollen and that for some reason is where I'd want it. I still like the idea of a lizard scampering up the leg like they do on a tree.

Third) is that I read a true story a year or so ago about a man who was talking to a younger man. The younger one said he thought it was against G-d to desecrate the body. The older man said yes, it was, but then bared his arm to show that he, too, had a tattoo, but one not of his choosing but foisted on him in the concentration camp he was in during the war and being Jewish he had been permanently, indelibly, marked – for life. All these reasons have stopped me adding the lizard. I love lizards.

In Sydney we had a rather large (by normal standards) lizard of about 15" long and 3" wide at his middle. Obviously middle-aged spread! He was called the blue-tongued lizard as he had an electric-blue-coloured tongue. An absolutely brilliant vibrant blue that darted out when catching his lunch. I remember "him" with fondness and would have liked to remember him in memoriam with the tattoo but I also remember the pain! People have since asked me if Michael would do the same for me and have a Mouse tattooed on him. I've said "Ha, no way!" His pain threshold could never handle it. I've yet to be proved wrong on that…

LISA'S BIG DAY

Nottingham was the venue for Lisa's 21st birthday and this time we did know that her father was flying in for the birthday! You can't pretend twice! Again, 20,000 km from Queensland!

I made a dark chocolate cake, enough for everyone; Lisa's then boyfriend Jai, a Pharmacy student, also came. And I decorated the cake with all Lisa's names: in the clock positions: 12 noon had Lisa, 3pm had Princess Possum courtesy of her Dad, and at the 6.30 pm slot I had/have my own special name for her, MLH*** (my own special greeting to Lisa) while Stuart used to combine her name plus her surname and got Leebees at 8.45 slot. It did look wonderful and tasted good, if I'm allowed to say so (it was, says Mr Mouse.)

Everyone had a lovely time and Lisa's Dad Gerry himself complimented me on the rich dark chocolate cake. Well, I had pulled all the stops out for that one. My goodness, eighteen years ago.

Do take photos. It all goes so quickly. A cliche, but that's why they are cliches.

HEALTH PROBLEMS LOOM...

My leg pains started when we moved to Buxton, a year away. Fibromyalgia is odd where I'm concerned as it doesn't make me think of doing something/saying something that occurs automatically with others. It's funny, IF I'm watching a scenario being played out it WILL occur to me what the other person should be saying precisely BECAUSE I'm not "in it." I'm able to see both sides as *an outsider*. Suddenly when it involves me directly I don't always say what should be said. That can be very frustrating. Lisa has been able to help here and there with it too (as has Stuart but he has done so much more often) although she incurred my wrath three years ago when she forewarned her friends prior to bringing them to the apartment that I had fibromyalgia and that it affected the memory. It made me come across as somewhat senile and it made them compartmentalise me. When people are not forewarned, I am much better and if I lose my train of thought, well, I'm like anyone else and appreciate the odd prompting.

FROM BUXTON TO TORONTO

Going back to London would have been a rabbit-hutch/shoebox existence. We did our research and made two reconnaissances to Toronto and read extensively (Neil said we'd gone "on a whim" but he was wrong.)

We bought a condo in downtown Toronto. The Canadian rules are that after the course one has to leave the country and re-enter when awaiting one's Permanent Resident Status.

After Michael's course, we were going to go and look at New York. I've been there before and loved it. Michael hasn't. He also had a mistrust of it…having never been! I DO feel one can have a "good vibe" and give off something. That way one isn't necessarily at risk.

Anyway, we had to go somewhere and we were advised to go back to England where we at least had a base. We were told that gaining what is called Permanent Residence status could take weeks - and living in a hotel in New York would be very expensive. Our old home at this point hadn't sold. So we went back to Buxton. Although what we found wasn't what we expected. The boiler decided to play "Camille" and do the dying swan act and most of the heating went off except in the hall by the front door. We still had TV but having only four stations in the High Peak area of Buxton and freezing one's tits off in the dining room didn't appeal at all. So we decamped to the hall where there was a small radiator on high. AND NOTHING ELSE!

This was Christmas of 2008 and I had actually thought we might spend Christmas lunch over at my mother's. That wasn't to be either.

Our house was cold, bleak and very soulless. Its heart had left when we did and the only good thing about coming back to it was the fact I was going to see my mother and brother on this trip I rang up Mother thinking we would get invited to Christmas lunch. We are not Christian but we still have a turkey dinner like everyone else.

Well, not this Christmas we weren't! They had been invited to Christmas lunch elsewhere. Mother said she didn't feel she could invite us to someone else's Christmas lunch and we understood that. So instead we walked over to the relatively new Sainsbury's in the market square and found some "basics." Certainly not Christmas fare: peanut butter, juice, coffee, cream, some fruit and biscuits, I think. And we huddled around the only radiator that hadn't yet seized up! This was the hall radiator so we didn't even have the TV although, with only four channels, we weren't missing much. We read books; we always fall back on books.

Eventually, we gained Permanent Residence status from the Canadian High Commission in London. We took a flight back to Toronto, not in limbo any longer.

Chapter 11

CANADA - "THE GOOD LIFE" OR OUR VERSION: BUT NOW IT'S MORE EXPENSIVE THAN EVER.

We first came on one good reconnaissance to Toronto in September 2005. A wonderful trip. One of two trips. This first was done without the stress of my Mother knowing that we were visiting, so we rang them beforehand to wish them a Happy Rosh Hashana (New Year) so that there would be several days of no calls but with nothing seemingly amiss. It worked. Less stress all round.

It's funny going to a city/town where you end up passing what will become your local stores but one doesn't realise it at the time. This first trip to Toronto was super. It was lovely listening to the Canadian accent although I have to admit I cannot tell the difference between Canadian and American accents but I am sure the difference is very much there. Not dissimilar to between Aussie and Kiwi!

At one point we were standing at an intersection on Queen West at Augusta St, and asked the way of a Chinese guy standing nearby. He told us and then added "Welcome to Canada!" A lovely addition that doesn't seem to happen in England. Yes, I know I'm generalising but I just don't think it happens a lot back there. I could be wrong, that does happen!

The weather, yes, Brits talk about the weather a lot, unfortunately, and for the moment I'm no different. Toronto's is much better. When it does rain it doesn't go on incessantly. It gets over itself quickly and bright sunshine comes out afterwards and stays here! (I've now got used to the fact that the world's weather IS changing, HAS changed and it is now MUCH WETTER!)

Shopping is fun in Toronto and they have two wonderful markets here, Kensington and St Lawrence. Kensington is a village with a very Bohemian vibe and with Rastafarians, Chileans and Portuguese running the fish and cheese stores (they're "stores" here not shops) along with Hungarians who run a crepe restaurant with the most delicious savoury crepes. Colourful characters abound of which Michael is one. No, I'm not biased, well, yes I am, but he was a character in China where he was virtually the only bearded male as earlier stated.

On the second reconnaissance we came with a mission: to buy an apartment. Technically a condo, but I love the European word "apartment" as opposed to that ugly English word they use in the UK – a "flat!" A flat what?! An "apartment" sounds so much nicer, classier, and sophisticated. Although I must admit some of the apartments we saw left much to be desired. We saw one that had a small balcony. This was only about 5-6' long and that's being generous. What screwed this balcony up completely was a generator of some sort taking up HALF that precious area in the first place!

We were also shown a wonderful apartment on the 25th floor of a block somewhere around Eglinton and Yonge which was too far out of the Downtown core for my liking (shame but one learns in retrospect.) The views were panoramic, which I love but the lounge was teeny. For a space that one is going to live in more than the bedrooms, that was odd, wrong and unfair of the architect – but as I've always said, nine times out of ten the architect would never live in one of their own (often) crummy designs, but we have to find a way to make them work. This did have a very spacious terrace and we should have bought it…

Hindsight is wonderful. I'm going to contradict myself now. The lounge was only small because I wasn't used to these apartments over here. It was "adequate." We should have bought that place…

I am very lucky indeed when it comes to "house-hunting." Or apartment/condo-hunting. Michael doesn't have a great amount to say on the subject and TG! He does not have design awareness and that is --- B L I S S! If I was married to a style guru I'd have to compromise – but I'm not and I don't have to and it *does* make things simpler. The downside to that is that if I do make some exciting change he usually doesn't fully appreciate it – but "them's the breaks."

The old/first apartment was lovely and bigger than this and faced west which is exactly what I wanted. I say "I" because Michael Mouse really couldn't care less where he lived and as he is no style guru I get to have carte blanche for the décor! I recommend to anyone to marry someone who doesn't have particular tastes! It's so much easier than having to compromise!

(When we lived in St Albans, Herts, UK, I painted the brick hearth wall over the hearth oven, a Raeburn, a lesser-known cousin of the Aga and an area about 8' wide and

10' high. THREE WEEKS LATER he comes home from work one day and asks, "have you painted that?!" Ah, my wonderful unobservant Mouse; but it does allow me a free hand and that is worth *everything*!)

STUART'S IMMIGRATION ANGUISH

We were wanting to live elsewhere, and outside England where we could actually afford (Mr Mouse here: we did not want to move back to London as ending up in a shoebox or rabbit hutch did not somehow appeal...)

Oddly enough, we first thought of Greece because of Michael being a Greek scholar but it is in the EU and suffering accordingly. And as Stuart pointed out to Michael, "Hazel will be really cut off if everyone's speaking Greek around her the whole time." I couldn't agree more.

And with that comment the scene shifted to looking elsewhere. Then all three of us (Lisa was away at university) were sitting in Buxton one day and watching "A Place In The Sun" and it was Toronto! This couple were looking in Toronto and it was summer and we have hot summers although Canada is only known for its winters. One of the reasons I loved it there. And they have TIFF here, the Toronto International Film Festival which Stuart is interested in and wanted initially to be part of (he was at the time a freelance photographer here in Toronto and is still available for commissions.)

Michael went online and got sent emigration papers for Canada. OMG! The ton of papers that arrived had to be seen to be believed and when one had filled them all in, and

115

checked them all, it was finally sent off. Only to be returned when one paper wasn't done properly. This can happen again and again. When it is officially correct – and you are accepted into the waiting queue - one finds out the waiting list is three-and-a-half years LONG! We thought *that* was long! Two mice and her one child out of two getting into a three-year queue. Then we found out that those from India have a seven-year queue, and realised we were lucky!

Stuart sat with us at the dining table as Michael went through the mountain of paperwork that had to be filled in for the Canadian High Commission. It was a MAMMOTH task and I was mightily impressed with Michael diligently going through it all with a fine-toothed comb. I found it overwhelming, and I wasn't the one ploughing through it!

Then the REALLY bad news came. Lisa, who at the time wasn't perturbed one way or another, got on the application form automatically because she was under 22 at the time. Stuart, however, was over 22 at a mere 23 and ineligible! The look of horror on his face is one I shall never forget: "You mean I have to apply for emigration completely on my own?"

It's a very daunting thing for a younger man. He had his degree but didn't have enough points being so young. There must be many like him that just haven't acquired the points because they haven't been out in the workforce long enough.

With this, Stuart decided to take his then girlfriend Sara to Australia and show her where he was born, and work their way around the country to some degree, stopping longer if they liked somewhere.

They did all that and went grape-picking in wine country. The Barossa Valley or Hunter Valley, I can never remember which; possibly both! Then they made their way to Melbourne and liked it a lot. They stayed there about a year and then Sara returned to England to study more for a speech therapist's degree and sometime after that they broke up.

GAY PRIDE

Whilst the sisters gave us grief all week and never letting up (see next chapter) we did get some respite, if one can call it that, during Pride Week!

Our condo block stood at the corner of Church and Charles Streets and part of the procession went down Church! And our sunroom looked directly onto Church… and we had ringside seats - for all kinds of people and these included transvestites wearing the most magnificent 18th century ballroom type dresses and looking absolutely wonderful. Could easily put many women to shame and their FIGURES - talk about me being envious!

In amongst these was everyone else, a real mixture, and, at one point men walking three abreast, and all nude except for their shoes! Talk about getting an eyeful! Curiosity would have liked binoculars, but we were close enough! We actually saw more from above than we would have at ground level.

I must add that living here in the Gay Village we felt very safe. As our neighbour John, of John and Wendy mentioned earlier, "if one ever got attacked, people would run to help you, not away from you."

They were all lovely people, including Jim Ayerst, our neighbour in the next building on Charles St East. He also had his dog, Herschel(!) named after Herschel's previous owner who had died but asked Jim to look after him and Jim did so, very willingly.

Jim often wore an orange beanie. Jim was gay, but not overly camp and came over regularly and had coffee with us. He loved all Michael Mouse's dirty jokes and often told us his too!

He loved the fact that the orange beanie looked to Michael as if Jim was wearing an orange condom on his head! I think he dined out on that one thereafter. He's now gone but never forgotten but he did leave us one lovely London story:

He was based in London around 1975. Walking across the concourse of Paddington Station, he saw someone who was obviously a friend of his family. He went up to her and said "Hello, I'm Frankie and Freda's boy from Ontario." She replied "I'm Margaret Thatcher!" Jim ran off back to his carriage and closed the curtains out of sheer embarrassment.

THE GREAT FURNITURE ACQUISITION!

I'm referring to having a nose and keeping an eye out for second-hand furniture. There's a buzz that comes from the "chase" or merely just walking along with one's husband, or whomever you're with and you spy a piece of furniture that has been put out by a home- or condo-owner because they no longer want it for whatever reason.

Michael was learning well from me! Michael had been coming back from RABBA, a chain of general stores but, better than that, open 24/7 all over the place. With hot food available too. Very handy places! And very pleasant inside. Wish they'd go international!

Well, Michael Mouse was observant (for once in his life!) He walked past a condo block with a wide driveway and, plonked at the side of it, was an extra-long double chest of drawers (approximately 5' long and 2' deep and about 3' high and a double set of four drawers.) Very, very handy and no sign of wormwood. Michael Mouse came home and told me about it so naturally and instantly I wanted to go and see it and maybe bring it home!

Which is exactly what happened, but Oh My Goodness! Michael's hands, as everyone will be aware by now, are arthritic, so his ability to grab is limited and that's being nice! We both went to either end and grabbed hold. And we shuffled and shuffled and shuffled, for about three feet, and that's being generous too! Then we paused because being Mice, it is tiring, and going that slowly we are *inching* our way home, literally! Home is very close, like a quarter of a block. We could SEE our apartment, but getting there was going to be at the proverbial snail's pace.

I have to add here, that I had imagined what we looked like doing this, and that gave me the giggles, which in turn weakens my muscles, and I can't do anything, so there were stops ALL along. Like every six inches! That said, Michael got me stopping often, too, as his big arthritic hands couldn't cope for very long at all.

Then a man took pity on us and, being broad, picked it up with one hand at one end and one at the other and took it to the traffic lights and across and onto Church St!!!! We thanked him profusely. We have found so many wonderful people in Toronto. It's a very welcoming city.

By now, we were on the street that our condo was on (Church Street) but the main entrance was on Charles St East, so we still had a little way to go, still painfully slow, about 250 ft. Then a couple went past, overtaking us. Not hard as we're back to snail's pace and they walked in front of us for about six steps if that. Guilt must have got to them and they turned around and offered to help which we very appreciatively took. We almost ran the rest of the way with suddenly four people doing it with what was two pathetic mice prior.

At our corner they bid us goodnight and we thanked them profusely. Then we had just 10' to go to our main front doors and then to the elevators. After which, we were at our floor and then had about 20' to our front door and another roughly 30' to our bedroom where it found its final resting place! K n a c k e r e d!

MISTS: TORONTO, SYDNEY, MACCLESFIELD. I LOVE THEM ALL!

It snowed all night and it is still snowing today. It has barely stopped and it's 11.30 am and it is soooooo beautiful. I am at the age where I prefer (mostly) to look out at it from behind glass! When it was snowing earlier it was actually snowing *horizontally* – something I've never witnessed till arriving here. And facing into a blizzard, wow, that's something else! Bitingly cold yet an experience I still wouldn't change. It also makes one fully appreciate milder weather. Don't get me wrong: my favourite two seasons are Autumn (Fall) and Winter in all their wonder and utter beauty.

There is a delicate "sea of mist" across the whole vista with a whole magical quality to it. I adore mist, hanging as it does, creating a wonderful, sometimes eerie quality about it yet utterly enchanting. Worthy of a good film maker to capture it! Yes, I have Stuart in mind suddenly and he's very good at interpreting.

(I *must stop* buying this rubbish cherry cake that I'm nibbling in between typing! It's rubbish but I like it but I'm *not* buying it again for a long time!)

No...... I've found other "rubbish" instead!

We never had mists in Sydney (before Mr Mouse's time!) and I did miss them. It's actually an attraction in England for me especially during Winter when England can look very gloomy.

When one sees Winter depicted in modern movies in England it is "done" with the right conditions. A lovely house/cottage/terrace/or mansion and thus cosy and with all the right implements, making it a very good ad for visiting but reality hits when those things are missing.

Mr Mouse and I watch TV programmes like House Hunters International and if they're in England it is the best way to see it for an hour, without a budget and without the weather intruding. Wonderful having a nosey around other properties and my itching to tell people how they could improve a place with only "tweaks" and being budget conscious.

In Sydney as I stated, we never got snow and I missed that but West of Sydney, in the Blue Mountains, the scenery is absolutely magnificent.

The Three Sisters comes to mind (and nothing to do with two sisters we meet later on.) These are Three Sisters so named because they are three magnificent peaks seen from a lookout point, and they are each slightly smaller than the last, and absolutely covered in trees, leaves and growth. And a view as far as the eye can see. Quite phenomenal.

Digressing as I do.

My Mouse says that you can make a small fortune in Canada: just as long as you start with a large one!

Chapter 12

THE UGLY SISTERS - AND NO FAIRY-TALE
OR
TORONTO'S 51ST
PRECINCT TO THE RESCUE!

O ur lives were about to be turned upside down by two middle-aged women who were sisters. I shall call them Nancy and Heather. They were friendly with us at first. We still have a photo of Michael standing with them up on the roof of the condo block one beautiful afternoon.

We didn't see them very often because there were 17 floors and seven apartments on each floor so one could go for weeks without seeing a particular person.

We got the initial complaint in October 2008. Security had two wonderful Sri Lankan men on duty who alternated shifts and both were very sweet.

The first most farcical call came from security one Saturday morning when we weren't even in:

"Are you using a hammer?" he asked me. He'd rung my cellphone as obviously the landline hadn't been answered. "No," I said, "we've just ordered our breakfast here at Paddington's Pump (part of the St Lawrence Market down on Front Street and nowhere near our then condo) and the only 'person' in the apartment is Holly, our Jack Russell. And if she's using a hammer, it's a World's First!"

Very soon after our first complaint we got a letter from Mr G S at the management's HQ who, ALTHOUGH HE'D NEVER MET US, AND STILL DIDN'T DO THE COURTESY FACTOR FIRST, sent us a letter: "if you do not stop banging, knocking, and moving furniture etc" they would take matters further and that we should respect our neighbours and not make any noises…We had *NEVER EVER EVER* made such noises and if you saw how Michael moves you'd see why!

It was Michael who devised, as only his sense of humour can, a special name for these people: the Tactical Weapons Advisory Team, aka TWATs…Yep, that's Mr Mouse's sense of humour.

Every single time they accused us we had been either in bed watching TV, or watching TV in the lounge or at our respective computers or preparing dinner in the kitchen or…out!

Unbelievable! This started to be a regular occurrence. Too regular for the likes of our very sweet security men/concierges. Every single week, several times and mostly at night we would get a phone call from security to ask if we were banging something or moving furniture around. Of course, we never were. IF we ever did it was during the week, and during the day, when making any kind of noise that might disturb the neighbours *was allowed*. And most of the time we didn't anyway. That didn't get believed by the "sisters" *but they never had the decency to check our floor themselves.*

They would send security up who would apparently listen outside our door for anything untoward. All they often heard was either the tv or washing up dishes. Normal sounds. We didn't use the dishwasher unless we were four

(my Mouse shares dishwashing duties but he's taken a long time to get good at it! I should retract that - he's never been "good" at it!)

This didn't stop and the sisters went on making complaints every single week and often in the evenings. It was to be a while before they started doing the same during the day, usually on a weekend. Sometimes when we were out; we found out from security staff later. From what I have read, when couples go through any kind of trauma they either buckle under the stress and maybe separate or they just find strength in each other and maybe the others around them. We were in the latter category.

(The funny thing here is that our old condo block is a very solidly built block and when an earthquake hit in northern Montreal we felt it here in Toronto. Both Michael and I were sitting at the table laughingly called a dining table but usually being utilised as a desk by both of us. At right angles to each other and we held hands and made Mouse faces when the earthquake shook.

It was amazing. The whole room gently vibrated but nothing fell off the walls or dresser and they could so easily have done so. It did tell me just how strongly the building had been constructed. It also made us realise (although we had already realised this) that this whole building was very solid. We might hear our neighbours opposite go out because all our front doors are wooden and that's where the noise DOES escape from. But hearing sounds from the next floor up or down? No.

What one hears directly above is not necessarily from directly above. Sound is distorted. But, oh yes they were if you were one of the sisters! They sent security up, they called the police out on us, but they never came up themselves: *That* was the most annoying part.

And still the complaints kept coming. Something like six months into this the police visits started. Those poor police from the Toronto 51st Precinct – well let's just say Michael now remembers many names: Brewer, Garda, Gillan, Holt, Holt J, Kalms, Kay, Mafano, Patton, Prevost, Recette, Scott, Snow, Waugh, Zborowski and several others we slept through (and not *with*, as one of our gay friends mischievously interpreted it!) There was even Linda Nilsson at 51st Precinct reception desk who heard us say we were being accused of making noise in our condo. She took one look at Mr and Mrs Decrepit – at which point she burst out laughing. They were all wonderful but what a waste of their time!

In all, the knocking on the ceiling added up to 1,249 times and went into a complete second year!

The police would arrive shortly after being called at let's say 11.15 pm and Holly, our Jack Russell, would get all excited. As a matter of fact, I found out that when these two officers (they always travel in pairs – very sensibly) arrived, they stand outside the door about 5' away to see if there's any real noise emanating from our apartment – and so as not to start Holly off. There was never anything remotely newsworthy and when we had been in the lounge there was the tv sound but it wasn't disturbing OUR floor let alone the floor beneath! Sometimes there was even less sound if we were on our respective laptops. As I said to one of the cops one evening, if we could hear downstairs and vice versa it would make for a very poorly built building and it wouldn't be as popular as it is. And it is.

The knocking continued on many evenings. One particular evening we actually had security in our apartment talking to us ABOUT the sisters when they started knocking on their ceiling which is our floor! It's lucky it never drove us apart. Those officers went down to tell the sisters it wasn't us but it didn't change them one iota. Michael and I are very strong **but we bitterly resented – and still resent - the fact that Mr G S of the condo board management NEVER came to see us for him to realise we were NEVER the culprits.** In fact, maybe that is WHY he never visited!? - in case the knocking started while he was with us and we would have used him as a witness to us being totally blameless! And we were/are out of pocket to the tune of seventeen thousand dollars because we retained a lawyer. What a waste. And, that goes for Mediation. The man in charge of that said "you're not alone," and we never saw him again!

Michael and I were told to keep a file and so we did. This went on for TWO full YEARS as previously stated! Then we were asked to go to mediation! Now, it's all very well going to mediation IF you're one half of the equation but we were NOT the culprits in the first place. And security and the police knew this. And it cost us $1,500 to front up to this farcical meeting and Mr Jones, I shall call him, was the mediator.

I had had a very good idea of how to prove it wasn't us. I suggested during the mediation process that any afternoon when one of the sisters returned home, whichever they preferred, instead of going straight to their apartment would come to ours instead. They could have a coffee or whatever we were having and just "BE." I followed this with, "then when the so-called noises from directly above you start, you ring the sister up here with us and say 'are those two doing anything?'" And she would have to say "No, they're making dinner, or watching TV, or on their respective computers OR whatever the hell we were bloody well doing." But they wouldn't be able to say more. I was half way though my point when Sister A, the shorter of them both, said "but you wouldn't be MAKING the noise then," and I said, "that's right I wouldn't be therefore my point would have been made" but at that point the mediator cut in and didn't even agree it would be a brilliant idea.

This was a very stressful time for my Mouse and me. Luckily it wasn't stressful all the time or we'd have gone stark raving mad. We had sympathy from our immediate neighbours John and Wendy. A sweet couple who lived directly opposite us in the corridor and who even wrote a letter of full support in case the authorities ever needed it.

Another time we had them over for dinner in the solarium and, lo and behold, we were interrupted by knocking on our floor *again*, through sitting at the meal with them eating, and knock, knock, knock, proving once again it was not us who were the culprits.

Around the time of the mediation we got a letter from their lawyers that claimed who was making most of the noises and I read to my horror that I was being singled out! I was the one supposedly moving furniture around at night, using a hammer, and generally supposedly driving the sisters mad. *They didn't need any help in that department!* When one set of cops visited them one evening the cops afterwards came up to us. As usual I opened the door not expecting two cops. You don't *expect* two cops outside your door. You expect a neighbour, or security, or even a family member.

We did get in touch with an organisation called St Stephen's Conflict Resolution Service. A young man and a young woman discussed the situation with the sisters and us. The young man then wrote to me: **"Hazel, I hear your pain. You are being accused of making noise that bears no relation to where/what you are doing at the time."** Game, set and match!

I had to hold Holly who used to get all excited but I asked the cops to come in so we wouldn't disturb our neighbours. They could see behind me to a darkened lounge which immediately told them we've retired for the night. Then they came into the darkened lounge and I immediately put the light on and they started telling me that they've had complaints. It's almost farcical because initially they don't want to say who the complaint is from, as is always the case in these things but with us it CAN only be these two "sisters," and we would tell them this. We must have been discussed down at the 51st Precinct, making interesting "fodder." In the gay village, as we all are here in this condo, and with at least 1/3 being gay couples, plus a few lesbians. We've never had complaints before and everyone on our floor knew us. Two gay gentlemen lived on both sides of our apartment and if we'd been making noises, they and John and Wendy would have been the FIRST to hear!

We even got a letter complaining about us, from the sisters --- when we had finally left the condo two months earlier!

Chapter 13

MY MOTHER, RR, RUTH ROLAND

Today of all days, here in Toronto, I'm starting to write this on Thursday, September 11th (Oy!) 2014. (I say "oy" because I remember September 11th, 2001 and the Twin Towers. For many you'll have to google it). And this month, on 23rd/24th, will be the third anniversary since my Mother died.

Unbelievable to feel she has gone. I do hope she is with Daddy, Russell and Cedric. I wasn't with her either when she died, this time being in Canada. If I'd have flown out that Saturday night I'd have landed Sunday morning and Neil would have taken me to see her body. I KNOW from our (hers and my) past that she would have said, "don't see me dead, remember me as I was, you don't want that kind of memory." So I flew out Sunday evening and arrived Monday morning. So G-d was very clever (as he always is) and had Lisa wanting to go - and going(!) – to a party that night. Which I thought was very wrong at the time but a blessing in disguise, aren't they all? And I didn't think to chastise her; I was a bit preoccupied.

At three months past her 90th birthday in June 2011 is when she actually went. I'm just so glad Michael Mouse and I worked out to do our trip and we had seen her in the April beforehand. And it was planned as a complete surprise with only Neil knowing.

It was lovely, really. I came around the morning room door and she was sitting on the sofa. Sitting upright and white hair done up in her signature bun. And she beamed with pleasure. It was so good to see her. I knew she was very old by this time but it still doesn't occur to me that I might be seeing someone for the last time. It's always a surprise even when it isn't, if you know what I mean.

When I was back here, three months later in September in Toronto I finally got *that* call from Neil. "This is the call you've been dreading," said Neil as soon as I picked up the phone. I felt quite calm really. My whole original family have gone now and, oddly enough, I'm an orphan. (Not an original idea but still appropriate). Odd to think of that at my age, but it's still true.

There must be a heaven. Or another planet that's only attainable through the passage of death because I feel we *have* to all meet up; otherwise what would be the point of our "being?" I have felt this for a very long time. It is the only way I can put it. But I'm doing it again, and going off on a tangent. I'm very good at that!

The first time that I'm aware of Mother having the chance to "experience" anything from "the other side" was years ago in 1982 when she was 60. She awoke at 3 am with the top of her head burning hot and woke Theo who went and got her a cold damp flannel. She put it on her head, and it dried out almost instantaneously. Then he did it again, and several times after that. It took about ten minutes for her head to stop being so hot.

Three days later Interpol had contacted the local Sale police in Manchester and they sent two policemen around to the house. "Do you have a son Robert Cedric Ward?"

(They sometimes get the names wrongly reversed.) Theo had answered the door and Mother's worst nightmare just became true.

The coroner's report came much later but he had "passed" three days earlier at 3 am when Mother's head was burning hot…I can remember it as clear as yesterday. She felt differently after that about the "hereafter."

I didn't know till I read a transcribed diary that she had spoken into a mike that Neil set up for her (this life of hers was before she had fully exploited her extreme brilliance as a painter that even LS Lowry, the late, great Manchester painter, acknowledged.) She had wanted to become a doctor! I never knew this until I read Neil's transcript of the recording. It obviously wasn't meant to be. She has paintings EVERYWHERE and all over the world. Also one, at least, on permanent display in Lodz (pronounced Woodj) in Poland.

She was very modern for her time. Before she painted so much, earlier on she set herself up as an interior designer specialising in kitchens. Our kitchen at Brooklands Road, Sale, was a perfect case in point. Before we first moved there the back rooms were a warren of three little rooms with none looking out onto the beautiful expanse of lawn and flowers that Theo grew. He loved gardening and Mother loved painting the flowers that he grew.

Well, Theo and Mother bought the house, even with this rabbit warren. Not having permission to do anything substantial to the house didn't stop Mother! Oh, No! And she went further than most and hired a man with one of those bloody enormous concrete balls that swung into the back wall of the house and helped "create" the start of the picture window that would go exactly where the ball went!

Yes, planning permission was granted! This was around half a century ago…!

She wasted no time in putting in two picture windows. One at the side which took in the flower beds there and a larger one overlooking the back, maximising the light and making a very decent size "morning room," something like 12' square.

The small room adjacent had originally been the morning room - and totally illogical that way round to mother's thinking. Mother switched them. Hers was not to have the typical American huge kitchen with an island but an easy-for-them smaller kitchen where they could produce *without* the distraction of other people!

Mother brought all her knowledge of kitchens to the fore with cupboards, for example, that were slightly longer than the bottom part of the cupboard; this way the door "became" the handle. Several companies now do this. She was the forerunner for this. For mixing a pudding there was a cupboard immediately next to the stove but lower. Sensibly designed so that if one is beating in a bowl with a wooden spoon one's elbows are not uncomfortably high as they often are.

One thing she did that would horrify most people was to rip out the old fireplaces and bury them…under concrete in the front entrance that she had created so there was parking…and a graveyard of fireplaces immediately beneath! They could be extracted as they won't have moved!!!

The only consolation here was that this was a twentieth-century house and not a Victorian or Edwardian house. Even Neil would have been up in arms about that!

In the morning room was my favourite carpet. A very clever mix of charcoal grey, black and ivory ocelot type markings that, as Mother stated, will NOT wear out! She had had it in Letchworth and had brought it here. How I would love to have a new version of that here in our apartment, or even a large worn piece! Talk about evoking memories! And I would still adore having it.

Mother once had a woman sit, well lie, on a sofa, and was painted in oils - in the nude, in their large square hallway. Later it was drying – lying up against the back of the couch for anyone who walked in the front door. Theo came in that evening and walked straight past the sofa with the reclining nude female form and down the hallway and straight into the kitchen. Mother: "Did you see her?"

"Who?" said Theo(!)

Mother took him back and pointed out a painting of a full-size nude on the sofa.

"I'd have noticed if she had been real…!"

Then I remember Mother and become achingly sad. It's funny how these thoughts and feelings suddenly wash over you with not necessarily the awareness of what triggered it. Then I started to think of her being reunited with Daddy and I was relatively happy again. Wondering "where they are." Are they in a parallel universe? And if they are, they must have Russell and Cedric along with them. I've always liked being the only girl with what I used to jokingly refer to as two-and-a-half brothers! In "normal" English law he'd be a half-brother whereas in Jewish law he's a full brother as we share the same Mother. You can always find out who the Mother is but not necessarily the father…

Once, visiting me in Sydney when Stuart was a very new three-week-old baby she said, "you know, not a day goes by when I don't think of Leslie." That said, to be fair, she did later say to Neil and others, "everyone should have a Theo" and that was used by Neil in his speech at Mother's funeral.

Theo and I *never* got on, but he DID look after Mother properly and to the best of his abilities and adored her. Freshly squeezed orange juice every morning and he became a very good cook mainly thanks to her. He said to us at a meal not that long ago that she taught him timing for the whole meal and when to put things on to cook, in the right order of importance.

I managed to get a piece of card written by Theo, but it's what she had taught him. So it's a reminder for me instantly of her. I have it somewhere. I'm an old sentimentalist.

For Michael's and my wedding she baked in advance the most gorgeous cakes, about ten of them, and a lovely homemade wedding cake with pink icing! All so delicious. Memories!

I've just remembered (again) Mother once saying that "you have no malice" to me and I've just this minute realised you, oh Mouse of mine, are the same! You are too sweet to have any malice towards me, even when I irk you! Mwah.

And I haven't mentioned loving my mother anywhere, have I!

MY LETTER TO MY LATE MOTHER END OF 2015

Dear Mother

You have shaped my life and being, much more than I ever realised and all in a good way. Well, mostly!

This is also not going to be in any order - just as I recall things.

I can now see more of your face in me as well as Daddy's face (January 24th, 2024: it happened again last night too in the mirror.) But it pleases me greatly as it makes me think of you and that warms me. For many years I thought I only looked like Daddy and that pleased me too, but since I moved to another continent, yet again, it cheers me no end to know I have both your faces within mine. It's very clever how G-d created genes to do this, and that's partly why I DO believe in a G-d, because we're too complex to have been created by accident, or by Aliens who I don't believe would bother! It's SO obvious. It's funny cos you'd look at me and see only Daddy whereas I can see you both now, although it probably irked Theo daily?!

Back to Mother. You did have your faults, and especially with me. Well, I was compared favourably to Sara when she would turn up to the house without Felix's required spare nappy, and an extra change of clothes. I even pointed this out to Mother. It was kind of annoying, *I was good in her eyes because of what Sara didn't do*! She did appreciate it being pointed out. That was gratifying.

Where Sara was concerned it was the little things that didn't come to mind for her as she has an academic brain (and a very good one too) that resulted in two degrees, one in Russian - she would later proceed to be Neil's guide on a visit to Lithuania and Russia to see where our ancestors came from.) The other was reading law at Leeds which is where Neil came into her life very permanently.

But I'm digressing from our Mother. It's funny because it's just reminded me of a conversation I had with Mother.

She said, "Oh, I don't ring Neil, he's far too busy and I don't want to pester him during the day." When I regaled this to Neil he just smiled and said, "What utter rubbish! She rings me at least three times a day!" But he was more amused than anything, and had an extremely good relationship with her. To quote him at our Mother's funeral, after "shiva" (ritual mourning) and several people had come over that evening: "…my exceptional parents."

Back to Mother, not that I ever really left her.

When we'd sold this recent condo, I put together clothes I wanted with me at all costs just in case they got lost in storage or that the storage facility went up in smoke. Highly unlikely but one never knows. I packed a wonderfully lightweight "jacket" but made of lawn cotton with something else mixed in. I chose the colour too, dark green with little purple and lilac flowers on it, with deep pink squiggles and dobs of white. Absolutely magical, and unique, and Mother helped me make it – about 47 years ago! Just my style, collarless and simple long sleeves. Perfect for in a restaurant when one wants something light. And it's in such good condition! That's because I've not worn it to death! It's being worn now and will take pride of place in my wardrobe and I shall leave it probably to Lisa - who might even like it by then!

Lisa looks most like Mother with her hair darker than mine. And Lisa's is wavy where Mother's was absolutely straight and long and always swept up in her signature trademark bun. Fairly high and beautiful, she was stunning all her life but in the fifties I think even more so. She just looked good. Period. I remember when she came down one evening dressed to go out with Theo to some function…

And wearing a full-length silver dress. Stunning "starts" to come close! Her dark hair swept up with her 1" strip of hair from front to back in a natural silvery white just adding to the glamour. (Daddy had loved that white stripe!).

Theo **knew** he had Wonder Woman on his arm! She pointed out that she was wearing the simple modern (silver and very simple style) earrings that I bought her in Manchester. Less is more and these were stunning and they became one of her favourites. She was always saying "less is more." When she had one of her many art exhibitions she would often wear a Philip Treacy hat and would wear it with aplomb. She was a very good ad for him and I don't think he even knew. I must tell him one day!

I'm very glad I came from these two, Ruth and Leslie.

Chapter 14

WHERE THIS BOOK STARTED LIFE!

H ere in our new (as of 2013) Toronto apartment on Front Street East, Toronto, it's the hottest day so far for this summer and it's hard enough to summon any energy to write. Ho, ho, ho, but I shall continue to give it my all.

We also have what I consider the best view in the condo: the top floor, the eighth floor, with a commanding view of the whole, peaceful, luscious atrium with its greenhouse-type roof of half-glass making us basically completely outside. We also have huge windows which make full use of the glassed-in atrium and it's just all very positive. The light is fantastic and we get reflected sunlight plus a western window in the lounge bringing actual sunlight in.

Couple all this with a small waterfall creating gentle gurgling and thus creating "white noise" that drowns out most city noises and one does have a brilliant set-up.

We have the equivalent of a penthouse suite and boy do I appreciate it. Every evening before I go to bed and first thing in the morning I gaze around in wonder at our lounge and the whole "feel" of the place and thank Him. We don't even need the lights on a lot of the time. Wonderful and I love it.

The people opposite have their blinds closed a lot of the time. Exactly what our friend and female builder Yohanna

("Me and My Tool Belt!") said would happen if we'd have bought a south-facing apartment. I'm so glad we didn't. Having one's blinds closed much of the day in summer does seem to defeat the purpose.

I'm reminded that before I became a Mouse, back in Sydney, I lived very differently. My ex and I lived in Sydney and it doesn't have distinct seasons. At least not in my view. Summer was long, hot and much of the time muggy. As mentioned, I hate muggy. I can't function in humid weather and if I was living there now I'd have to be at least getting sea breezes to write anything including emails.

I actually have what I consider to be the perfect conditions to write a book: our kitchen/dining table doubles as my desk and I got it from the St Lawrence antique market here. Almost haggling. The man had it marked as $125 and I adored it. Still do. A country-style table with ornate legs and a small drawer in the middle. It had my name on it and was just beckoning to be taken to its new home – mine, well, ours. I said I didn't want to insult him with my offer – to which he asked what that offer was. I said $90. And it was mine!

I have also painted our antique Parisian double bedroom doors which came from an architectural salvage yard and I adore them. I started painting that last night too and finished late. When I finally came to bed, I'd taken my amitriptyline but it didn't work and 45 minutes later was forced to take a strong 500mg Tylenol. Michael Mouse curled up with me in bed which was so lovely and tried taking my mind off the leg pains.

"Think of a deserted beach for us to walk along," is as far as he got. I rejected it and Michael said, "yes, it is a bit of psycho shit!" Beaches for both of us are just hot and sandy. One combination neither of us likes and here he is trying to take my mind *onto* it!

HOW TIMES CHANGE

We've jumped now. It is noon, Tuesday 24th February, 2015. We have this wonderful apartment on the market. Yes, how times change. It has high monthly maintenance fees which I think are hindering the sale. Last night Tony (Prochilo, realtor and good friend - and the most RELIABLE realtor anyone could *ever* know) helped me unpack the new dishwasher. A beautiful gleaming white BOSCH enhancing the kitchen beautifully along with my painting of one upper wall.

Summer 2015 found us having just sold our condo - and Karma coming to bite us hard. We had asked for three weeks move-in when we bought the place from an elderly couple and now we had become that couple. So, they had to get out and "so it was" that when we finally sold we were given the same three-week notice. The only good thing about that was we had actually sold. That said, I did love that condo and I will always remember it. I got a huge pleasure every evening for the first six months, just before bedtime. Standing at those $600 double glass and wooden original antique Parisian doors and just standing in awe of the sight of the lounge, with its beautiful white floor and the fireplace opposite, with the built-in china cabinet at the side. And my chosen flimsy thin curtains at the west window in a very delicate pale pink and green/grey leaves. Utterly beautiful and just adding to the picture I had created. I can picture myself back there too.

We had had to do quite a few things to get that sale, and "staging" was not one of those. Bit by bit I decluttered and tried to "see" the apartment through a stranger's eyes. We'd have sold it several times over except for the fact that we had such high monthly fees. That was a killer, to quote my Mouse. Then we thought of "improving" the kitchen, although I adored my white open shelving with black metal wrought iron brackets with interesting filigree - along with small round white lights at intervals creating softer light at night when one doesn't always want overhead lighting, or indeed need it.

My under-cupboard lights went up, under each shelf at three-four-inch gaps and on a separate circuit, and at night looked utterly magical. Tony, our realtor and now very trusted good friend, mentioned it might be an idea to "invest" in cupboards as most don't want a "country" kitchen, which in effect was what I'd aimed for. So DOWN came the shelves AND all their lighting, now still attached to each other, but in storage ready for the new place! That said, I'm very tempted to put them up in the bedroom and create a mini-library with our bed as focal point! And all the small white lights set at intervals will make a pleasantly softly lit bedroom without having to drill into the ceiling because no one will do that here. All old buildings have asbestos in them - but if it's left well alone it doesn't cause problems so no one wants to drill into it, fair enough. So, a bedroom that's easy to read in is a real must for us, with our books initially adding up to 900, but we have culled it to about 400!

So my then builders went to IKEA (they have wheels and we have limited funds so it seemed like a good idea), and brought back a brochure which gave me a choice of real wooden cupboards at very affordable prices. Blonde, mid-brown or dark-brown. I actually thought the mid-brown looked brown till I saw the dark-brown. I was VERY good and hedged my bets and DIDN'T go for what I would have preferred but went by what I thought the masses would have gone for.

I must say, the new mid-but-really-dark cupboards looked very smart and I chose brushed stainless steel knobs to go on. Again, trying to please the masses. Coupled with new wooden lighter tops and a very expensive new faucet that cost almost $400 on its own, we had really tried to make the kitchen sit up and sing.

And it worked, to an extent. The couple who bought it liked it. And promptly took up ALL the good new natural, air-dried pine floor planks and instead installed a real wooden floor but narrower planks, and REMOVED all the kitchen cupboards that had gone in five weeks earlier!

Actually, I'm glad we never got to see our newly renovated old apartment/condo for ourselves. I shouldn't be annoyed in any way as we got our sale but it amazes me that anyone can immediately undo some of one's hard work and change it all. They're hoping to put it on the market in a "quick turn over." It'll be interesting to see if they do and if it sells.

Side note: It did sell - it was just that the subsequent owners discovered the inferior quality of the work perpetrated by the people who bought off us and who sued the latter for around C$100,000! These "newbies" had had the stupidity to take out the marble hearth and put wood there – near the fireplace!!!

Well, it was lovely living in it whilst it lasted and we were very close to St Lawrence Market and the Antique Market that was on every Sunday. We still have the two stuffed birds I got there! One pheasant and one Mallard(?) duck.

When I'd bought them a tall elderly guy sidled up to me and whispered in my ear that these stuffed birds can carry all sorts of diseases. No, I wasn't buying it. It might be true but if done properly it shouldn't be a problem. I figured he was trying to put me off in the hope I'd turn around immediately, get a refund, and he'd snap them up.

Wasn't going to happen! And Michael Mouse and I walked happily out with them both, and we have them still, on display, in our dining room. Love 'em! Michael Mouse still remembers the looks we got carrying them out!

Chapter 15

AUSCHWITZ

My Mouse and I went to Krakow, Poland, in 2012. I wanted to visit Auschwitz, the concentration camp for those who don't know their history (pronounced Ow (as in pain! + Shvitz). One of the most "infamous" for the uninitiated, the other three being Dachau (the "ch" as in a Scottish Loch) and Belsen and Treblinka, in my humble opinion.

I once met one of that rare ignorant breed here in Toronto. His parents had turned the channels anytime something came on that was remotely upsetting, in the attempt to not let him witness anything and to shield him. The result is, he looked like a complete idiot, and he was nearing 40! There were, unfortunately still many more concentration camps, and they held political dissenters, gypsies and Jews and anyone gay. Basically, anyone who wasn't considered pure enough.

I had asked my son Stuart if he would like to come with us. I wanted to share my visit to Auschwitz with him. He sat me down on our sofa in the lounge and as gently as possible told me that he'd seen enough documentaries and knew all about these camps to know he did not want to visit it. I did not say a word. I saw in his face that I had to accept what he said and totally respect his wishes and that's exactly what

I did. He had added that he would have nightmares if he had come, and I would not put my son through that for anything. After all, it's not as though he's oblivious to it all.

As a matter of fact, I wish he'd have properly met our old neighbour, Elly Gotz. Elly lived in the same condo block as us in Downtown Toronto with his wife Esme. Elly was a young survivor of Dachau. Elly had been liberated at the age of 17 from *one of the worst concentration* camps in the world. You can google to find the right number of deaths. It's quite the eye opener. When I first met Elly he had a long striped shirt on, and I came to recognise that as his virtual trademark.

The first time we spoke he showed me his inner wrist, with the tattooed numbers on him (Sophie's Choice, The Odessa File (actually a favourite of mine - connected to a camp but set after the war) and a more recent *very* clever film Remember, featuring Christopher Plummer and with a superb twist.)

To see tattooed numbers on an elderly man's inner arm in real time is something I *haven't even got a word for.* What that man has seen - and guess how he uses his spare time… visiting different towns and giving talks to all kinds of people to explain what he and masses of others went through. To willingly relive it every time he goes away for a few days, in the hope to teach and prevent future "hatreds," my coined word. I don't know any word for that - a special resilience for him to keep talking.

I wanted to visit Auschwitz because I read somewhere that it was our duty to those who had lost their lives to visit these places in person and to prove to those neo-Nazis and many others that not only did this take place all over

Europe but many turned a blind eye and thought it too far-fetched to actually be happening. Nothing was too far-fetched as far as the Nazis could go. Nothing was too far "out of bounds." THEN I read about a lampshade made out of human skin. It's a revolting thought but *nothing* they could think up would surprise me.

I was an avid reader of True Stories of World War 2, both in England growing up and later, back in Oz, as well as BMM (Before Michael Mouse!) and had left most of my books back there. Boldness Be My Friend by Richard Pape was such a good one, as was Carve Her Name With Pride, the true story of Violette Szabo, shot by the Nazis three days before hostilities ceased. Then too Reach For The Sky by Paul Brickhill, the story of my childhood hero Douglas Bader, the legless pilot that all German soldiers knew of! Kenneth More played the title role there and very well too!). And I'm betting history lessons don't even touch, barely, on these people nowadays. If I'm wrong I'll be delighted.

BACK TO AUSCHWITZ...

There's an eerie calm atmosphere just standing there, in this large room with silence all prevailing but the contents seemingly whispering their past.

This long room at Auschwitz had long "seats" (benches, wooden and longer and deeper than most) on one side of it, in tiers. An enormous room, about 40' in length and these seats numbered about eight rows and covered - with shaved hair from those about to be gassed. The hair piled up and all along these seats. One couldn't even see the seats - too much hair. I have very good spatial awareness. It's a sight that doesn't get forgotten. I was there with 30-odd other Japanese tourists all clicking away with their cameras. I was the only one who didn't feel the need.

There is something very disquieting about the many clicks of so many cameras. It's invading the privacy of those who have died, and yet, as someone pointed out to me, these photos taken will be shown to others, and thus *might* take root in someone's memory NOT to have this repeated ever again, against ANY race or creed. That alone made me realise it was worth putting up with those clicks. Not that I could have changed it. Not that I now want to, on reflection. This whole place would have had a stench of death pervading it every hour of every day. And we are now in 2023 and Hamas has invaded Israel; and anti-semitism has surged again, even more so if that's possible. Not forgetting this camp had others deemed inferior in many other ways too. They should never be forgotten either. ALL life is PRECIOUS!

And in a large glass case on the other side of the room was a mound - of children's shoes, all now a stark reminder, a heap. Never to be walked in again, but a very vivid reminder that children were included in this vile extermination. Boxes of spectacles, too.

In another long wooden hut were bunk beds. There's an eerie atmosphere merely being there. Surrounded by these long wooden structures that were the sleeping quarters of many more than they were built for. Three to a bed, and that's two too many. The beds were there. The place would sap the mindset of the most fervent "hopeful-ee."

We were taken to the steps of the start of the partially underground "showers." Where no one was "cleaned" per se, but instead ZyklonB cans were opened up and tipped into the various small "entry" holes made deliberately for this purpose from the rooms above. One can only imagine what that fear and cold combined would do when the sudden realisation of what they were really there for became all too apparent. It really doesn't bear thinking about. They undressed as ordered, under the impression there was going to be a real shower. Unfortunately, they realised too late that it had never been the plan.

And my son Stuart *would* have had nightmares. I'm so glad he sat me down. He's at least seen the pictures and heard all about it at school. That's a very good start (I'm sure I must have told him more, too.) The more we have of that kind of teaching and the less of the kind that David Irving spouted the better. Putting it down as lies only makes those that died die in futility. Lest We Forget. So true.

I'm so glad I shared this trip with Michael. It reminded me of an early visit by him when we were dating and he'd come up to Manchester in his car.

He took me to the Jewish cemetery in Urmston, a miserable place if ever there was. I don't visit it very often, and don't feel that Russell or Cedric are even "there" as such, and the same goes for Daddy and Mummy too.

Michael did a very sweet thing - he said Kaddish, the prayer for the dead. I hadn't asked him to. I hadn't even thought of him reciting it. We're not overly religious. He just started it. It's not very long but it was the gesture that made me really warm towards him, even more than I already was.

WAR, whether it's in the Middle East or Russia invading Ukraine and many who have lost their homes in the ensuing fighting and lost family members and all for what...

Chapter 16

MY TRANS - SIBERIAN RAILWAY DREAM - FINALLY!

"**I** want to do the Trans-Siberian," said Hazel. "Why?" was my Mouse's response. "Because it reminds me of Doctor Zhivago" came the counter-retort - my favourite movie of all time.

So there we were ready to do seven days on a train. Except that one commentator said he would have gone rather stir crazy BUT he only said that because he was referring to people who did the Trans-Siberian Journey *all the way from Moscow to Vladivostock in particular*. We decided to have the best of both worlds and do the Trans-Siberian, through the Urals and as far as Yekaterinburg, the scene of the murder of the Romanovs, the Russian Royal Family.

Then we hopped onto the Trans Mongolian, a relic of better times between Moscow and Beijing, for another train journey going south east and through Mongolia and the Grasslands which have a raw untamed beauty all of their own. We even saw a herd of camels in the distance, near Ulaan Baatar. Pity they were quite a long way off. I willed them to come closer to no avail.

So we booked our tickets, not too difficult, got our Mongolian transit visa (*obnoxious "toe-rag" on the other end of the line, Michael Mouse's word choice!*), got our Chinese visa (now there was courtesy, a smile and efficiency!) and then we got the Russian Visa (despite the office in Toronto closing for six days over and above the Christmas break…). Talk about cutting it fine!

Actually, our first attempt to see Red Square was a short one as it was -40 degrees (it was that cold that my fingers were tingling with pain, and those fingers were in gloves!) Much better – and warmer - was the guided tour by taxi which we grabbed before succumbing to the bitter cold. For all that, the monuments, and church spires of Moscow are inspiring and we have the fridge magnets to prove it! Those are lightweight……as opposed to what was stupidly later bought!

In Moscow, a wonderful totally unexpected rustic Parisian Cafe (!) which did exquisite mushroom soup. Wooden tables and the rest! Exactly the same as my late mother's mushroom soup and instantly transported me back to her. I have to make some mushroom soup! I've even taken some internal shots of the place, it was so lovely.

Then the railway from Moscow thousands of miles east. Yaroslavl Station was something out of a Russian fairy-tale. Getting onto the train was the nightmare – one foot off the platform and eighteen inches up – thank goodness for the porter!

The steps up to the platforms were concrete and wide like in a grand hotel minus the carpet, but the fascinating bit was the slope right next to the stairs where porters pushed up heavy metal trolleys with our luggage on. *This at an angle of 45 degrees!* And they didn't just push it up with difficulty… they pushed it with ease and virtually RAN up with it. Un be li ev able!

Nobody from the west sees things like this normally. If that 45 degree angle had even existed in the west it would have been deemed too much for any human to push *anything* up it! And would be classed as a "ealth and safety 'azard'. Maybe it's causing heart attacks daily that we never read about. I, for one, would not be surprised. It was tiring just to be a spectator!

We had set off on the initial section of the Trans-Siberian. We actually had a very smart compartment. Much better than we could have imagined. The lady who fixed our adaptor plug told me the secret to happiness was "sex, sex and sex."! And we hadn't even broached the subject!

Yes, well, I can tell you that was the LAST thing on our minds. The image of doing a "no 69" on the upper bunk with the "stop-start" action of the train driver's ability would have made for some very interesting sex, especially with arthritis playing its part, not to mention the possibility of either mice falling down to the floor!

And getting off at Ekaterinburg (Pronounced Yekaterinburg) to see where the Tsar and his family got murdered. Even if the actual house where the executions took place was demolished in 1977 through fears that it might become a shrine to royalists. It was demolished by some local official called Boris Yeltsin!

Ekaterinburg is a beautiful city and its restaurants are not too bad at all, including the Uzbekistani one. The city has a pastel pink tinge to many of its eighteenth-century-style buildings.

The train was rejoined at Ekaterinburg at 1am – again with the help of the porter. This was now the Trans-Mongolian to Beijing. Our understanding was that the Russian trains were bad and the Chinese sections good. Ho, ho, ho. The Chinese compartments were tatty and cold as the wind found a way in through a draft in the window frame.

In all fairness there was no hole per se. A sliver of a gap meant air did get in and when we were both up during the day this did not impinge (during the night it was f ing cold! – Michael). It was merely noticed by us both because we shared the sleeping berth and while one slept the other tried sleeping in a chair with a huge pillow and felt this gap more keenly. It was very cosy in our little "home away from home." That's what you think, Dearie – Michael). Yes, well it didn't stop you sleeping, oh Mouse of mine…!

And on the subject of ho, ho, ho, the train pulled into one of the many stations. A man on the other platform waved to Michael. He waved back to him. Next, Michael turned round to put his Santa Claus hat on. (Where did we even GET that hat?!) He duly photographed him and gave a double thumbs-up. That was a highlight…and with his white beard he looked just like Santa! (Once upon a time, back in England Michael was walking in Nottingham and a little boy asked him if I was Santa Claus. No, he said, I'm his brother!). That kid shouldn't have even approached a stranger!

Our compartment was someway from the dining car (they got the fish right).

That fish was MELTINGLY good. The heating for the carriages came from coal which was loaded onto areas at the ends of the carriages. Coal produces coal dust. Very cold weather produces snow and ice and frost. To change from one carriage to another we had to open doors and hold onto handles. These latter were sprinkled with coal dust, snow, ice and frost – not a pretty sight as our hands testified, but another experience I wouldn't have missed but Michael would happily disagree!

And we'd be "jiggled" along the tectonic metal plates that were the train's links between carriages. This in midwinter and in the far east. What could be more magical and in the RIGHT season? A FROZEN Siberia and Mongolia! It doesn't get more romantic than that! Boy, did I appreciate Michael's natural warmth! I've often said he could be a natural incubator for premature babies at any hospital!

Michael: My sleeping patterns were slightly eccentric (like the rest of him!) Having got no comfort at all from the chair in which I was supposed to sleep, He spent quite a few supposedly waking hours sleeping on the lower bunk. He slept through the shore of Lake Baikal (mistake) and the changing of the wheels on the train from Russian to Chinese gauge. This, from my "train nerd!"

More inspiring was the brief *glimpse* of a Bactrian camel in the Gobi. That's a camel with two humps!

Beijing was once again highly enjoyable. We stayed in a hotel in a hutong. This is an old quarter and utterly fascinating. Some of these are being specially preserved. I went slightly down one narrow alleyway with my camera but I didn't have the heart to be so intrusive and came out again.

The hotel was very attractive and we were upgraded to the bridal suite! Our room was in the theme of an imperial bridal bed-chamber! Red silk curtains around the bed and much wooden carving. Absolutely magnificent, although rather OTT at the same time, but it made for an interesting place to stay. Very red all through.

The flight back from Beijing was via Warsaw. Once again, Michael's beard was the subject of attention as many Chinese don't have facial hair and was snapped along with some very charming young ladies… but it made Michael a temporary celebrity and he loved it and I was happy for him.

BACK TO LONDON AFTER CHINA.

We made a journey into London, as baby brother Neil (Roland) is an exceptional photographer; his photographs of London grace the walls of one of the key law-court buildings in the City, the newly opened Royal Courts of Justice. Friends, both of whom Michael had worked with several years previously, joined us for a lovely reunion enhanced by the photographs and lunch in the Cheshire Cheese.

A few days later, a reunion with someone whom Michael had known through his Birmingham Uni days. Viron (the Greek version of Byron) had been writing a PhD but had for many years worked with the BBC Greek Service. A typical phone call was "Can I speak to Viron, please?" "He's reading the news at the moment."!

Michael reeled off a number of British officers who had served in Greece with the resistance and one or two of whom he had met on his travels. Viron was most impressed and said that Michael was reminding him of the happiest period of his life! All Michael's studying had not been in vain.

A little here by my freelance Mouse writer, Michael himself:

"My writing has made a detour into consumer writing. I wrote about Mastermind and also about British F1 drivers, published in Evergreen and This England Annual respectively. Available from all good newsagents or in pdf from your humble servant. My love of motor racing remains unabated."

Mrs Mouse here - My Mouse is a natural when it comes to public speaking. He's very good at it, and it comes naturally. He can write on anything! He can speak on UK politics, politics of many countries' history and their politics. And he makes it fascinating!

Michael, I'm SO glad I did this trip with YOU. Mwah.

Chapter 17

LIFE IN A TRAVELODGE
THAT ACCEPTS PETS!

I t had been my son Stuart's brilliant idea to find a hotel that accepts pets, dogs in particular and that's how we came to be at the Travelodge near the airport.

Six weeks have passed since we left 812 Front Street East in 2015. We are in a temporary home in the form of the Travelodge Hotel near Toronto Airport. Holly, our elderly Jack Russell, has settled well. We have, in effect, rented out a studio apartment with only a very small fridge as a nod to a kitchen. No cooking facilities but we eat at their restaurant and try and keep costs down by not having a full meal. We definitely don't have desserts or an hors d'oeuvre. I also usually hope that Michael Mouse doesn't have a beer either as that really pushes up the bill by CAD$7-8. Just as well I never acquired the taste for beer.

We've also quite often bought bread and cheese and pickles and had our own indoor picnic or any other "take outs!" It all saves dosh. (Half dollars half cash.)

My Mouse and I talked it over thoroughly. He would have had to set up wifi as an extra cost but he is on the hotel's computer with wifi a lot of the time. When another hotel guest is on it he catches up on his reading or plans out the questions he wants to ask for his next email interview.

This is a very smart Mouse, well - he did marry me! We get on extremely well which might account for why this hotel set-up does work. The only flaw is that we're far out near the airport but that too has a silver lining. It has brought home to me just how much I don't want to live "out in the burbs" as they say here on the news. I hate that phrase!

Same as I think it's ridiculous to talk about 'erbs and not say herbs. It's Canada's only nod toward French here besides the signs in shops being in both. They don't say 'opital instead of hospital. No, they say it properly. If you put a French accent on with 'erbs, it's fine but then you should be dropping beginnings of all words not just the one. In addition, "calm" and "almond" get pronounced with the "l." All very bizarre.

It's now the last day of July. Yesterday was not a good day for us in more than one way. It started off with us getting the cleaner for the room. There are quite a few cleaners here but the building is very big. 99% are lovely. There's always one that can spoil things and we had our turn due and yesterday was "it."

The cleaner arrived and was greeted by Holly who, because she is very old and half-blind and half-deaf, reacts by barking at what she can't quite see. As she's also wagging her tail, most realise she's fine and some even stroke her. She likes that. Anyway, cleaner -----, I don't know her name and I don't intend embarrassing her - but she's in the washroom and I ask her if there's a plastic bag for the bin. It's not a big deal but sometimes they have gone without doing it. Maybe they've run out of the bags. The response I got was not very nice. She said, "we leave a bag there out of courtesy." OK. I asked from the hallway if "everything was alright" and she responds with, "Will you please let me get on with my work!!!"

Bloody rude! I hadn't expected to get a line like that and we have got on with ALL the other staff, from laundry to reception and to the staff at the attached restaurant. Ten years ago, or maybe even five years ago, I'd have simmered with annoyance and not said anything but I also felt that IF she was going to clean our room again I wasn't going to be intimidated – ever again, by anyone!

I wrote down the whole short "episode" whilst it was still fresh. My Mouse recommended that I took it to the Housekeeping Department because he's used to dealing with all sorts of things in his time as a magazine editor of one sort or another.

I intended to do just that but ended up in the lobby telling it all to one of the managers. Then handing the whole written piece to him. I also added I didn't want to lose her her job. I would hate to lose someone their job as I don't know her background and don't know whom she's looking after or anything else that might well totally rely on this job. I think this woman has a huge chip on her shoulder, but it's only a guess on my part.

The best bit was today when I could hear the cleaners nearby and they hadn't touched our room yet as there were those vacating – their rooms are given priority. Makes sense.

So I rang down to ask for a cleaner and darling Sima arrives. Proof positive. She was asked to go and clean and when she found out it was us, she was delighted and said so to the Housekeeper. It felt good.

Today, shortly after the cleaner had left, the supervisor came and asked me about what had happened and I told her. She is very nice too. And it was a good conversation. She apologised for the other cleaner. I said you don't have to do that. And I added I'm perfectly happy to add a bag to a bin. Being treated like royalty is not always a nice feeling. Both of us don't need everything done. That said, Michael is always appreciative when anyone helps him as his movements are quite limited. He's almost become part of the furniture as he goes down to use the computer in the lobby but comes off it when someone comes to use it temporarily, as most guests do.

Three days ago I was walking through the lobby and someone who works here asked how our search for a condo is coming. They are all very lovely here.

We're known to most as a lovely couple, which is fine by me!. I once told my brother, "I want to be eccentric." He said, "If you think you are, you're not!" THAT deflated me somewhat. An eccentric couple, maybe…but also maybe not. We're not yet odd enough!

We got into quite the routine at the hotel. We got onto first names quite soon and were regularly seen by staff when we took Holly out. The foyer was large and tiled. Perfect for dogs who have accidents! That said, Holly was pretty good and didn't poop too often in the wrong place! We're also lucky that she is now very deaf because she would have freaked out had she been able to hear the planes taking off and being fairly close as they made their ascent. Having our room at the back was another blessing as we were disturbed less and no street lights either. Also they had lined the curtains with black-out. The first time I've actually experienced that and it does work very well. Holly settled in too. I didn't expect anything else. They like routine and we were into our routine, just in another surrounding. Michael made the joke that Holly was a dog being looked after by two little mice.

Everything is "mouse" orientated with us. Mr Mouse has often remarked that he "likes shopping with Mrs Mouse." The feeling is mutual. One thing we've never managed to get – wait for it – are two tails! No, I'm not completely mad, it just seems that way! I'm sure that there would be mouse tails at some costume store – and one day we might buy two - BUT we'd only wear them at home - in Mouseville! Michael bought me a small mouse candle once. But I've never lit it, nor do I ever intend to. Whenever we buy cards, as in for birthdays, or Valentine's Day, Michael always seems to find a cute one with mice depicted on it.

Getting back to the hotel. I asked about pets at the Travelodge and found out we had accidentally chosen very well and they accepted pets, after Stuart suggested we try finding a hotel accepting pets! She, Holly (or rather we) were charged $25 as a one-off fee which I thought very decent of them. On top of that, the then manager, Jason Unger, helped us even more by giving us a 10% discount after I'd asked to speak to him and had explained our situation. He said at the end, "just concentrate on finding your new home" which we were both very touched by.

The three of us settled into the Travelodge Hotel; Holly came to assume we had our new home! After all, what does a dog know in that regard except that the room has changed completely. There is less furniture but there are 22 Metro bags as I decided to bring a few things with us that were precious to me…"just in case" (of what I don't know. Maybe that the storage facility might suddenly burn down and I'd lose many precious things including a cardigan of my late Mother's.)

Whereas before Holly had her own pillow to sleep on in our room, I felt we couldn't do that there as they still had carpet in each room, but not in the bathroom! So her new bedroom became the bathroom at night and she was tethered to the door knob. It worked very well as I/we couldn't risk her messing the carpet up and nine times out of ten she didn't because she had a large bathroom to mess in and being tiled made it a doddle.

Most cleaners very soon found out she would bark and wag her tail at them and then it was a case of "OK, I've announced your presence, I can now go back to my pillow and go have another snooze. I do a lot of that nowadays." If I'm not careful I'm starting to write this from a dog's point of view and that wasn't the idea! It was fun sometimes for Holly to meet another dog in the foyer. Having a dog is a very good conversation starter.

The staff at this Travelodge were all lovely, including the then Manager Jason Unger but there has been a take-over and Jenna and many were let go and all Mr Mouse and I can say is "thank you" to all who were there at our time. You're all remembered.

That said, the vegetables were often the same and I personally got to the stage where I (almost) never want to see broccoli again! There were variants and I got them, but eating out can become a drag! And I never thought I would ever say THAT!

BACK TO THE PRESENT DAY...

It's not a problem being together - just being here! We know all the cleaners by sight and mostly a lovely lot they are. Holly still barks at them initially, especially when she wakes up to them at the same time they're coming into the room. Yesterday was very funny though I had to take command of the situation.

I was busy emailing someone and suddenly I hear Holly barking. I've just realised, it's like one's own child! One knows one's own dog's bark! I got up quickly from my perch at the little round table near the window, where I type and read and watch planes take off and land. I followed the noise out into the corridor to find that the cleaner had one towel in her hand but had made the mistake of holding one corner of it and letting the rest hang down! This, even for a half blind dog, was lovely - and a game! She promptly caught it in her teeth and caused the cleaner to back off shaking the towel not realising she was actually encouraging Holly to continue the "game!"

I came out of the room and was quite amused but quickly got the towel and managed to get Holly to go back in the room. Dealing with a half-deaf dog is similar to that of a deaf person and I have resorted to using my hands and arms, trying to gesture where she should go. Explaining that Holly was quite happy as the other end of her body attested to that. I added that all this would tire Holly out quite a bit and she would soon be back asleep somewhere on the floor. Usually right in the road being TOTALLY oblivious that she's plonked herself down in the main thoroughfare and we now have to step over her. But she trusts us/me completely and usually facilitates that. Other times she goes totally illogical and gets up IN THE MIDDLE of one stepping over her. THEN not the most logical and THAT's when I feel she most takes after Michael...not the most logical man in the land!

THAT said, if logic can grow, he's grown *some* in the last 27 years! I never thought it could be so but I HAVE been witness to it! That said, my late mother Ruth *did* say, "Leslie taught me logic."!

WE MOVE TO A BACHELOR

We decided to rent a small bachelor and on one occasion we looked at what we thought might have worked. It was, amazingly enough, on our old first street when we initially arrived in Toronto and bought: Charles Street East. This time it was in the new-build that we had seen under construction: I never thought we'd be looking at it from the inside! This studio was a let-down. Don't get me wrong. The 35th floor had amazing balcony views – IF I could stand to actually *be* on the balcony! It must be vertigo – I get a very peculiar feeling through my bottom and I've recently discovered I get the same effect if I see the same kind of view on tv! Seeing a clip from the forthcoming movie "The Walk" intrigued me and gave me this feeling at the same time. Very odd in one's own home. Well, a temporary home anyway.

Then I discovered not only very thin curtains letting the evening city lights (although in a high up window (!) in to a bedroom that only just took the double bed, and to exacerbate matters, it was pushed up against one wall to allow more space. One of us was going to have to clamber over the other! Not even I relished clambering over my mouse! We'd have made a REAL farce of it. No, it wasn't going to happen. We were *also* told after the viewing that the rent would go up at the end of the first month because wifi was only free for the first part! That was a put-off and we continued our search.

English Electric Thunderbird Missile

Leslie Ward (Daddy)

Daddy (Leslie) in dinghy

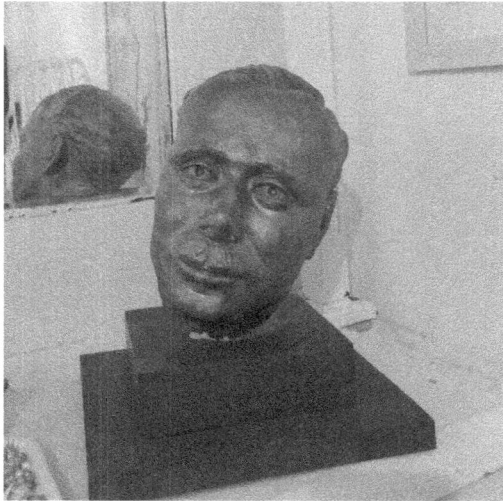

Leslie Ward, Daddy, sculpted by Ruth Ward 1961

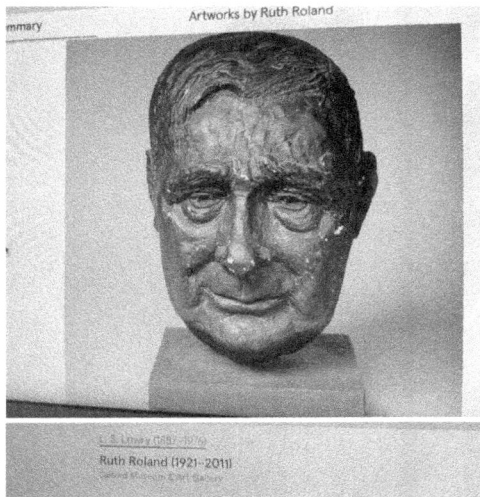

L S Lowry
1887-1976, Ruth Roland 1921-2011

Mummy, the then Ruth Ward

This just reminds me of the ONE time my son wanted to share some weed with me ('only' cannabis) so that we could watch a movie together in our apt...He did NOT expect the reaction he got. Hubby and I both tried it. (I'm laughing as I type!).
Hubby managed to walk to his armchair and virtually pass out/went to sleep. I sat for a very few mins in the lounge (I'm still chortling!) and then said I need to lie down.. son walked me to the bathroom where I undressed privately and as quickly as I could muster, (still chortling now whilst I type!) and FLAKED into bed without even washing my face! He watched the movie alone!
He's not offered any since...!!!!!!!!! Not surprising. What a waste he was likely thinking. He's very careful and has since cut down, but it IS funny on reflection. My life story is coming out soon and I've just realised I forgot to include this! Doh!

I don't encourage drug use at all but it reminded me of this time and it was so not what Stuart expected!

Me (first time round!) with Cedric (L)
looking like Abe Lincoln and Russell

Cedric, 33

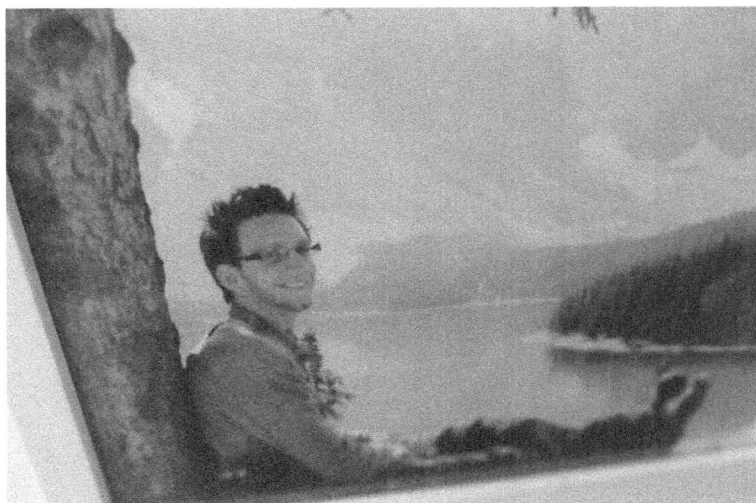

My son Stuart in the Rockies, 2011

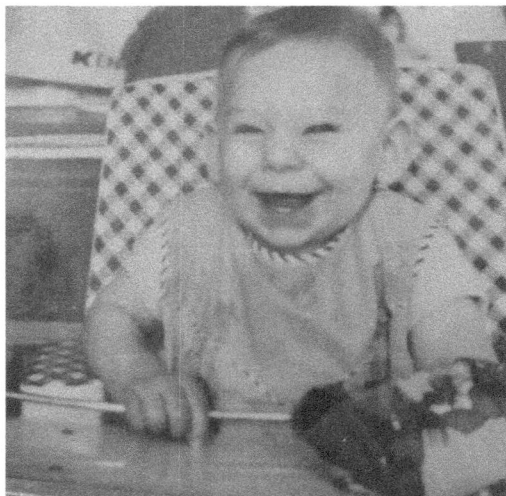

Stuart in high chair at ten months, Sydney

"Lisa as a two-year-old"
Lisa Esme Blain aged 2 in Sydney, SO utterly adorable.

Granddaughter Aurora

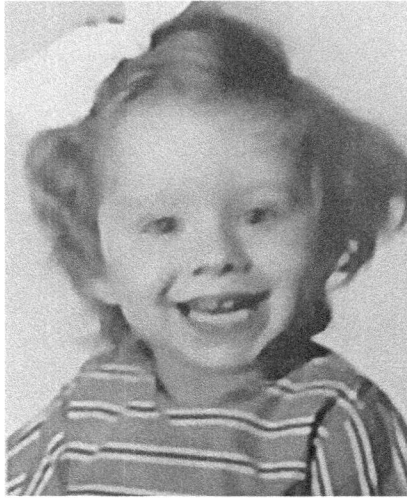

Me aged 3

Our house at 33 Broadwater Avenue, Letchworth

Mr Mouse
Photo by Stuart Blain

Mr Mouse with mouse face

Smiling

Mouse face

Mr and Mrs Mouse on their engagement.
I'm trying to sit on Michael's knee, hence my laughter!

Mummy, Ruth Roland (now) with me, Hazel, on my
wedding day to Michael Mouse, Feb 16th 1997

Neil at my nephew Felix's Graduation in Zoology
from Bristol, with Sara

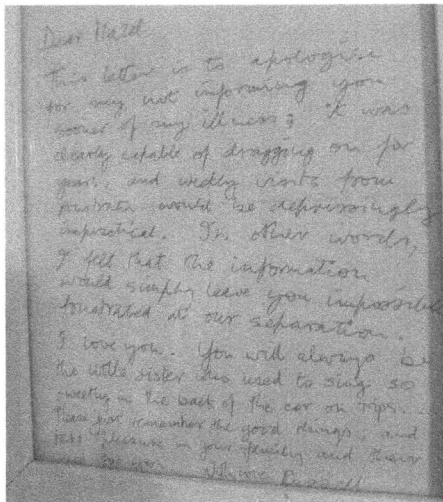

Russell's letter to me

Jesse, Lisa and Aurora

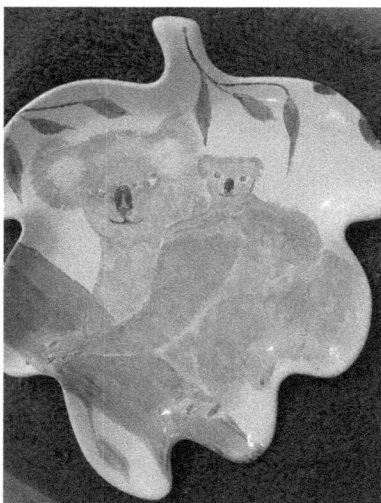

Koala dish, painted by me. In Jan's kiln!

Chapter 18

DOWN AND NOT OUT BUT NOT IN
BEVERLEY HILLS, EITHER!

We are *so* going to enjoy that new condo when we get it and it cannot come quick enough.

We moved, lock, stock, and no smoking barrel to 100 Pembroke Street. Right next door to a very dubious street or, rather, the characters who lived there are, to put it mildly, "not the kind you'd like to bring home to Mother!" How they didn't overspill into Pembroke I shall never know but am extremely grateful for that!

Indeed, Michael was coming back from his Internet café, but without the coffee(!) and wearing his army style parka and with his head dipped because that's how he is now and with his beard a bit disheveled - he gets approached… from a man trying to sell him crack cocaine! That's not a day either of us will forget. No, he did not succumb. Tea is his strongest "weed!"

I feel almost like a turn-of-the-century writer, living in a high-up garret with gloves on without their fingers, so that I can still type. A Parisian garret with a roof-top view of Paris. There are a few aspects missing: it's the third floor only and it's several back gardens/yards, and none of the wonderful rooftops (Parisian or otherwise) that I so adore. In fact, we have a boring factory behind with storage rooms for whatever and they leave their lights on – all night. Thank G-d the curtains are thick enough to block that out and because we're at the back it is a whole lot quieter. I almost forgot to mention Holly in all this. How many turn-of-the-century writers in a cold cramped room without the Parisian view had an elderly half-blind dog with cataracts? Also very deaf into the bargain, that slept most of her days as, next month, mid-March, she'll be nineteen-and-a-half!

Michael went to the internet café again after we'd done the supermarket. I came back to our tiny apartment ahead of him and I'm watching him subtly trying valiantly to untie his shoelaces which he can no longer bend down to do. That's been the way for a long time now. Sometimes I offer to help because the "picker–up" stick is very good at many things but holding onto a soft narrow article that is the shoelace is not one of them. But for $1.25 for most things it's pretty wonderful and helps him hugely get ready in the mornings, and later for bed. His patience is quite something. Last week the weather had gone back to normal. Normal for a real winter here I mean. It was minus 13 with a wind chill factor of minus 23. That is bitingly cold and if you're walking into the wind, well, let's try not to!

This new bachelor apartment is quite sweet (so is Brixton Nick! – Mr Mouse.) It's smaller than the hotel room as it only houses one double bed instead of two, but we have gained a small kitchen, if one can call it that! After a tiny fridge in the hotel room only and a slight "upgrade" to this kitchen which only has a sink unit with worktop space of about 18" square, maybe not even that, followed by four old electric rings (and a small oven with a cock-eyed front door) next to an old but working fridge. Talk about being inventive on how to use what kitchen space there is! By the time we get our own little kitchen it will seem huge regardless!

I am managing in this very small apartment as is Holly. The same can't quite be said about Michael. He's very able 85% of the time to overcome what he feels about this apartment and the end of living here has to surely be in sight. Last week he had to leave to go out for some fresh air. He suddenly got all claustrophobic and needed to get out quite quickly. And did. To the ground floor which is colder yet it's still *elsewhere* so it helped. So I'm doing what I can to make his life easier. I've done that all along, but especially since he has stiffened up somewhat.

On this very Saturday evening, February 20th at 6.50 pm Michael was about to go to the Brits Expats get-together, and I chose to stay at home. It gives me a chance to do more of this book and also to just have me-time. That's not to say we don't enjoy our time together. We do, and we're in each other's pocket almost 24/7 and we do that very well but money is tight and we're worried how long we can go before we get this elusive condo that's yet to come on the market.

I give Michael seven kisses on his lips to which he said. "I rather enjoyed that." He has got the most velvet of lips. The pleasure is all mine, too. He's going to this pub get-together because it gives him a chance to have a break from this room. He's getting quite claustrophobic at times now which I do understand. He just needs "out," so he's getting it.

Today is a lovely yet another cold day. The sun is shining, very blue skies and I'm sharing this apartment with a wonderful, loving Mouse and cockroaches when they dare show their faces. They are half the size of the ones we had in Sydney. It is rather disconcerting when I'm trying to make a meal/snack, and I see something move out of the corner of my eye. I try and have the attitude that all Buddhists have. All life is sacred. Someone should tell that to ISIS!

That said, my natural revulsion for cockroaches has the result in that I quickly take a swipe at them and to hell where they land! I'm sorry G-d but I do not appreciate cockroaches with butter, crackers, avocados and tomatoes. They do not mix! I actually hadn't seen any till about three weeks ago. I'd heard about them from another temporary tenant but we hadn't had the pleasure!

I have a new respect for writers and that especially applies to Neil. I asked him how long he took to write his book. SIX weeks at SIX hours a day! I just cannot apply myself that way. Life gets caught up in the middle!

We moved into this very small rented "apartment" about four months ago. For Michael it has seemed like an eternity. The building has a very cold entrance with marble floors but on the upper floors where all these tiny bachelor apartments are it is instantly warmer. There's also a distinct pong that I cannot put my finger on (nor would I want to)! The walls are my favourite soft blue/grey, a very lovely colour. The carpet has this colour in it as well as black and, wait for it – poo brown! Very sensible with an apartment block that accepts pets!

We have one of the so called larger apartments, which have an 8' long hallway which houses the kitchen on one side. This is far less than a galley kitchen in an aircraft, only not as well designed. The radiator at the far end under the window puts out a MINUSCULE amount of heat but we add to that by having the oven door open! It works very well considering the oven door opens skewed.

The bathroom however, is an interesting one. If one sat on the toilet facing the door, slightly bent head over the book or magazine, one's head would come into contact with the door! That actual act of sitting on the loo is akin to being 30,000 feet up! Not a lot of space at all. And at the right side, partially in our way on the floor, is Holly's pillow, her bedroom if you will. All this reduction in size is going to make the third home and condo seem VERY spacious. NOW we've just got to find the bugger!

The fridge is better than the hotel's tiny one was. Anything would be! That said, this has the old setup, the freezer at the top, where we hardly ever use it and the rest further down making most things hard for Michael to get to. Certainly not the ergonomically designed kitchen that I tried to create in our last place.

...AND HOW MR MOUSE IS COPING

I have found myself watching Michael subtly, when he uses his picker-up stick (he usually has about four from Dollarama.) I watch him slowly go about doing whatever he's doing, but taking so much time to do it.

I must be doing something right nutritionally because he still has an all-dark hairy chest, whereas his head is completely silvery white.

VEGETARIAN
LEANINGS - TEMPORARILY

And thanks to my son Stuart, we - but me a little more so - are leaning towards vegetarianism. I don't think I'd go 100%, but I am finding myself drawn into his way of thinking. He doesn't want anything to die so that he can eat and I think that is admirable, and to a large extent I can follow it, and very willingly. That said, If I'm in England at the Railway Hotel in Buxton where we lived for four years, they do a mean Sunday roast lunch with all the trimmings. Yorkshire pudding etc. Oh, dear, my vegetarianism has already temporarily gone out of the window! That said, a lot of vegetarian meals look absolutely yummy! All those differently coloured vegetables, and garnishings and the creation of a gorgeous abstract painting! Yes, many a time I have photographed a meal or a glorious dish. May that never end! Think of borscht beetroot soup with a dollop of cream dropped on it and left to its own devices. What a glorious abstract that would make! Almost a shame to delve into it and mess it up! Handy having cell-phones/mobiles with cameras!

HOLLY GETS A MAKE-OVER

On Friday April 22nd 2016 we took Holly for her nails to be trimmed. They are so long any woman would be proud of them! Michael likes us going to places together and I love being wanted. He'll ring up if we're in different parts of town and say "Mr Mouse is missing Mrs Mouse and wonders when he will see her and when they can both have a Mouse snack lunch." This is talking to me in the third person and I love it. It never gets old. And if I'm annoyed with him for something it has a very good chance of making me melt. It's called schmoozing, and I'm pleased to say it works most times!

He likes to put his "paws" up and pulls a face not unlike a werewolf, or as we have said in the past – a Weremouse!

Anyway, back to Holly's nails. We're in Diane's pet store near us in Downtown Toronto. She's an Asian sweetie pie and so lovely. She had two Chow Chows, mother and daughter, who have both died now. Both had electric-blue coloured tongues. Very vivid and quite fascinating to see. Diana does Holly's nails herself with a hand from someone else in the back of the store.

I saw a small packet of treats with a price tag of $7.99 and, *for the real first time* I just said to myself "that is a good price." My point is – accepting the price in Canadian dollars and not converting it back into pounds mentally. I was told to do this in our first year here, but it doesn't work that way. It's a thing that has to come naturally **but it has to take its own time**.

Same applies to grief when you lose someone. The pain is so unbearable you think you'll never get over it. And in a way you don't: your mind just starts slowly accepting it and you don't even realise that this is happening. I've had plenty of experience with this having lost two brothers and a Mother. Daddy died when I was eight and I don't know about my grieving process from that time. I didn't and no one to ask either, except Neil and he wasn't even thought of then! I might ask him anyway, as Mother talked to him a lot over the years whilst I lived in Sydney.

We've now been in this cockroach-infested apartment for too long. It was a novelty at first but even that's worn off now. It really is too much when I'm making dinner and two cockroaches join me in the preparation. It's quite disgusting but I also know that it's good to have some germs freely around so one builds up a natural immunity.

What a way to get it though! I had visions last night of a cockroach sandwich! No, I could NEVER do "Get Me Out Of Here!" They make you eat disgusting things that apparently do have protein. If I was in a desert or forest, I'm afraid, then besides water, I would be *very* hungry.

Thank G-d again, we are now into cold weather and have the heating on only very slightly. That's because it's controlled from elsewhere! I was very surprised to hear this as I've never come across it but it works very well. If I felt the "radiator" which is not a radiator as we know it but this grille in a long low metal contraption that has warm air coming out of it – fractionally above tepid but I have two windows open in the lounge and we're lovely and snug. Very odd but it works. It stays on round the clock costing pennies.

We have been complimented, though. Being here I mean. Our friend Joanne has said she doesn't know how we've done it and that she could not live in such close quarters with her husband Howard. My son Stuart has said the same. He likes his space and "copes" with visiting us occasionally. That said I do attempt to declutter even more than usual before he comes. We moved into this bachelor apartment and brought quite a bit of what I didn't want to lose into the bowels of the storage facility which has two units with our stuff in it! Apparently we have "more boxes than most," said one of the removal men. We brought 22

Metro supermarket vinyl bags with us with various different things that I didn't want left in storage. PLUS my darling daughter Lisa's three suitcases which she "has" to dump with "Mother's storage facility." At least she knows they're safe, (and free.) If a bloody pain in the arse!

We were coming back here one day early on in this place and someone had put out a wooden three-tiered shelving unit. Very basic but it IS most useful and I shall off-load it when we leave. Shame to let something like that get smashed up. I hate things broken for breaking's sake.

I keep saying this but I AM very lucky with Michael but I don't think luck has anything to do with it. We were meant to be paired up. We don't get irritated by being here, not for the most part. When we go out to the movies it's a break we need, making it easier to come back.

ESCAPE FROM PEMBROKE

We have temporarily given up finding our "forever" home this side of Christmas 2016. To that end, my Mouse and I have found temporary Mouse Holdings(!) on the longest street in the world, our very own Yonge Street (pronounced Young)!

As we're now finally moving out next Thursday, exactly a week from today, we worked out that we'd have to pay (based on a month) $50 per day for the last four days starting this Sunday. Up till Wednesday night. We're moving out Thursday morning. Yeh!

Our landlord? I used to call him "Hamas!"!!! Not every time I referred to him, just when I'd gone blank! And not to his face, either! I shall call him Said (pronounced Sigh Id). It was he who told us, "We have to charge you the daily rate of $95 daily rather than the 'pro rata' rate!" Yeah, like that's going to happen! He said that if we wanted to leave sooner we could and not incur that charge! I pointed out that a hotel at this point defeats the purpose and also pointed out that he was making a situation more stressful. $95 for a daily-cockroach-infested room! "You must be living in cloud-cuckoo-land if you think we're paying you that!" Bad enough paying a $50 extortion fee - even at that price!

We were at a stalemate but I *was* going to win. Fact! This situation stayed that way till the last week when we knew finally we were moving out on the Thursday. We went to Hamas's office and he'd gone out and left the female "holding the bag" as a fob-off - passing the buck. I'd said to her three days earlier, "$95 for a tiny room with cockroaches and you think we're paying $95 per day for the privilege!!!!" When we went to her the day we left, she had put four times $50 ($200) in the machine and we paid. I won. We had finally signed papers and were moving out and into the newly renovated rented apartment.

I told my Mouse (it should affect him too as he is a diabetic Mouse!) that he should buy what he wanted but to not let me see it and I was going to concentrate on having "savoury" foods when any urge came. I've actually changed my eating habits and I *never* thought I'd been able to do that. The mammogram has definitely played a part there! Knowing that cancer cells feed off sugar helped me go cold turkey on that. The only sugar I HAVE had is a small amount of coconut sugar (very low on the glycaemic index, onto my own home-made muesli and very good that muesli is. Michael loves it and it really keeps us going well past lunch time!) Unfortunately, that sugar-free lifestyle has not been completely maintained... Well I AM human...

It's now been three weeks according to Michael since we bought desserts at that supermarket. I am very pleased with that. NO I have not weighed myself yet, nor will I till I see the GP again. I'm too worried nothing good will show up! What I HAVE achieved is eating only savoury and still being careful. I've not even gone for anything sweet in the evenings except for a hot chocolate with sucralose. I know, not good, but it's better than sugar at the moment. And it's working! Michael buys the odd mint new Kit-Kat but eats it elsewhere away from me to satisfy that urge he has. That said, I think he's eating less sugary stuff because he's often in my company, which is lovely.

Well, last Saturday it was eight weeks or two months since Holly died. This is now Wednesday October 5th and I think we're officially in the Fall, or Autumn as Mr and Mrs Mouse know it. Looking for a new Mousehole has taken a very long time. On this Monday morning I got a call from our very good friend and realtor (1,000% integrity) Tony Prochilo, a sweet, lovable easy-going Italian. On his "search" that he'd set up for us, had come another corner condo in the building I had coveted since deciding we liked this part of Toronto city. It's not in the downtown core which I've always loved, but further out. This building has exactly the stores one wants/needs most and makes life comfortable.

Last night was cinema night because Tuesdays are $5 nights for a movie, and proper mainstream movies. I have kept my cell phone on whilst we've condo hunted. Last night was no different and half an hour into the movie at 4pm Tony rings. He knew we were at the movie but said this was a special call: "Congratulations, you've just bought your condo!!!" Our offer of full asking price was accepted and we're finally on our way! My Mouse said, not for the first time, the only time he wants to move out of this new one will be in a box. Oy!

We've even joined a new (to us) medical practice. He said, "Yes, I'll take you," as soon as I said, "we don't intend to come too often if we can help it!" That clinched it for him. He will be across the street from us. He couldn't BE closer! We will now get to have our long-term home on the longest street in the world!

The highlight was the kitchen – actually bigger that the one I'd lost. Complete with white-goods which I prefer! And blonde wood cupboards that were lovely. I'm not one of these that always say, "no, these have got to go, it's a real total gut job!" I wince, and think how sad something has to be ripped out when a good paint job and new knobs would work wonders. Some people have no vision Michael's a GOOD case in point! Back at home in St Albans, the UK one, I decided one day to paint the chimney breast wall. Something like 5' across and 12' high. With a hole in the middle where the Rayburn sat. I did it in some lovely colour. My Mouse came home that night…. And THREE weeks later says, "have you painted the chimney breast!!!"

No, I don't usually consult him on décor. As Rhys Ifans said in "Notting Hill" after discovering Julia Roberts in their bath and coming outside, looking to the heavens and mouthing the words "Thank you G-d," I DO thank G-d for Michael Mouse's total "obliviousness" if there is such a word.

We've taken "the scenic route" to find our last condo. Holly came to all of these temporary abodes of course: Stuart thought it would upset her and disorient her but I think completely the opposite. It's probably been stimulating of sorts, yet she's still had me looking after her, but found new different things to look at (what she could manage to see!) and different smells. That's what they like! A good old sniff up another dog's bum!

Chapter 19

HOLLY, OUR JACK RUSSELL

A Mouse takes a dog for a walk…I took Holly out last night at 10pm. It was rather cold again, not really surprising for February but me still with my only coat, my Shopping Channel forest-green suede jacket (that I adore! I only wished I'd bought a Tan one too!) only just keeping me moderately warm. Thank G-d we're not out for long. There is an island out the front of this Pembroke Street apartment block. An oval patch of grass with what I think is one grey birch tree. I certainly saw enough of them on the Trans-Siberian Railway. Is it really two years since we were there! It feels like only six months ago.

This grassy patch is quite large and has the street lights lighting it up. It's a whitish very pale grey lumpy looking carpet of snow. The lumps are caused by tufts of grass underneath. It's really very pretty in an odd sort of way. I do feel guilty though for taking Holly out in this extremely cold weather. My son Stuart feels she should get this little outing for some fresh air and the chance to do her business and to sniff around. The thing all dogs love to do. That said, when the wind is in her face and there's no respite for either of us, and the wind is making her face look a little pinched and makes her white eyelashes stand out, I do wonder if I'm doing her any favours. After what is only a few minutes she's as happy as I am to go back into the warmth. Even this place takes on a different cosiness when it's become one's temporary home. It's good to be back in the city after being near the airport.

Holly turns 19½ around the middle of March! The vet gave me permission to increase her pain meds to two broken pieces of tablet in each feed. Her teeth had started to chatter again, and that is apparently a sign of pain especially if she's inside and we're not talking of cold weather.

It's not surprising that neither Holly nor I love the cold anymore. We're both older now. The news said, "minus 13 – windchill factor minus 23!" Well, I do love the cold - to a degree!

HOLLY'S GETTING OLD

Holly is VERY old now, and we know each other well. She has finally learnt that if I move her bowl when she's eating, I'm actually trying to help make it easier. She is getting very tired. When she eats now in the temporary studio apartment she gets her food in a bowl on the tiled floor. I see her doing the splits whilst trying to hold herself steady. It's achingly sweet but I don't leave her like that. That would be cruel. I had the bright idea of standing over her with both feet of mine – one on each side of hers, stopping her sliding. She's aware of it, and I know she's appreciative, dog wise. I had another idea to put a small bath mat under her feet which works very well too. Then she does the illogical thing of moving to another side of the bowl and losing the mat in the process!

Michael Mouse used to like to say that in this family he was a Mouse taking a dog for a walk. That changed several weeks ago when she moved suddenly. Maybe seeing a black squirrel. All I know is that Michael didn't react quick enough and his arthritic hand got yanked. He was in pain. That has finally gone down and I'm sure he's now over it but I've taken over taking her out and it will stay that way.

She had a dark "lozenge" triangle on the top of her head which has faded considerably, along with white eyelashes. And her sight is so much worse than it used to be. If I drop a piece of food on the floor, regardless of its colour, she is searching the 6" away from where it landed. It's very sad, but she'll get a surprise tonight. We're all going over to my son Stuart's place. And a dog called Chilli. A two-year-old pug. The difference in energy is a lot, not surprisingly. She has a lovely temperament. They both do.

It's funny, Stuart thought she would find it confusing being in another place yet again. I think she's taken to it like a duck to water. I feel very strongly that as long as she knows I'm around and that our belongings are around, albeit slightly differently arranged, that as long as she gets fed and watered, and a little fresh air every day, and quite a lot of stroking, then she seems as happy as a clam. I've reassured both "children" that if I thought she was in pain I would do something about it.

Luckily, as she is deaf, she is no longer afraid of thunder and when we were frying some fish last night and the coconut oil and sesame oil got too hot it set off the mandatory alarm. Shrieking its noise off while Holly slept blissfully through it. I was amazed. I thought high-pitched sounds could be detected. Evidently not necessarily the case when one loses that sense.

HOLLY - MAY HER DEAR
SOUL REST IN PEACE

For the last few months Holly has gone from pulling the lead (and me with it!) out of the elevator at 100 Pembroke Street on the third floor, around the corner and into our tiny bachelor apartment. This was for "breakfast" or "dinner." She was equally excited – it is, after all, FOOD, and her love of food only waned when she wasn't well. Even then it didn't last.

I'd been told by the vet (and I've read online) that when pets are coming to the end of their lives they sleep more and also don't necessarily want their food. Holly stands out for being un-textbook like! Everything started to slowly break down inside her. She was also diagnosed with a heart murmur.

She now also had cataracts that were in both eyes, prompting the vet to comment, "for Holly it would be like looking through a dirty windscreen." She also told us Holly could only make out shapes. I can't IMAGINE how that must have felt. Coupled with failing kidneys, a huge thirst that the other day, last Thursday (August = hot = thirsty) had her going to her water bowl. I didn't count for the first ten licks of water, then I started – and counted 165!!! Within 45 minutes (it was somewhere between half an hour and 11/2 hours (I've hedged my bets) that she came out of the bathroom/ her "bedroom" and promptly dropped her load

- one almighty swimming pool! We should have had shares in kitchen paper towels!

To start at the beginning is to start when Michael and I had been married only a relatively short while. I wanted a dog and had never had one in my childhood. I made up for that in Sydney. I only found out relatively recently that Daddy had had one when I came across old photos in black and white of a dog and it was his. I never knew!

When I last took Holly outside to the front where there was a small grassy area with a black railing around and she'd walked along until her front paws crossed over each other causing her to lose her balance and she leaned against the railing looking so forlorn I had to pick her up and cuddle her. She had an expression that just said, "I can't keep doing this."

Her age had finally caught up with her.

I had made our appointment with the vet for noon on Saturday, August 6th and my son Stuart was coming with us in the taxi. He came to Pembroke and asked if Holly could go on his knee and, of course, I said yes.

I took Holly down in my arms. I only wish I'd taken her down more often, lately, in my arms. That said, she was very tired and slept a lot. She knew she was loved and I think she stayed longer because of that.

(Today, August 17th, I've received an email. Holly's ashes are ready for collection. Stuart is getting them.)

DEAR HOLLY...

We loved you very much. Still do, and always will. I remember buying you from that old lady whose daughter had bought you for her. That old lady had cancer and really couldn't look after you. Her loss was our gain. A cliché but so true. She opened her front door and put you, then called Lady, on the ground and you wiggled your way towards us. I can remember it like it was yesterday. I had brought Amey Montgomery with me. A school friend of Lisa's and as Amey was hoping to be a veterinary nurse, she had the contacts and came with me in our car. She also held you in her arms as we took you to your new "home" and you've been with us ever since! As Neil said to me in one email, "she has lived in many places." Starting your life with us in St Albans, then to Buxton in Derbyshire, then emigrating to Canada and to your first apartment at Charles Street, followed by Front Street, followed by the Travelodge Hotel near the airport, and then to here, 100 Pembroke Street (which NONE of the taxi drivers can pronounce properly. They all say Pembrook, when there is a distinct difference between Pembroke (as in shire) and Pembrook as in a river.)

You took to every new place as a duck takes to water. Stuart said a couple of times that he thought you would get disorientated. I don't think you did at all. I think your sight started to go and the cataracts were forming for a long time but you were good at finding your way around. This tiny apartment has been relatively easy for you. I have to think that way.

It's funny you were called "Lady" initially as you were anything but! Your name should have been "Pro" as in prostitute, or "Tart because you were one! You happily laid down for any dog, in the "submissive" pose and promptly opened your legs! "Come hither" is what *that* said, so "Lady" had to go! As we had got you near Christmas I thought "Holly" was reasonable. It wasn't the most original but a simple lovely one and fitted you well. And much better than someone else had thought up – Osama! As in Bin Laden! Yeh, I can just see myself running around the park shouting out "Osama," especially near a Muslim suburb!

I remember your little "jaunts." In Buxton we had lived in Hardwick Square South, with the back facing north. We had put in a white picket fence as we "thought" we could restrain you slightly! Ha, that was a joke! I can see you now, looking around to see if we were visible and watching and, on realising the coast was clear, promptly jumped up and onto the top of the picket fence, balancing precariously across the top. You "hovered" at the top and then jumped down on the other side and went merrily on your way. A good look around and without your lead. Thank G-d we'd had you microchipped!

Then there was the time you nearly gave Michael Mouse a heart attack. He was walking you over The Slopes, a park across the road from our back gynnel. You decided you wanted to go home. You dashed cross a fairly busy road, Michael Mouse accidentally losing his grip on your lead! – How you avoided being run over, Mr Mouse will never know – and dashed back into the ginnel. Mr Mouse was left in a state of shock.

We loved having you as part of the family and you will always be remembered as a loving member. I really cannot believe you've gone. We've had you for eight weeks shy of

20 years! We will still salute you. You won't be forgotten, ever. Not by a long chalk.

We have some pictures of you and in time I will have Stuart print off one or two pictures of you, both when you were very young, then as a middle-aged female, as in one photo that has you newly arrived at Charles Street at around 11 years old. I never imagined you would be here this long. I have been complimented many times on your achieving your age, and I do feel pleased. Pleased that you loved me enough to want to be with me. That shouldn't take away from Michael, Stuart and Lisa.

I've just remembered - Lisa took you a few times when she went rollerblading up Church Street, Toronto, (and Cavendish Street, St Albans) and she just had you running with the wind in your hair! How you must have loved that! Everyone who met you loved you and I was always so pleased about that. You were friendly to everyone except for smokers. You didn't like the smell of nicotine on their fingers, and rightly so. Lisa didn't see you before you died. Maybe that's not so bad. I didn't see my Mother just before she died, or even after he'd died and before the funeral. Mother would have been glad I hadn't seen her in that "passed away" state. She would have wanted me to remember her alive and with those memories intact and I like to think Lisa has that of you, too. No memories of her last 24 hours. That's alright too.

Even when I was just making a sandwich. Your sense of smell never left you! Or maybe that you KNEW I was doing "something" with food and that if I could, I'd give you some. Another good name for you would have been "Scrounger!"

Holding you in my arms at the vet was a very precious time to me. To help you in your passage over to those who have gone before. Thank you for allowing me that; for holding on and giving me that opportunity. I had wanted you to die gently in your sleep but you, or G-d, chose to let me help you through it and I really appreciate that. I would still like one extra cuddle. I have to retreat into my memory for that. I am so lucky I had you for the best part of twenty years. Not many dog owners can say that!

You slept on a pillow in the bathroom here at this bachelor apartment. I loved walking in and seeing your chest going up and down as you slept deeply. I was glad for that, because it meant you were not in pain. I stroked you often, over and down your spine too. In these last few weeks you've lost 30-40% of your body weight. That's what the vet said (I should be so lucky!) With you I felt every vertebra. Stroking you with absolute love. It was actually, and still is, surprisingly easy to love you. You had a lovely temperament. When you were younger we played with you quite roughly but you loved it. THAT brings back a sudden memory. Us holding a rope knot for you to grab in your teeth and we'd lift you up in that moment and you stayed holding it fast! You were so strong and so utterly wonderful. Your only "fault" if it can be deemed that, is that you "shed" (a Canadian word) or moulted. We could have stuffed a cushion with your surplus hairs!

I will never stop loving you, Holly. Or as Stuart nicknamed you, Holly Wolly.

AND DEAR HOLLY - THE *FINAL* LETTER

On Saturday it will be eight weeks. Although you lived up till our last place I can see where you'd go around here. You'd have had more space here. Well, that wouldn't be difficult after the last place, Michael "charmingly" referring to it as a "dung-hole!" It wasn't quite that bad, except for the cockroach family that joined us in the kitchen. Even the cockroach family knew you weren't to be feared with those cataracts in both eyes.

I could cuddle you at will. I also had to give you your pain meds by dropper, directly into your mouth and you hated that, but we (you and I) both got you over that very quickly. That pain med was supposedly beef-flavoured. Obviously from a chemical lab - and you found it FOUL!

In your last few weeks I took you downstairs and outside to be in the sun and fresh air although, according to the vet, you could only see shapes, like looking through a very dirty windscreen.

The other people down at the front of these apartments, on the grassy spot, had their dogs with them. A lovely husky dog with those blue eyes and a little white fluffy thing. All knew you were into your last days and left us to be just you and me. They were all very sweet.

EVERYONE, including strangers, was amazed when we told them your age. I was complimented on your longevity many times which everyone put down to me loving you and looking after you. You must have loved us/me too, otherwise you'd have given up long ago. Jack Russells have a longer life span than many but even at 16 you were "past your sell-by date!" You were ten weeks shy of your 20th birthday. I will remember it and you very soon on October 12th and I will text both children. I loved your presence. You only stopped greeting people, including me, when you stopped being able to see properly.

One big plus for you, you went very deaf and thus were not frightened any more with thunderstorms as you were quite oblivious to them! I was very happy with that for you.

I love you very much, and so did everyone else. Gone, but never forgotten.

Holly, I do hope I helped your passage through into the next life. When you lay like a baby in my arms on that last day, Saturday August 6th this year (2016.) I stroked you. A lot. I hope that was truly recognised. And Stuart was stroking you too. Stuart was like me, a mess of cried-out eyes.

Holly, I cried so much. I cannot believe you've gone. After virtually 20 years. G-d could have taken you during any night. Or you could have "chosen" to go any time. I think you hung on so Stuart and I could say our goodbyes properly. By the way, Lisa wanted to be there too, but it was too far and hard for her at that time. You've had an impact on everyone and all who met you liked you. That's quite an achievement in Dogland! One day I hope to see you again. Enjoy your rest.

Holly (Wuff!) WARD, just shy of your 20th birthday!

Chapter 20

I AM NOT THE SUM OF MY TITS!

Our new local GP sent me for a mammogram but not till I told him I wasn't happy having one after all that I've read. That said, I also have my opinions of vaccinations, babies and cancer. When Dr S…was sending me, he asked would I accept "digital mammogram" and as I didn't know any better, and assumed that what he was offering was different, I said yes, only to find out that my boob was going to be just as squashed as before and that it would therefore be just as painful if not more so with my fibromyalgia, as that (with its nerve endings situation) makes this most painful and it certainly did. And to top it off I had to hold my breath!

When one holds one's breath in one raises one's chest, too, obviously. That pulls on the now-fixed-in-place boob held in by two pieces of plastic from the machinery. When you pull your body away but part of it is "trapped" there's going to be pain. I know, better to find out, etc.

So this so-called digital imaging didn't change a bloody thing. And to add insult to injury, a week later I get a phone call calling me back for a re-check! To me, not a good sign and worrying. I haven't told the kids yet as it's no point worrying them yet.

The mammogram recall was the kick I needed and that excess sugar is no good for anyone. So I cut out sugar from my tea. I'd already gone cold turkey with coffee. In fact, sugar shouldn't even be in our diets but manufacturers do not care about the consumer one iota, only that we buy their product. They would care if they all got sued but it's simpler just to boycott their products and hit them where they feel it the most. In their hip pocket, except not enough of us do this.

PATIENT 26328 OR HOW I CAME TO EAT HUMBLE PIE

How life changed suddenly and I joined that "elite" group that are diagnosed with breast cancer, and now I'm one of them. Not something I was thrilled to join but then back in 1994 I wasn't too happy to join the then "recently separated wives" club either.

Yesterday was my first day of chemo. So much for saying, "CHEMO IS TOXIC" and me vowing for the last 25 years at least that I would NEVER TOUCH CHEMO! I've just blown that one out of the water! Now is the time to eat humble pie!

It actually really starts three weeks ago, when I was sent for another mammogram. I had been asked when I had had the last mammogram prior to that and I had no idea. Yes, I'd had one but G-d knows when. It has to have been on a significant day, like someone dying, well known or family. Or anything else similarly big, then I'd have likely remembered...

190

My mammogram showed a mass in the left breast. The one Michael had named Caress. He named the right one Adore, and there they "stood." Or rather, hung. Well, Caress had a mass in her. Dr S had sent me for a mammogram and although I hadn't wanted any such thing done it had shown up the mass (as I said before, I never liked these procedures because they squashed the boob and with having fibromyalgia I feel pain more than normal when it's applied.) I went back to see him briefly before anything official started as I wanted to thank him personally. After this I got an invitation to go to Sunnybrook Hospital for another mammogram, followed by an ultrasound and then a biopsy. I must admit they are very lovely there and, more importantly, very efficient. I went in for these three procedures and they proceeded one after the other and quickly. I didn't even have time to pick up a mag and dive into it. It might be because this second mammogram was deemed "fairly aggressive" which is not very nice!

Apparently a benign tumour has a smooth outline which I likened to a blown-up balloon. The malignant one I "saw" as a tree in the evening with a full moon silhouetted but this time with a craggy/rough outline. This was on a monitor - and inside Caress too! Well, I would remember Caress with fondness.

I was telephoned to be given an appointment at Sunnybrook and given Patient ID 26328. A couple of appointments later I resorted to writing in biro on my left hand 26328. I'd also discovered here in Canada they don't know the word biro which is used everywhere in England. They have the ball-point-pen here, but don't know its origins. Actually, he was Hungarian, says my Mr Mouse.

I've now had several appointments with one particular doctor. Every doctor, well, it seemed like that, one now "my" oncologist, and someone else too that I cannot recall, that ended up feeling the left breast. I mentioned lightly that it would make it easier for everyone if I just sat upright on the examination couch and they all filed past and had a grope!

The amount of times now that I have been to Sunnybrook is at the point I've lost count. Michael Mouse had worked out the route. Like many *former* nerds (what's a better word for you, oh Mouse of mine?) he worked out such a simple route. Bus outside our new home condo to Finch subway, four stops to Lawrence subway station and the 124 bus directly from the underground bus stop to Sunnybrook and into its grounds! Same route reversed as the bus does a loop. SO straightforward. One doesn't need complications when one is fighting cancer, and obvious but not always followed through on (not unlike all the spy holes in our former studio/bachelor appointment at Pembroke St! These spyholes, and the ones here, are often not looked through and I can attest to that because the TALL person who put them in did NOT allow for shorter people, only put them *all in at his own height.* Idiot! Digressed again, sorry!)

CHEMO COMMENCEMENT

That was yesterday, Friday 24th February - only eight days after our twentieth wedding anniversary. I had to be at Sunnybrook Odette Cancer Centre. While I'm a patient, queueing up will be the thing each time we go, passing my ID over a machine and then waiting to be called. I was due there at 9.15 and we were on time, as it should be.

By 10.10 I'd finally started with the chemo coursing through my veins. I find I'm being wry towards myself after how vehemently being opposed to chemo for so many years. Don't get me wrong. I still am, and it IS still toxic, and it still kills non-cancerous cells too, in its wake, but apparently fewer good ones and more of the cancerous ones. Well, it should be. With a "fairly aggressive" cancer I didn't feel I had much choice. Neil didn't want to lose a third sibling. Stuart claimed that he wanted me to be a Grandma too, one day and I do too, to his children as well as Lisa's!

The chemo is doing its job too well, and I don't mean in shrinking the breast tumour. No, it's done a very good job of weakening my hair so that if a brush so much as looks at it I start shedding. I usually wash my hair every other day. I decided it was absolutely no point in washing my hair this morning as I would end up with a handful of very clean but loose hair in my palm. Which is exactly what happened. I'd forgotten about it being weakened. I looked in the mirror and started to gently brush my hair and suddenly, in amongst the hair, seemingly hiding, was this thick softly matted mass of what looked like your wider-than-average dead RAT! A thick wad of meshed hair that just came away in my hand. It fitted my WHOLE hand and not just the palm! A mouse losing her hair. My linguist Mouse said earlier "chauve–souris" or bald mouse was Bat in French! I can't imagine being bald but I think I'm about to find out quite soon…

I have been collecting lovely scarves for years now. Now, will they come into their own? I would never have guessed this way. They would suit being in Paris with me looking very chic and nobody guessing why this woman had that many scarves. Yes, Paris would be a gorgeous place to forget chemo for a day or three. No, I'm not wearing scarves on my head. They don't stay on, I prefer the warmth around my neck and I think it is good to teach people in any town that there are people fighting cancer, so I'm not covering it up after all. It gets too hot for me anyway and too quickly, so it wouldn't work.

Well, my son Stuart came around on Monday night, later than planned but we have had blizzards here in Toronto and temperatures plummeting to minus 7 but with wind-chill factors making it minus 17. Very cold by anyone's standards.

My hair was still here, as in thin but still all here but looking rather "see through." Something I've never had in my life. I went to brush my hair in the washroom with my hairbrush, and again this great swathe of hair, lurking in amongst my other hairs, just came away like another thick, fattish, elongated dead rat. I still have it and I now have eight of these. When I held it, before I pulled it easily away from other hairs it was like watching something from a horror movie. A very good premise in the first opening credits. It's certainly creepy and I've experienced it. I have a ball of hair that has the dubious honour of being the first hairball to leave my scalp and it's a reasonable size. Four-five inches in diameter, and thick dark brown with wisps of white caught up in it. And it's soft. As I've been saying for the last 36 hours, it would make a very good bird's nest. As would the subsequent ones…seven more and one of those is the elongated one. Incredible how much hair I've had. This has got to change me emotionally, definitely physically, and

194

neither Michael nor I can think of a third one. I thought "spiritually" was one but Michael said that was the emotional factor again. These things are sent to change us, presumably for the better. One would hope all people can do with being improved and I'm no exception. I have also realised that my hair probably wouldn't suit a bird's nest as the chemo has permeated through it and the birds would sense that.

I can snooze at the drop of a hat and I now look every one of my 63 years. I am now regularly knackered (an old English word for having the old horse taken to be chopped up for horse meat - 'Knacker's Yard'. The horse being very tired has come to mean knackered.) My Mouse is taking Mrs Mouse out for dinner over the weekend, or Sunday lunch and I don't think I can wear a scarf all through lunch. I will get too hot. I overheat very easily (chemo drugs again?) so it'll be interesting to gauge the reactions of other diners. That said, I actually tend to forget what I look like unless I see a reflection. It's a surprise every time.

My hair is now pretty much "no more." Like the Dead Parrot Sketch. With seven "nests" and one thickish tailing thinner, which is the aptly named "dead rat" that I suddenly brushed out of my hair, over a week ago now. It's actually incredible to brush one's hair and a whole swathe of hair comes along with it. There's a completely surreal feel about it. I've kept all my eight nests so far and I intend keeping them for quite a while yet. That hasn't changed. I still have them. They're not going anywhere.

Chemo is exhausting. It's tiring just to "be!" My brother Neil is very sympathetic and also tries to bolster me up. It's good to get his emails. Three thousand four hundred miles away but emailing is very good.

ULCERS ARRIVAL: 18TH MARCH 2017

Well, they had to arrive, I suppose. Pain in the form of two mouth ulcers on my tongue - one on each side. I felt one just now and it's more raised than it was before. They're not huge but what they lack in size they make up for in pain and tenderness. For the first time since this started, I've rung the Sunnybrook helpline and a doctor rang me back very quickly, which I really appreciated.

Michael's going across the road to Shoppers Drug Mart to get me what amounts to a mouthwash (it gave my Mr Mouse a chance to buy himself some chocolate. He likes dark chocolate, with a very high coco count. Better for diabetics…!) An antibiotic and other ingredients that help calm mouth ulcers. It's a gargle. These ulcers have really got me down. More than the hair, this is pain and it even makes swallowing interesting. One doesn't realise how many times one swallows just in the course of any 24 hours. The only time we don't is when we're asleep. Actually even speaking is made harder and my huge sneezes - I just did one - don't help. A sneeze that creates pain - who'd have thought it! Michael not hearing me first time in *almost everything I say* and that makes it harder. Selective subconscious deafness. Luckily I only *contemplate* killing him!

These mouth ulcers take energy, or lack thereof, to a whole new level. It's come very close to making me miserable. The hair is something else. I can forget I've lost my hair except if I go outside with it, or rather, without it.

I still have hair down both sides of my face, actually framing it. It's fine, pale, blondish white with about 30 strands on each side. Blonde and cool; Why couldn't

I have had you when I was younger!? Looks odd but I don't see that.

We went to St Lawrence Market today. Harry's fish stall was SO welcoming. The lady there hasn't seen us for months, and Michael with his neck brace from his spinal surgery and me looking like Fruma Sarah just got the biggest hug from her. It was really lovely. She grasped me around my waist, from behind! It was all very sweet. She is Harry's Mother and also works the fish stall, a big one. They are so lovely there, Valerie too, who'd never sold fish before! Fish is so healthy, especially wild caught.

First time in a long time going to St Lawrence Market and mostly to buy some Manuka honey. It's expensive anywhere and this tub is going to be gone through very slowly. It has real medicinal properties and is revered the world over. Can't hurt.

The Sunnybrook doctor on call is ringing through to the Shoppers here and Michael is going over to hopefully pick up my prescription for the mouth ulcers. It cannot come too soon! It's a special mouthwash that is going to do some healing, I hope. With Michael I have to spell things out: needing more talking and that can be frustrating. The severe backache of a week or so ago was OK because painkillers dealt with it. A mouth is resistant and we use it, if only to swallow and breathe. Meal times are not something to enjoy any more at present, just to "get through with minimal discomfort."

FAST FORWARD...

...to my third chemo session. This time I was joined by my Stuart. I am EXHAUSTED, and from "just being up." I've not washed my hair – what's left of it - since this whole "journey" began. I have blondish hair down both sides of my face in a soft, thin bob, but none at the back. Only soft "down" on the back of my head. Rather like a brand-new baby - except with an older face!!! A "boiled egg" look front on. Not the most alluring. In fact I could pass for an inmate at my late mother-in-law's former old-age home in South London!

Eating habits have changed too. I bought chicken filleted thighs on Friday. It's a favourite, and I cooked baby potatoes with their skins on, for added nutrients along with carrots. I couldn't be bothered doing extra separate veg so those two cooked together. Simple and delicious but I couldn't face the chicken. There's this "I just don't want to eat that" feeling and I'm just picking at foods here and there. You'd *think* I could bloody lose weight on this regime, but oh no, G-d forbid! What happened when I bought the Atkins diet book? I bought the book. Michael Bloody Mouse lost the weight!

Fruit is a G-d send as it doesn't require any thought or decision-making. Seedless oranges are almost my saviour. Pomelos I adore and are a wonder, but they don't seem in season as they are not as sweet as they should be. Raspberries: now there's another saviour. Also kiwis. I need all the enzymes that one gets from fresh fruit without any enzymes being lost. The extreme tiredness is here though, and not going away any time soon. I later found out that I cannot eat citrus after all because it interferes with the cancer-prohibiting drugs!

My mouth sores seem to have returned, although I can't see them and I'm having difficulty swallowing. So "back to that" which makes me feel despondent.

I just want to go to sleep till all this is over. My oncologist has told me she'd like me to meet with the radiation guy. I've agreed to meet him. End of!

To explain, I was already hugely against chemo but because Neil ("baby" brother - then at 51!) said he didn't want to lose another sibling and between us we've both lost two other brothers, Russell and Cedric, as earlier mentioned; and my son Stuart said he wanted me to be around as a grandma - when he's ready, I didn't have the "luxury" of looking around and trying alternative therapies that might well have worked. I already feel that half the processed junk that people put into their bodies does a superb job of encouraging different cancers to "go forth and multiply."

We're already eating much healthier than many and the supermarket bill attests to that. I could be trying expensive drugs that we'd have to contribute to, OR eat very health giving foods, and I know which I'd rather sink my teeth into. You get so many more nutrients with real foods because they come from nature. They're in abundance!

I've read the two brochures on radiation and it's not a pretty picture. It's all very well if someone is "recommending" it but they are not going to go through with it and have what could be devastating side effects. After reading the two fairly comprehensive brochures I'm even more put off than before. Secondary tumours are not unheard of when people add radiation to their "therapies." I've put my body through enough already and next Friday I will be half way through the chemo. At the end of May I will finish and then I get four-six weeks for my body to slowly recuperate from this onslaught. Then I will be scheduled for the bilateral mastectomy, ie, both. I'm sure I'll be subjected to more questions, AGAIN, on why I've chosen this method over a single one. I'm also getting somewhat tired of trotting it out. Each medic wants to hear my reasoning. I think part of it is a psychological evaluation done over time to see if I change my stance. Not happening! It actually gets boring after a while because one starts to try putting it another way and there's only so many different ways to phrase it!

I was also asked to meet this radiation doctor and didn't really want to meet him at all. On top of that I was asked to meet him on the Friday of the week I wasn't even going in for my regular chemo! So, with my huge lack of energy I was to be going into the hospital that was on one of the days of the week that I didn't have to be in there for! And he does go in every Friday! HE could surely come and see me whilst I'm tethered to the drip that was giving me so much "wonderful" chemo, couldn't he? It's not the end of the world to ask him to visit me, is it…it may seem a bit of a chutzpah, but I AM there, on a Friday when he's there too. So how about it?

I'm going to sound a total hypocrite now, because I'm going to add "you shouldn't be put off." If your radiation doctor says it'd be good for you, you have to decide if you agree with him. Each person will feel different and will /should read masses on this. I feel I've gone along the "established path" (thank you, Michael, my literary editor that I can wonderfully ask any question even at 3am! - it does have its benefits!)

I've also looked into "breast reconstruction" and don't much like the sound of that either. (now eight years later I've changed my mind about that but I think it's too late, shame.)

I thought my mouth sores were back but I think it's just the swallowing mechanism that is having a hard time. Plus my thigh grew another "angry" pustule. Well, that's what my Mouse called it. Btw my Mouse is now giving me the daily injections to build my white blood cell count up again. I swab the area we both decide on (after looking at the diagram I was supplied with) and we keep alternating the area. I swab it and then pinch it hard on both sides to give me a slight pain which overrides the injection going in. And it works! Michael has to come in with the injection at a 45 degree angle and he does it well! (bloody miracle!)

My tiredness has arrived again. I WILL finish this book, just not sure which year!

KOJAK BUT WITHOUT THE LOLLYPOP! (MAYBE GOOGLE HIM!)

I can easily forget I've lost 90% of my hair when I'm out. I could now pass for someone of 70+. I have a new look. The hard-boiled egg look. Not the most flattering but it does get me a seat on any bus and the subway and for that I'm very appreciative. Everyone in this city of Toronto is so kind, welcoming and helpful and that was before I was diagnosed with breast cancer.

I joined an "elite" group when I first separated from my ex husband. That was in late 1994. Suddenly I'd go into the supermarket and every checkout woman was a divorcee, or about to be, or had been for years, or whatever their situation was and I'd suddenly joined their ranks and not willingly either.

This new breast cancer group is another case in point. I haven't met any others yet, except those I've seen at Sunnybrook Hospital. The ones I am seeing there are either wearing a wig, or a knitted bobble hat, or a scarf covering their entire head but I am not caring who actually sees me like this.

That said, I do have a hat. A black peaked hat that doesn't cover all and I'm fine with that. If I look tired it is realised why and what's wrong with that? My peaked hat has "POW MIA (Prisoner of War - Missing In Action) Their War Is Not Over." I used to read true stories of WW2 and left many back in Oz. Boldness Be My Friend by Richard Pape and Reach For The Sky by Paul Brickhill (this is the true story of my hero Douglas Bader - the legless pilot) and last but not least Carve Her Name With Pride . The true story (as they all are) of Violette Szabo. I must get three second hand copies again!

The hat also reminds me of my (and my ex Gerry's) very good old friend Terry Boardman. Himself a Vietnam Vet and a lovely guy and my partner in the 1981 Castrol GTX International Car Rally. Terry had his VW Golf. A rarity at a car rally, well, it was then.

Chemo is tiring. Very tiring. Exhausting actually. I do small jobs around the apartment in small increments. I can't wait to have this apartment ship shape. The light coming into it is wonderful. We are technically only south-west facing but because of Yonge Street not being exactly north-south we are getting east, too. So West, East and

South sun in four windows, resulting in much light which is phenomenal.

Our 20th wedding anniversary on February 16th. Where was I? Getting a mammogram, an ultrasound and a biopsy one after the other in that order and very efficiently done, and then shown on the screen where the malignancy was. I didn't cry then and I still haven't. I have no tears and I have no idea why. IF they had said it was all inoperable and I only had six months to live, that would have made it very different. I would be crying, horrified, angry and shouting at G-d but I have also read, in more than one place, how He only gives us what we can handle. I think there's an element of truth there. If I had been diagnosed with bone cancer in the leg or arm and faced amputation, I would be a lot worse off emotionally now. Losing a limb and getting used to putting on and taking off a prosthetic limb would be too much for me physically, I think, (although my Lymphodema is truly getting me down now). I've seen young men on the news after they've lost a limb in Afghanistan and they are fitted with a new prosthetic one. They learn to walk with it. That's different though.

I have lymphatic fluid in both legs and feet that has built up and no way of releasing it (now, seven years after my bilateral mastectomy, the lymphedema *is* releasing all the bodily leg fluids and I make a mess around both shoes daily. They (the lymph fluids)have to find an "out." Isn't that lovely - not!)

I'll deal with what I have to and appreciate that He knows who he gives what to. That said, I am looking for ways of improving the lymphatic system within me and hope to offer myself as a guinea pig...

Now I'm tired again. It comes in bouts. Now my Mouse and I are even more complimentary to each other than we already were. We both tire from totally different things but both in legs! and get pleasantly tired together.

THE HARD-BOILED-EGG LOOK AGAIN

Just now I took the recycling down. I don't bother putting my peaked hat on then. It's really not worth it and my head still gets too warm very quickly. I really don't care whether people choose to look. I know I would if I was in their shoes. It's a natural curiosity and it does show life from a different angle. Also, because I'm not seeing it I tend to forget what others see. I only feel it if there's a sudden breeze or worse!

Yesterday after alighting from the bus I found it very cold. Even more appropriate now: the "gills" are exposed! I haven't washed my head or brushed my hair since 90% of the hair has gone. My head feels quite nice. It has a light coating of down on it. I guess I'm lucky this started mid-February. Still Winter and freezing but going in the right direction!

I am still exhausted, daily, but just lately not "needing" naps but I don't claim to understand it. I have had a "partial cold" for best part of a month and it's REALLY BORING! It's obviously part of a now somewhat suppressed immune system. I want to use oil of oregano, but I have another mouth ulcer that popped up again on the side of the tongue and I know that oil of oregano stings somewhat - but oil of oregano is THE turn-to whenever I feel off colour. It's my FIRST port of call. There's a hint there. It's bloody good stuff. Do its instructions in 1/4-1/2 glass of strong juice and stir it, and swig it. Get it in early and head anything off at the pass. Now I buy Oil of Oregano gel capsules and they're even better and easier to swallow and no after taste.

My whole life almost revolves around hospital appointments. Actually, that's an exaggeration – my life revolves around chemo, injections, and extreme exhaustion. I've also found that many foods that I fancy, e.g, fried chicken pieces, lose something when I finally serve the food. That said, I can start cooking with extra virgin olive oil and a diced onion and it smells heavenly. I've also gone off many drinks. I found a new one lately. Brewed iced tea with raspberry infusion or peach infusion and have been on that for several weeks. Now, suddenly, that's waning and I have found skimmed milk is doing the trick. I cannot stand most water but iced water with a wedge of lemon is passable, especially in a restaurant.

Today Michael went for an early morning blood test after a fast since last night. I went on ahead and we'd catch up at Odette. My session was "only" Herceptin today so only half-an-hour in being hooked up to an IV and the Herceptin coursing through my veins. G-d knows what it's doing to the rest of me but apart from extreme exhaustion and a persistent irritating cough (I am taking headache tablets with codeine in; as I found out years ago caffeine is a cough suppressant and unfortunately I recently found out that it also makes for constipation!) My bone pain started to put in an appearance this morning but I took Acetominophen and nipped it in the bud.

Michael gave me a cuddle the other evening. I was sat on the side of the bed needing a cuddle and he came around to my side of the bed and I just put my bald head against his tummy. "I've never cuddled a hard-boiled egg before!" He said. I actually found that funny. And very sweet. You had to be there I suppose.

We are still "complimenting" each other. Michael has diabetes and not very good circulation and that results in sore feet and a limp and walking v e r y slowly. *If he went any slower he'd be going backwards !*At least we're not (mostly) getting impatient with each other. If we do, it's me. I have unpacked a picture, framed, of our wedding. Of Michael standing tall and resplendent with his terracotta bow tie that I chose and just a wonderful picture. How I wish I'd realised how much he hunched over the computer so often. He *cannot* be the only one who has done so, to the detriment of his own not-infallible body.

REFLECTIONS ON RADIATION

I haven't cried at the beginning and I still haven't cried now, three months later. The tumour has shrunk to a golf-ball size so that is good but according to what I have read online the chemo is worse for the body than the actual malignant tumour. And don't even get me started on radiation. I googled Ten Things to Ask Your Specialist Before You Go Ahead With Radiation and up popped a complete article. Very illuminating it was, too. I was already off the idea: I did *not* want to go down the radiation "therapy" route and now I'm even more sold on that idea – to avoid it. You *must google this and choose this for yourselves*. You have to do your own leg work and be happy with your own choices.

There are those who have *not* done their homework and who blithely say, "Well, my doctor recommends this and he/she knows much more about this than I do so I'm placing myself in their hands; they know best." Do your own due diligence. Some doctors would not put their own families through any of this but they will *never admit to that in some cases* and would actually say the opposite. What do we, mere plebs, stand a chance of, when it's all stacked against us? Many would actually get into trouble if they put us off radiation.

CHEMO - HALFWAY HOUSE

We left the condo this morning, 7th April, 2017...in a BLIZZARD of snow, winds, and biting cold. This afternoon is Spring. Mild, bright and absolutely gorgeous. One would never get such extremes in the same day in England but here in Toronto anything is possible!

We have just returned in the last half-hour from my fourth chemo and halfway point. We got to Sunnybrook at...9.15am and left at 4.30pm!!! Blood-work first, as is the norm, because if that's not "right" the chemo doesn't go ahead.

I was also "assessed" as in: "Have I had any nausea and/ or vomiting?" As well as other such questions? It was no to all. Funnily enough, this nurse we knew from last time, who was very sweet and allowed Stuart to stay when I pointed out I didn't see him very often; there had been TWO seats last time, very rare! Otherwise, he would be kicking his heels outside in the large waiting area. So, thank you

Carmen!!! Not going to forget her! Well, the blood-work didn't take more than five minutes but the results of it, and thus allowing the chemo to start, took another three hours!

We met with Dr Icannotpronounce! He checked out the mass himself and then proceeded to tell us the advantages of radiation. Oh, I love that word. No, I don't. I hate it and all it stands for, but I have two reasonable booklets on radiation and its side effects and how it's done etc. I said they were reasonable. I mean in their explanation, not in how I perceive them. I read both booklets, properly too. Michael's going to read them this weekend.

It didn't help (well, it did for Me!) when Michael's cousin Gerard rang him to tell him that his Uncle Basil's wife, Barbara, had secondary tumours brought on by the radiation she'd had years earlier. I remember Barbara fondly because one of the very first sentences uttered to me when we met was, "don't let the buggers get you down!" She was referring to Michael's late Mother Doris who wasn't thrilled when he started dating me. A divorcee, and with two children in tow, and, "she's older than you!" Yes, by ten pathetic months and two days according to Michael Mouse! Michael reasoned, "I have my own life to live," and wanted it with me (I did explain to Doris that I knew EXACTLY where she was coming from and that if my son had done the same I would have felt exactly as she did). Not forgetting Michael also pointed out that Doris had been 13 months older than her late husband Sidney - so total hypocrisy there, too.

Dr Icannotpronounce said that they usually recommended chemo followed by surgery followed by recuperation followed by radiation. After chemo and surgery, chances of the cancer returning were reduced by 75%. "Very few" have secondary tumours returning. That's very good, if one isn't in that minority and if one is going to follow the oncologists to the letter.

I'm not at all happy. I met with him because Dr J had requested it. I've heard what he's said. Michael's Aunt Barbara through marriage was diagnosed initially at around 40 years of age, and had chemo and an operation and radiation. Now she was in her 80s and suddenly these secondary tumours reappeared. Admittedly, she didn't get these secondary tumours until her 80s as Neil (baby brother Neil Roland) pointed out. All this for her started in her 40s and ended in her 80s. Mine started in my 60s and I want to see what all these experts have to say when I'm through the chemo and the recuperation, followed by the bilateral mastectomy and through *that* recuperation.

Dr Icannotpronounce has indicated we'd meet up after the chemo is finished and likely before the operation and that's fine by me. What I hadn't known till today was that in most cases the patients do the chemo and the op, and finish up with radiation that "scoops up" stray cancerous cells. That said I thought THAT was what chemo was supposed to do. If that is the case why aren't we all just having just radiation, for that matter, bypassing chemo altogether. Also, because radiation on "microscopic cancerous cells" cannot be guaranteed as they are by definition microscopic and therefore cannot be seen, so the radiation beam targets random healthy tissue. Thus equally producing ensuing pain and not necessarily getting rid of cancerous cells - by my reckoning.)

The one thing I'm glad about is that my Mother Ruth didn't go through this and that Lisa hopefully won't ever go through this. It happened to my Grandma, and has come to me. I'd rather me have it than Mother and it looks like it's done the jumping of the generations, as it apparently does. Also means my granddaughter could be next. We'll have to cover that bridge…

Just before we left Sunnybrook we had to go via the pharmacy to pick up the meds and - oh joy, my favourite bit, the injections that bring my white cell count back up to normal. This would almost be the blind leading the blind except Michael *has* to look what he's doing! TG I don't have to! Swab the area (choose one of several each morning and alternate) and I pinch myself hard so I feel *that* pain rather than the needle, and it works! Michael has to swab and then go in at a 45-degree angle and that's it! We also took the anti-nausea meds. Not because I wanted them; indeed, I didn't AND I still have the same from the first week of chemo, unopened. And before you say, "well, if you feel queasy you may be glad you had them." Yes, but I already have the very first lot and I'm unintentionally stockpiling them!

On top of that I have TUMS in our bathroom cabinet and - how can I explain this…TUMS must have less in them than a made-for-chemo treatment, so I've managed very happily to suck on a TUMS when I HAVE had queasiness, but those times have been few and far between, thank goodness. Any chemo med HAS to have more in its makeup than brands such as TUMS so by definition I have to be putting less medical crap into my body…TUMS have to be more carefully made up, surely, because the general public has access to them. Am I so wrong here?!

I was actually getting tired mid-afternoon whilst the chemo drug was coursing through my veins but then late lunch arrived. No, not Room Service but Michael Mouse Room Service! And very well he did too! A completely raw salad including mushrooms, broccoli, purple cabbage, carrot, beetroot and cucumber. Not only was it filling but the enzymes that have not been totally destroyed by heat HAVE to surely help my fight against the tumour? Well, I'd like to think so. Although the raw salad would have been better prepared by me earlier at home because as soon as one cuts into raw veg they start to lose their nutritional value when it gets exposed to the air. Hence a serrated plastic knife is best for lettuces or rip them up yourself.

Chapter 21

KEEPING ABREAST - OR NOT

7 am Saturday morning on 26 April 2017. I had been warned that yesterday was going to be a long one as I was now having new drugs,and they wanted to monitor me very slowly as all were being administered, to be instantly on the ready for any adverse reactions I might have. Actually reassuring and frightening at the same time. So one that took one-hour-and-a-half yesterday will only take half-an-hour next time. A bad headache started, and didn't improve. It went in the wrong direction and I ended up on painkillers.

I had been also told I'd be on a proper bed because of any sudden reactions and that also didn't happen, but curiously I wasn't unhappy about that at all. It was nicer to see the "old familiar reclining armchair." Everyone is so lovely there and can't do enough. Bessie was also there, "our" Greek nurse and I get a huge kick out of hearing Michael converse in Greek with her. He enjoys practising his Greek and everyone (any Greek we ever meet here) is always impressed with his Greek. It's always better grammatically than theirs.

The one big minus with how much fluid is being drip-fed through my system is that the amount that "has to go somewhere" and soon I was "peeing for Canada!" OMG - if I could have moved the armchair into the washroom I would have, because I would barely get resettled for about ten minutes and back I'd go. Of course I left it as long as possible but that feeling of REALLY needing to go is no fun. TG I was the only one seemingly doing it *that* often. I really resent the others' needs for going less and yet am very envious at the same time. Relieved (no pun intended) that they don't need it, the end result being that a washroom is not blocked! Also, seemingly being the only one that makes that trip stands out too, for all the wrong reasons. Almost an imaginary banner above my head reading, "Look, I'm off to pee again." Horrible, but no getting around it. I know it's only in my head, but it doesn't change anything.

There is a tv above my head in the recliner if I wanted to watch tv but we've both brought reading equipment - in the real meaning of the word. Printed paper, not an iPod or whatever other electric gadgets we don't possess or want.

I'm now going to be going every week to Sunnybrook's Odette Cancer Centre as I will be on Taxol and, to be administered every Friday, Herceptin (which is apparently for a year!) plus seeing Dr J every other Thursday so my calendar has filled up. As Stuart would say, "what else are you doing?" Well, apart from writing my book - not a lot. What else do I do? Try and muddle our way through an apartment which is still looking very unpacked and yet not put away? Certainly we could "almost" pass for a couple on the programme Hoarders, but TG I have learnt to "cull" some of our stuff but looking around, the untrained eye would be hard pushed to believe me! WE, well, 'I' know what I've thrown. Michael would never notice till months afterwards. SO tempting to get rid of what he might keep but I'm not that mean a Mouse.

Yes, we've been Mice since the start of it all and that is our status. Mr and Mrs Mouse since February 1997. The only thing missing are our two tails!

We finally got our "get out of jail card" at 6.30 pm last night, here at Sunnybrook Hospital. Later than planned, and next week will start somewhat earlier but as my better sleeping seems to happen between 4am and 9am so we'll see how much it does change.

Trass Too Zoo Mab (other name is Herceptin!) "No side effects, maybe flu symptoms but nothing big" is a quote from my nurse, and she seems right. She's very sweet. She adds they'll also check my heart every three months for up to that full year, so till April 2018! And every other week blood-work is done with the Taxol.

Paclitaxel (Pack-li-TAX-ell). Thank you - spell check is taking a rest! A clear solution mixed into larger bags of fluids. I can attest to that and so can the toilet, although I must add it's lessening slightly. I've also decided to sit in the recliner as an upright armchair and that has made a difference!!! I can snooze better too, as I do that at home in my armchair there. It's recommended most daytime snoozes don't get done in the bedroom. Makes sense otherwise I'd seemingly never leave the room and would get very fed up with it. The pillows they have in Odette are pathetic hence upright is simpler all around.

Side effects can be numbness or tingling in hands or feet (the latter never arrived.) Heart or liver problems, also not yet but scary, thanks for nothing! Bone pain is raising its head again. Got that briefly weeks ago and felt it as if eating a cooked chip that had a point which got stuck half way down. Not nice at all but two strong painkillers got rid of that in about 45 minutes. Still creepy knowing this is going on inside. I saw my doctor on Thursday and a newly-introduced-to-me female doctor had a feel of the mass. Now it's 3 cm, so seemingly smaller. They didn't make a big fuss about it but I guess that's going in the right direction? Stuart, you could enlighten me when you come to this, please. You would anyway. You know your centimetres. You're a sweetheart. Lisa, you'd be good at centimetres too, wouldn't you?

My nurse also mentioned, "use these numbers (the telephone number she wrote on the back of these particular printouts) if you get diarrhea." I wish I'd left this alone. I was fine in hospital with "number twos."! How "gracefully" can anyone be typing about such things? I will keep it brief! (Ha! says Stuart, she doesn't even know the MEANING of the word!") Well, I do - whether I can execute it is another matter.) You'd THINK if one did number twos in the hospital one could continue doing same back home... no. Finally home at 9pm and immediately had the runs. Probably shouldn't be surprised after SO much fluid but I DID TG for it happening at home when it could have struck at any other near loo (and home is always the nicer familiar one) OR, WORSE, in-between, maybe on the subway and I'd have been - MORTIFIED!

I rang the out-of-hours number and a male receptionist passes my name onto the doctor. I was told he'd need my patient ID number but he says no and just asks for my name. The doctor usually rings back immediately. This didn't happen and it's now 12.10 midnight and I'm regretting even having rung. I rang back to cancel as I decide to take some Pepto Bismol, that pink stuff, wonderful. The same receptionist tells me that he can't cancel it and that if he did and something happened to me, his head would roll. I said the only thing that could go wrong here is if I don't make it to the bathroom and end up having to change the bed at midnight! We both laugh. And that I WILL get a call from the doctor, whenever. Great! Now I decide Murphy's Law: if I plan to go to sleep, I guarantee he would ring. So I did, and he did! Ringing shortly after, while I'm chatting to Michael in the dark. Bismol is fine. Just as well as I've taken it. The night goes without a hitch.

Now I just need home-made real fresh coffee so I'm off to put the pot on. I like my little rituals and I'm still around to DO them. That's the best part.

Yet to finish all Odette hospital visits by June 2nd and the four-six weeks to respite in warmer weather on our first-ever balcony, before the big operation. Then real recuperation and then nothing. I'm NOT going down the radiation route! I'm sure things have changed but *I still don't have to like it or want it*. Radiation gives me even more of the willies, and can give secondary tumours - even if they take a long time to grow.

SHORT BUT SWEET: 29 APRIL 2017

Thursday I had blood-work done again. It really does make me think of vampires. Just as well we remake the blood, or our bodies do, because otherwise I'd be drained by now! No snack for any blood-sucking handsome young Frankenstein.

Last week we were offered papers to fill in if we were interested in getting a car that would pick me up and deliver me to Sunnybrook and do the same in reverse. I talked this over with Michael very briefly. It was a sweet thought but as it's quite a simple route (and with no carbon footprint making things worse, which it would if we accepted a car) we've decided not to take this offer up. I think it's good that people see people like me on the subway and that we're not hidden from view and that they can offer their seat. Many do, and I'm extremely appreciative of that. With a car getting caught in traffic I saw no real gain and in fact the subway does indeed probably get us back to our vicinity much sooner, and with a clear conscience.

Immediately on the return train journey yesterday, Friday, a young man tried to tell Michael he could sit on a proper seat - he was resting against those "bum-buffer" things that people just lean against. Michael joined me at the next stop. He doesn't ever risk walking when the train is moving. Just as well with his newly fractured - but now healed – spine.

The same young man then came up to me sitting on a seat with space ahead of me and knelt down and looked me straight in the face and asked if I had cancer? I said yes. He said which one? I said breast. He said he was a student of mental health at U of T. He said I was looking "illuminated." I took that as a huge compliment. A woman in the queue yesterday at the Odette Centre happened to also say I looked very well. That was lovely too. She didn't need to make any compliment and as I have the Kojak look (if you need to - google Kojak, plus lollypop!) It's doubly boosting getting a compliment especially when one doesn't know it's coming. I've had very few ask anything. Most have known what a hairless woman's head means and the many people in Toronto on the trains have always been so lovely and helpful. And this was before my diagnosis! It makes me well up.

I took Michael for a haircut this morning and went to the supermarket. THAT has taken all my energy. Sapped of energy over basic daily needs. Roll on the end of this month when chemo comes to the end and I am supposed to get four-six weeks R&R. Later this month I see my surgeon, who is hopefully going to give me a date for the operation. Also, for the time being, I have finished the daily injections!

I cannot wait for the end of chemo. I've had no mouth ulcers for a while now and I try to keep that at bay, too. Swallowing and mouth ulcers are wretched. I'm hoping to find a juice bar not too far from here where I can choose all very fresh fruit and veg and especially kale etc that have very good anti-carcinogenic qualities and as long as it's not too thick (as in a smoothie) I am really looking forward to finding this type of place. Stuart is also visiting tomorrow and I am *really* looking forward to that too! It's real nourishment for the soul and the rest of me. The old-fashioned word used to be a tonic and it is so true.

This whole chemo/cancer/breast "situation" I've involuntarily found myself part of has humbled me like no other thing. I didn't think I was exactly cocky before but this has a very sound way of humbling one. I also know it's fascinating to look at a person bald, who obviously didn't choose to be that way. I would try not to stare too, and not manage it. I would also talk to that person because it helps pass time, and it takes one's mind off the sheer exhaustion that chemo creates. It's certainly an experience, and I don't want to sound cliched...but I'm glad I've gone through it.

Well, that's based on me surviving and then some! G-d, if you take me very soon I warn you I will go kicking and screaming. I *want* to see my deceased family - but NOT for many years yet!

19 MAY 2017 SAW MY SURGEON TODAY

She's very pleased with the progress so far. The tumour has been shrinking. It's now the size of a golf ball, makes you wonder how big it was in the beginning! I'm scheduled for early July. She'll know closer for an actual date. We (Michael went with me) were told about the dye they will inject into the lymph nodes in the left armpit that deal with drainage, the lymphatic system etc. If the dye shows any cancerous cells she will want to take all the lymph nodes. I'm praying that is not the case because it creates complications. We need lymph nodes for drainage and if we lose them there's a strong possibility that the left arm swells up as drainage has nowhere to go, and stays there - horrors! I did ask: "Couldn't the right arm's lymph nodes take over," and she said possibly. They try to if they're aware. How they 'become aware' I have no idea. (my legs have swelled up as we now know, big time, with no end in sight).

Although there's apparently only a small minority who get this breast cancer reoccurring in the other breast, I'm not prepared to go through all this again. I didn't want chemo in the first place and if I could have - I would have opted for the operation only. **To that end I am having a bilateral mastectomy, ie both.** I've already said my goodbyes to them, my breasts that is. I've also decided emphatically, after reading that piece I wrote on radiation that there is no way I'm touching radiation. I am not going down that route. Final.

I'm also not having reconstructive surgery. I've read online, and yes, it was only one person's experience, but her experience included some "intense pain" when the space was "created" in the chest wall for two new "boobs." Pain is relative, so maybe her "intense pain" wouldn't be mine, I don't know. I likened it to my children (when they were younger) going to the orthodontist and having to re-screw tighter a little bit weekly. Many people will know what I mean here. Others might just realise adjusting screws on any part of the body is going to result in a pain of sorts. On top of that the two new boobs (I saw online) didn't look particularly feminine or boob-like and it seemed a lot of pain to go through after the pain and discomfort and all the side effects of chemo that I have already had. The sooner I'm free of all meds and can start really recuperating and NOT have my life revolve around hospitals the better. Maybe get back, given time, REAL energy even, wow. I've forgotten what real energy was!

I was given two large brochures today about the surgery and the lymph nodes side of things and much more besides. I mention this because it mentions all the things one has to do immediately after the surgery. It mentions no heavy lifting. All obvious stuff but specifies it. All good to know - and my Mouse manages to help me where he can and TG he does.

OFF CHEMO - ER, SORT OF

Last Friday (2nd June, 2017) was my last chemo! I'm still having to go to the Odette Cancer Centre for the Herceptin in the armchair. Luckily it is only half an hour each time and as they don't need blood prior I don't feel I'm in Dracula's department any more. I have to have it for a full year.

Sunday (June 4th) was my birthday and we had planned a restaurant outing and I had hoped to have Stuart and Lisa join us, to share the evening rather than just Michael and I. Stuart said he was working all weekend and would be absolutely knackered by the time dinner came so I suggested we put it off till the Monday evening as I wanted a son I could talk to and not a zombie and he very much appreciated that. Lisa is in St Catherine's still (just outside Toronto) and she wasn't feeling well but Stuart did come and share it and it was wonderful. He also brought the most gorgeous bouquet of very delicate pale pink roses and babies' breath together. He knows I prefer delicate colours in flowers, usually. Oh, SO gorgeous. And the scent is divine. My favourite coloured bouquet and flowers. They are the best!

Since finishing chemo last Friday I have found myself even MORE tired than usually. Sheer exhaustion is a better form of words, and ongoing. I have since found out that the chemo I've been having is cumulative so it's no wonder. On top of this I am "trying" to get the kitchen reworked so that when I am completely out of action, as in after the operation which is sometime earlyish in July, Michael will actually have a "relatively ergonomically" designed kitchen.....I have requested from Michael that it is *not all scrambled eggs* or sandwiches because he can cook - fish too - but he does leave the kitchen looking like a tornado has visited it!

Michael is restricted in arm movements because of the arthritis of his spine and can raise his arms only so high so this kitchen has to be designed accordingly, or as much as I can in the time I have. He can lift up to 'so far' and only down to 'so far', so moi does most things around the home. (At least I know they get done......!)

I have been booked for yet another MUGA test. A heart test with me two-thirds "into" a machine. Not strictly accurate there. I had to lie down on my back which, since the 1987 car prang, left me with a back that doesn't like to lie flat on a firm surface (as all hospital surfaces are, barring beds) and this bed was also rather narrow which doesn't help. Then these three pieces of separate machines, all around the size of an old original deep tv from the 50s - actually slightly less so but you get my drift - move slowly around me for best part of half a bloody hour and I have to stay *motionless*(!!!) With fibromyalgia pain which is "encouraged" by my lying in a position my body doesn't like. Also, as if that wasn't enough I was told to put my arms above my head, and they had to stay there! Talk about being a contortionist! Well, it did make me very uncomfortable and I had to HOLD that position. *I promised myself never again.* Then I got this phone call just a few days ago now telling me the surgeon had booked me in for another, so soon after that last "jolly" one! Yey, I'm rushing back for THAT. NOT!!! We got around that. I can't remember how, but we did.

I realised I was going to be worrying the whole time before that date and I wanted to avoid it at all costs. The surgeon wanted me to have another heart test so soon after the last one! I hadn't heard any bad result from the first one and I'd like to think they would have said something if that was the case.

I decided I had nothing to lose by emailing my oncologist and outlining my points and putting forward that *there must be an alternative* that she could order instead? I also didn't hear back from her, which didn't help so I sent another email to my oncologist with a virtual twin email. She responded back within about a week. I have been redirected to get an "echo" done (the MUGA has been cancelled!!!) I had one of these before too, mentioned in an earlier chapter (the power of writing an email - and it worked!)

The "echo" was the one with the cold "goo" that was smeared on my legs by the woman doing an ultrasound on me last time. Hard to forget that! Also hard to cope with when she presses very hard on a vein in an upper thigh with her monitor(?) in her hand, to get a picture on the screen in front of her. (I voiced my pain...!) Anyway, the whole thing was easier to handle than the MUGA and that is what I'm having instead. I emailed my huge appreciation.

I also have a persistent ineffective cough that has been with me almost since the start of this. It might peter out finally as I discovered from the nurse (who rings two-three times a week to find out how many symptoms I'm still coping with) and how they might be relieved. She said it was one of the side effects of chemo and as that has now officially stopped so might the cough! Caffeine and codeine are ingredients of one Life-Brand pain med and when I have had the bone pain return, as it did last night, I've taken two of these. The bonus I found out years ago in England is that codeine is a cough suppressant! What I *didn't* realise at the time is that it also causes constipation!

Tomorrow is the first Friday in a very long time that I have to myself and don't get hooked up to a drip!

I'm trying to make sure we eat healthier than ever before, and to balance out the constipation...more veggies, *not*overcooked. Over the past weekend I made home-made mushroom soup. Exactly how my late Mother Ruth used to make it and a replica also of the superb French rustic bistro we found in..... Downtown Moscow, of all places, in 2014!

Well, I'm very tired again. I haven't cornered the market on it but I feel I rate up there with the best for tiredness. Today was a small Hallelujah - 'twas my last chemo! Unfortunately, not completely the end as I will still be going to Odette for Herceptin every three weeks till April 2018! And not forgetting Letrozole for the next five years MINIMUM! That's to stop the cancer returning - at least that's the idea.

Michael came with me today. This time I got registered, so I was "in the system," and then we went to Druxy's Deli which is cleverly downstairs in the Odette Centre. Really very handy and brought brunch back to the waiting area where we sat for the next two hours. Shame, because I had had blood work done to supposedly speed up Friday's getting hooked up to the chemo again. That said, there are other patients who are still connected to drips and I have to wait till one is completely finished, understandably.

Still can't get over the fact that all the empty, strong, plastic bags that had all our collective drugs in them in one form or another, and *masses* of their connecting tubes

- there were a lot just for my drugs! - are NOT going to be recycled and that just isn't right! Multiply by about at least six rooms and four patients to a room, comes to 24 times however many bags and all our connected tubing. And this is *only one hospital and one day's amount*! Masses going into landfill because they apparently can't recycle any of these because of what they've had through them! There surely could be a way to incinerate?!!! - or maybe make car tyres or similar out of all that mass of tubes.

After all, *no one* is going to suck on a tyre!

I faced three hours today which was slow. I also had a headache that didn't help and the drips we're all tethered to keep bleeping and that is quite annoying. I try and bury my head in reading to block it out...and I'm almost there.

Reading and having a coffee are OK but the cold reality of being a cancer patient has well and truly reared its head. It's certainly happened to me. If Dr X had said I was going to die within six months, or Dr Y had said you've got about a year at most, THAT would have been my reality. I was stoic (according to a lot of people), even to my own surprise I guess.

On our wedding anniversary, on February 16th of this year, when, instead of celebrating, I was getting a mammogram. Immediately followed by an ultrasound and then a biopsy which instantly showed up a mass with a serrated edge. That was my reality and I had no feelings one way or the other. I didn't immediately collapse in a heap, and I wasn't howling. I think one of the worst parts was that it was deemed "fairly aggressive" and I didn't have the luxury of looking for and trying a slower, more natural method. I think it's because I truly do not feel I'm going to die. I've talked with G-d quite a few times. Well, over the years, many times but if he wanted to take me he could do that anywhere, anytime. I have requested not to be taken for a long time yet. I want very much to become a grand-mother - to both adult children and not just for the first five minutes! There are things I still want to do and people I want to see and be with and places to visit and I'm simply not ready to go. "Gone" has no return ticket. I don't like one-way tickets, not in this department anyway.

I was SO glad to get home today. Even to get back to our area and briefly go into the supermarket was a pleasant, "normal" thing to do. I'm back to injections again tomorrow, but only for the next eight days then they finish too.

Our apartment is still looking like a very messy outpost of the Salvation Army with some surplus stuff here and there. I wish I was Mary Poppins and could magic it neat. The one good thing is that when I have the operation it will be summer and I can recuperate on our balcony.

27 JUNE 2017

Michael and I went to my appointment with my surgeon. Appointment was 11.15 am this morning and with the train suddenly having signal problems twice we finally got there at 11.25. Rush up to the sixth floor at Sunnybrook, well, OUR version of rushing...to end up waiting TWO hours till seeing her at 1.10pm! It really pisses me off and one doesn't like to say anything. (I know,there are other patients and they're equally important. Just annoying to rush like a blue-arsed fly!) At this point she's pretty sure she'll not have to take any lymph nodes out from the left armpit. So I'm blocking that out too, and praying that is going to be the case.

Also found out answers to the questions I put forward (in an email) courtesy of Stuart, who cares enough about me to put his thoughts into words. As I'm not having a lumpectomy I won't be subjected to radiation afterwards which is exactly what the surgeon said. So that's another reason for my not choosing a lumpectomy. I "shouldn't" get nerve pain across the chest as they will have been cut. There should be numbness once all the healing has finished. I'll be monitored afterwards every few months for the cancerous cells - seeing if they migrate to other parts of the body. If they get it all, that shouldn't be the case. That is a big part of why I decided to go for a bilateral mastectomy. Taking a wider radius forces the medical team to go wider than they would otherwise do. They would go for "medically wide" which would be X centimetres around the tumour and which, as a layperson, would seem very close to the tumour for me. To them it would be a large enough area.

I don't want to be back when stray cancerous cells rear their heads and not only have more surgery but chemo all over again prior to it and a second operation and the subsequent anaesthetic. The idea here is to not be returning to the hospital. They have all been wonderful, *but I'd like to never see them again!*

I've also decided not to go for reconstruction. I've read a fair bit about it on the Net with personal testimonies, and it's another painful process and I just don't need this. They have to "create" this space in the chest wall. I want it all over asap. The sooner the healing starts the better. If I ever want reconstruction I can have it in the future, if we can afford it… but at this point I don't see myself changing my mind. **I've not regretted my choice to have a bilateral and no reconstruction, until now.**

I do believe that fighting cancer can be done through nutritional ways. It shouldn't be a surprise to anyone that we in the West have more cancers of every kind there is and we in these western countries, especially UK, Australia, Canada and the USA, have more than most when one looks at what the "average" person buys in their trips to the supermarket. They are so laden down with carcinogenic foods and don't even realise it, and the some that do, don't really want to know - as they are so hooked on their "garbage" till they get diagnosed.

It's funny, in Japan they eat very little dairy and have very low incidents of osteoporosis and yet in the USA where they have ads pushing "dairy for bones and teeth" they have much higher incidence of osteoporosis and other related diseases, *because those that promote dairy are wrong to promote such but will do so for the dollar and yet* dark green leafy vegetables have calcium which is *absorbed better than dairy* is and one also gets the added enzymes if the leafy dark vegetables are ingested raw, for the most part! Some veg are better cooked. You have to do your own homework.

My nutrition books number about 33 and then some. And the theme becomes the common thread: the "cleaner" way of eating is apparently the way to go and I have a small booklet that says just that: "EAT CLEAN." Getting more live enzymes is the way to go and is what I'm constantly trying to do with Michael Mouse, and myself, of course. The booklets fit into my handbag, although even I don't have to carry them all the time now.

One good note to end on is the small "payot" on both sides of my head. Well, not quite. Payot means corners and in this context sideburns. My slight sideburns, really just the hairs that didn't get burnt off by the chemo and are longer and frame my face and...are blondish/white/pale grey and I DO like the colour! Please G-d it stays and more follows suit! Funnily enough, in that photo of me with this pale hair the pale hair seen is the only hair I have! That, sadly, is not in this book with its photos. My bald, chemo styled head was photographed on the subway, with Spiderman, and I had the "hard boiled" egg picture too. They're now in cyberspace because no one has been able to find them for me! Those pictures were dated 2017 and they're now lost. They would have been in this book. I was very upset to lose those pictures. Do photographs live on in cyberspace?!

Michael and I are eating much fresh fruit and vegetables, salads, and nuts plus other stuff too, but I think this has helped enormously in my not having pain daily from fibromyalgia that many other women DO get.

30 JUNE 2017

Today I was back at the Odette Cancer Centre for a half hour of Herceptin.

Shortly after I returned home from Odette I got a call from Sunnybrook telling me to report to the hospital...at 6 am on Tuesday July 4th! This was for *the* op! I may as well take my bed there and stay over somewhere in the hospital! It would certainly be easier, really! Now we'll have to take a taxi as public transport doesn't start again till 6am.

Michael came home on Wednesday from a (lately rare) conference - with a COLD! I told him I don't want him near me, and I've put us both on organic oil of oregano, the best and ONLY thing for flu. Every half hour can really kill the cold in the first day or two. I'm on the preventative dose of three-four drops, and Michael's on five (if you're curious, google Dr Cass Ingram and his book The Miracle Of Wild Oregano. Bought at Toronto's Green Show several years ago now.) He's written several excellent books and explains a LOT......

I'm officially nervous. It's major surgery and I just want it over and done with and for it to be successful. The sooner I wake up later in the day of Tuesday July 4th, and it will still be America's Day Of Independence, the better. Easy to remember for future for it'll be the anniversary of me getting rid of my tumour. At least we're in Summer so taking it easy on the balcony really appeals.

My hair has "started" to grow back, albeit fine and wispy and whitish blonde. It looks like a small, very thinned out messy mass, if indeed it can even be described as a mass!

I'm very tired again.

Chapter 22

JULY 4TH: AMERICA'S INDEPENDENCE DAY
OR
MY OP DAY - SO, EASY TO REMEMBER!

July the 4th dawned and we were up with it! Awake at 4.15 am for a 5.15 am taxi to Sunnybrook Hospital by 6 am even though all had different operation times! Mine was for 9.20 am but it started slightly later than that and I was still wide awake when wheeled into the operation room! It's quite daunting. I would much have preferred not to have seen that room. It's a bit like seeing a torture chamber with the exception that you ARE (in most cases) going to survive - touch wood.

I had my left arm stretched out and someone was getting the back of my hand ready and putting a needle into it. As I have fibromyalgia it makes all nerve endings more sensitive so this was felt and quite a bit. I cried out. The more they learn, the more little things they'll improve on over time, I figure, and that's a biggie!

I had very good BP and they've taken it very regularly - much to my dismay. Even with a bigger cuff it squeezes my arm so tight that I'm in real pain, more than the average because anyone will tell you fibromyalgia makes all the nerve endings twice as sensitive. So *any* arm cuff is giving me hell. Then I try to stay calm so the cuff relaxes but I hate it.

I was taken down on a gurney into the theatre and then oozled onto the operating table. While they were injecting my left arm, a woman put a mask over my nose and mouth and told me to breathe deeply in and out. Well I'm not going to do anything else in that position, in that room, am I? The mask was awful, very close on my face with no space inside so it felt very claustrophobic. I've not experienced that very often. Then the male was administering dope (!) and it hurt - well, it was the back of my hand and it did. Then suddenly I was asleep.

When I did awaken in Recovery, absolutely knackered, there to prove to me I was still in the Land Of The Living were Michael (Mouse) and Stuart. Stuart helped me to the washroom. Just as well, as I was very dizzy then and it has stayed with me, lessening as we've gone through the week but still here. Shannon (my son Stuart's now ex) dealt with organising my meds and she was super...considering I had read what they said about not bringing valuables in, including money, so I left my wallet at home...and in the process left my OHIP card! (like the NHS card.) Shannon had a lot of explaining to do on my behalf but she was brilliant. I was later brought some lunch but too exhausted to eat and then it was taken away.

Unfortunately, so were the two jellos, red and green, which I would have appreciated. I didn't take them off the tray and thus they were whisked away to the kitchen. When I later asked a nurse for some food, she said there wasn't anything! You'd think those staff could think ahead that those foods could be left for later. Anything that might help a patient later! NB *Learn to put them elsewhere in the room!!!*

This is a hospital with *several food areas* but nothing planned to come up to Recovery! She found me a turkey sandwich, which I had one small bite of but suddenly I couldn't swallow properly and slightly choked. The next food was 6.30 am for "breakfast" if one can call it that! This was an airline-type breakfast except an airline one would have been better! Joke. A cupcake that wasn't, and MARGARINE! (see NB the chemical labs) and a jam with nothing for them to go onto, and a bowl of Rice Crispies with skimmed milk. I had that. I hadn't eaten since Monday evening and this recovery unit has no food in it - yet the whole hospital has several "watering holes" but no food available in Recovery, and *no-one to get it from elsewhere.* Totally nuts! Now nuts would have been nutritious!

It's now the fifth day since my bilateral mastectomy - I'm not going to forget this day! The "district" nurse (not called that here) has just been. Up till today I have had four numbered little plastic bottles attached to different parts of the large incision through four tubes, each draining whatever would be leaking excessively from my chest area. Up till today the "look" has been a grossed-out version of an Australian billabong hat which has the corks hanging from it to keep flies from annoying the wearer. This was similar except further "south" at tit level!

I was really expecting a full bandage across my upper middle and if that had been the case it would have been my virtual boob tube but the way it is I have to have a proper top on. Shame, because in the real heat which we haven't had much of this year, I'd have been out on our balcony resting in the breezes. That said, we only have upright dining chairs out there and they are not conducive to sitting out there for long periods.

I was operated on yesterday and only kept in overnight. I thought it would be terrible but the bed was SO good, I asked if I could have a queen-size version!

By my way of thinking, having a lump removed the surgeon will "only" take a certain amount. They extend the radius of the lump by X centimetres and that didn't mean anything to me. Even when they converted it to inches that didn't make me feel relieved. I wanted them to do a much wider circle, especially as, after radiation was explained, it struck me that a beam of radiation that is going "roughly" where they want, but was not going to necessarily hit a stray cancer cell and there was a definite message of "hit and miss" about it. There has to be, if these stray cancer cells are "microscopic" and they are and these radiologists will tell you they are. IF they could all be seen they'd zap them easily, but they aren't.

This surgeon and presumably all others, will do the circle around the malignant tumour *as wide as they see fit*. So the only way I saw to force wider, was to go for a complete bosom removal. And, as I didn't want to go through chemo all over again, (I hope!), I opted for what I think was the same reasoning behind Angelina Jolie's bilateral mastectomy, and decided to say goodbye to both (though she did have the Bracka Gene.) No guarantee I would have had the cancer return but no guarantee it wouldn't either.

Back home Mr Mouse greeted me with messages on large sheets of paper (remember the film Love Actually? with Andrew Lincoln holding up cards for Keira Knightley's character who had just got married?) after Stuart and

Shannon took me home by taxi, saving Mr Mouse from going to hospital at 5am, and to which Mr Mouse was gratefully appreciative. As for the written notes, lovely and sweet and typical of my Mouse!

Today, Sunday, and the nurse came two hours ago and took out all the drains! She had said she was leaving one in but hasn't and all seems OK. The "corks on the billabong hat" have now all gone. She asked me as she was leaving if I felt lighter, because of boob absence. I said no, not yet. Possibly because I can still feel sutures and generally because I've been "worked on." That lighter feeling will come later, I expect.

I still feel light-headed and dizzy so I'm not leaving the apartment yet. I'm actually too exhausted to. I am sleeping better than I was, and that was with those drains in! I was sleeping at a steep recline to allow the incision to drain properly and as I was so tired I was sleeping. Normally I prefer the foetal position which many adults often do.

I start to feel tired about an hour after being up! Even helping with an evening meal is exhausting. All things are quite the learning curve. Thank G-d Robert the handyman has done the kitchen shelves because what I'd have done without that heaven only knows. And TG it's summer and my sutures could almost (pity it doesn't fully) resemble a "boob tube." As the malignant mass has gone too I should feel psychologically lifted but I think the tiredness is masking everything at the moment. Just too early for any monumental realisation…

I have had no regrets. As far as I'm aware, there's no recurrence of breast cancer and if it's about to rear its ugly head, I'm not aware. The only thing I do wish I'd done, but I really didn't want to back then, was to have a reconstruction.

Now, seven years later I wish I had, but it's taken that long to feel this way. I'd love to have a pair of baby boobies! Or as my daughter, Lisa, once referred to hers as "quarter lemons"! Probably too small but I'd settle very happily for two large peaches! And have tattooed nipples too, whilst I was "under..."

Chapter 23

MY TITS HAVE FLOWN THE NEST!

Tomorrow (11th July, 2017) will be exactly a week since the operation. It did go as expected and I'm now home. I'm still having dizzy spells and prefer to stay at home as I get tired very easily.

Back to Sunnybrook Hospital this morning to see the surgeon for my first real check-up since she operated. Before she came in, the Registered Nurse came in accompanied by a medical student (female) and a doctor who said, "there is no cancer left," which was good to hear.

The doctor who carried out the surgery finally arrived. "You've responded well to the chemo and to the whole thing." Usually, people accept having extra radiation but she's well aware I don't intend going that route. Everything has healed well. They found some "fluid" on the right side that the doctor offered to drain, saying it would only take two-three minutes so I naturally said yes and it went ahead and all was mostly fine. As I'm mostly numb where surgery took place, I didn't feel the needle going in, not until the other doctor went a little too deep and then I squeaked, well, I am a Mouse.

Last night, as on all nights, the feet have felt like they've been put into socks that are three sizes too small. Memories of the movie Inn Of Sixth Happiness (1958!) in black-and-white showing how many Chinese were forced to have their feet bound and mine feel similarly and very tight (this has still not left me seven years later and no one has been able to help.) I'm very tired of having such tight feet (and legs) with no letup in sight and no one medical has anything ever to add to my comment. They really don't seem to know what I'm even on about. That's demoralising.

The best bit, apart from getting the virtual all-clear, was when I realised I had a golden opportunity to hand Dr —— a copy of what I have found on the net when I googled "what to ask your oncologist BEFORE you have radiation?" A recent study done at UCLA Jonsson Comprehensive Cancer Centre found radiation actually induces (leads to) breast cancer cells to form more tumours. Plus malignancy in radiation - treated breast cells was three times more probable. Radiation actually promotes malignancy in cancer cells instead of killing them, and it allows cancers to grow back with even greater force!!! That did not inspire me to change my mind!

That was the end of the printed-off piece. Dr —— confirmed that this *was* the case (!!!) but added it was felt that what the radiation does to the cancerous cells already there (if any) outweighed the fact that it induced more cancerous cells. However, I was blown away that a medical doctor admitted such. She also pointed out that the radiation route for more cancerous cells took about ten years, which was supposed to be a good additional fact.

I thought my hair would start to grow back and the light, pale golden and white hairs on my head do not stand out. I just hope the colour stays as it is now. I really like it! Natural blonde! Doesn't everyone like that! The "sideburns" that I had up to three-four weeks ago, all 30 hairs on each side of my head, decided a vacation was in order and left! The other hairs on the top are barely there, so to all intents and purposes I am bald. That's what it looks like if I look in the mirror. I also have "steri-strips" along the whole incision across the chest but keep finding they've dropped off which is another good sign. I haven't taken any off myself. I'm seeing how long they last! I hope the hair has started to grow properly by the time Autumn/Fall has started, otherwise I'm going to be rather cold around the gills!

I have 1/8th" of hair growth on my head and can only just catch it with my fingertips. Definitely less "hard-boiled egg" and I'm not impersonating Telly Savalas anymore! I said I thought I looked like a lesbian to the Virgin Mobile store gentleman till the young man (in the Eaton Centre) assured me that a) I didn't and b) said that they dress differently to me (that wouldn't be difficult!) and that c) they don't usually have their (male) husbands in tow! We laughed at that. Squeak! My naivety knows no bounds sometimes!

I was expecting to have to possibly turn up tomorrow for my "next serving" of Herceptin introduced intravenously as before. Glad to say that isn't happening for now. Dr J saw my ankles and could feel that they're very tight. The skin is taut and looks it, and is in fact downright uncomfortable. She does point out that this is not her speciality which I'm aware of (and it's not anyone else's speciality either!) I'd also taken a painkiller and that didn't touch it either. I tossed and turned from about 12.30 till about 3.30 am getting nowhere in slumberland. Then, as Michael was half awake, I said, "I'm tempted to go and watch some tv," to which he said, "do so, just close the door."

I had been in – well - very real complete discomfort and actual pain which was totally preventing sleep. One of the side effects of Herceptin is insomnia. So I am wide awake at midnight, and apart from property programmes that I love, I'm on my laptop. Reading and laptop are two things that don't wake Michael. I then may go to sleep around 1 am. It has been later. Michael is wonderful and is not disturbed when I come to bed or, when he is, adjusts himself and goes back to sleep. Lucky in that way. Bastard Mouse! In many ways he is very easy to live with. He has his difficulties but just works around them. He has said he tries to be everything his father wasn't! And he achieves it admirably.

I finally did get up at around 4 am and went and watched some TV. Feet and legs still painful but at least now I was distracted to a degree. At around 5 am I had the pleasure of watching two reruns of M*A*S*H. If you're unfamiliar - google it. It is B R I L L I A N T - anti war theme and brilliant scripts and humorously executed. It doesn't get better and should be "de rigeur" in ALL schools in ALL countries with its anti-war theme. There'd be less loss if this was on all curricula worldwide and children brought up on loving one's neighbour and not always "anti." I don't mean pushing religion on anyone, just "Live and Let Live," for *all* creeds.

Dr J has asked me to see another vascular surgeon, to get a second opinion. I agreed after establishing that I wouldn't be getting another immediately-prior veins-ultrasound. I pointed out that it's not as though my last one was three years ago but approximately three weeks ago and the results won't have changed, but having fibromyalgia when they do these tests, they press a monitor's thingummy onto one's veins and press very hard in certain areas and I really have shouted out. The air turned blue. I wasn't backward in coming forward. Dr J said it would just be meeting the specialist to get another viewpoint so I agreed.

She also asked if I would start on the Letrozole and I said yes to that too. I'm not happy about either of these meds, especially as I am supposed to be going on the Letrozole for "at least" five years! This is apparently to help 50% of the cancer from returning. The printout on that is three sheets and two of them are filled with side effects that one could have a reaction from and we had three lists: one could react to all, some or none but the list was frightful.

I'm having my Letrozole with freshly brewed coffee every morning. I nearly bought three months' supply which was going to be about $78, but I suddenly remembered Odette's pharmacy rule which is that once you've bought those tablets and taken them home you can't bring any unused packet back. Even if for some reason you decided not to take any as you have left the property, they will not risk using them.

A bit extreme for an unopened packet but that's that. They will incinerate any you bring back and you don't get refunded so instead of accepting three months' supply that I might get an early reaction to, I decided one month's supply was more than enough. One went down this morning and only 29 to go!

Because of my recent pain/huge real discomfort that doesn't let up, especially at night, Dr J offered me sleeping pills! I hadn't seen that one coming. She did point out they can become addictive. I'm aware of that and said no immediately. I don't intend to ever go down that road. A slippery slope if ever there was one, and more meds in my system all with their added possible side effects. I'd be a walking pharmacy! No thanks.

Hippocrates made the best statement when he stated "let food be thy medicine and let medicine be thy food." How apt.

People must know instinctively, when they've offered a seat on the subway or a bus, and many have seen my head or they've had cancer pop up in their own family somewhere. Another reason I won't wear a wig or a scarf. Both are too hot for me anyway. I cannot cope with standing, standing, standing, as all it makes is varicose veins and *for a very tired body*. My son Stuart has always offered his seat and I'm very proud of every aspect of his being, not just that.

Michael is walking with a limp which is slowing him down something rotten. He's had several jabs over this year, so far, and very recently one blood test, all related to the limp but it has to be ascertained whether he's had TB or not before they can fix his limp!!!!! Don't ask us for the connection between the two! We have no idea. We have to google it later and see why they do what they do. Result was - nothing!

I have discovered last week I have lymphedema, hence the swelling of both ankles. I also have an infection in the left ankle area. The antibiotics finish today…I had a little of this a few years ago and when I mentioned it to son Stuart who was in Oz at that time, he said he'd see what he could find. he got a wonderful pocket size book and sent it to me but it's now that it's coming into its own. It endorses proper food combining (as in either carbs and veg/salad

OR protein and salad and veg but NOT carbs and protein together.) Apparently easier on the system and a lot more besides, so this eating formula is not just a newspaper fad.

After we had finally finished at Sunnybrook Hospital we took the subway downtown and had a breakfast snack. This city is cheap for breakfasts although by the time we got there it was around 1 pm. Walking back to Queen subway afterwards a young woman walking behind us that I hadn't realised was there suddenly whizzes round to be in front of us and says, "you guys look so cute together." I felt this was said because I was holding Michael's hand and was the one leading. Not going too fast for him. She asked how long we'd been married and I said guess. She reckoned about 50 to 60 years! I just mentioned we'd only been married 20 years this year (2017) but said to Michael afterwards we must have looked like 70 and 80 respectively! I didn't think I looked THAT old but it was coming from a young woman in her 20s we think. Michael is always amused by this and it doesn't seem to faze him. He used to internalise problems and that is not the way to go but we laugh a lot. With each other and at each other. It makes for good pairing.

CANCER - THE GOOD NEWS

I'm wide awake on 5th August 2017 and just starting to write this chapter at half past midnight!

Michael went with me today to my appointment at Sunnybrook to see my oncologist Dr J who hasn't seen me since prior to the operation. From Dr J's own lips are the following statements verbatim: "There is no cancer!!!!!!!" The best possible news. "The chemo worked extremely well." No cancer anywhere in the breasts. She also added there was no need to offer me radiation! That WAS good to hear! That made sense, too, as the radiation wouldn't have a target, but it was VERY good to hear that nonetheless. Unfortunately, to further reduce the chance of the cancer coming back she added they want to put me on a hormone therapy course that would be one tablet a day, probably for good. Not too thrilled with this one: taken at the same time every day, and keeps the oestrogen low. For those interested this tablet is called Letrozole/also Femara. They're letting me digest all this and are planning to ring me next week.

A funny thing to share, yet very willing to share and also, possibly, one of you too could be diagnosed any time with same. Yes, men can also get breast cancer; they just don't have quite the same physique as us. Maybe one day these chapters will help someone else, male or female.

I am not too thrilled being told about this hormone therapy even if it is only one tablet per day hereonin. My best friend in Sydney (Oz, naturally, the REAL Sydney!) Jan S gave me a book years ago: Hormone Heresy. It promoted avoiding medication and doing things a more natural way. That said, this is apparently "lowering" my hormone levels and in that way it helps a lot to stop cancerous cells starting up again. That does make sense, but it comes also with a list of side effects. Dr J added that if I accepted this and went ahead and then had one or more of the side-effects they could look at changing it to another doing the same job. Several choices doing the same thing.

The side effects are as follows: headache, muscle pain, cramps or stiffness, constipation, mild swelling in arms and leg puffiness (I digress for a minute if you don't mind; as you're all aware I've had very tight-feeling feet and ankles as though I'm wearing bandages around both feet AND they've been done far too tightly. This is all day, but more noticeable at evening.) The side effects continue: tiredness and feeling dizzy, with advice to rest often and be slow to get up. *Do not drive a vehicle - I should be so lucky!* Probably the only female in Toronto to have a Canadian driver's licence with...no car! Although they DO drive on the "wrong" side of the road :)

Side effects continued: bone pain and bone loss. It's just dawning now that this cancer treatment is ongoing and is going to be a part of my/our lives whether we want it or not. A sobering thought even though I don't drink! I was lucky, or G-d was watching, or both. I have had that bone pain during chemo. Well, instinct told me it was the bone pain. And it was short lived, TG again! It's almost "punny" - I felt it in my bones. A pun even on a pun!

Another possible side-effect could be bone fractures (long-term effect). I could be asked to take calcium and Vitamin D supplements which I'd much rather get from deep green leafy vegetables as their calcium is better absorbed. I now take Vit D, one per day but I'm making sure we have plenty of green veg too.

I was told today by Dr J how there were NO stray cancerous cells at all and that included the back "wall" of chest muscles! Re - reading (proof reading) this makes me feel even better! Also, none found in the lymph nodes during the operation hence no removal of said same, which I was very relieved about.

I've been asked by different people if I've had any pain. The answer has been a resounding no. I've had peculiar feelings across the chest but not pain per se. BUT It's also been very hard to scratch an itch if it's "inside" the numb area. By rights one shouldn't even get an itch. I don't understand either, "but if that's all she's feeling she's doing very well." I am. I still get tired during the day, and if I go onto this hormone tablet then the tiredness will become a regular part of life. There are worse things, I guess.

Whereas men have "fuzz" growing you-know-where, I have an 1/8th" of an inch growing back on top of my hard-boiled egg head. Getting up close and personal it's very short, a slight gingery blonde and I'm really praying the colour stays as it is now. When I run my hand over it, it feels like a velvety piece of fabric, although from a short distance away I still look like the egg one is used to. Now it's 2.07am and this bare-headed-looking Mouse is really going to bed.

AUGUST 2017: ON THE WRONG FOOT - BOTH

I was in yesterday having that ultrasound all the way from the jugular to, and including, the toes! Even during the whole procedure both feet were tight. Today, they're even worse. I've been sorting in our bedroom and moving around, which is supposed to be better for the circulation. I got to the point where I HAD to sit down. Both feet feel very tight, the right even more than the left, although earlier on it was a tie.

The right feels like it's in a vice. Earlier both felt exactly the same. Also, although Sunnybrook is not aware of this, I supposedly have "arthritis of the left ankle." I had it x-rayed sometime last year. I mention this because quite often I get up from my armchair and I CANNOT put the weight onto my left foot and it is excruciating. I then hobble very slowly and very carefully, holding onto furniture until the ankle "comes good again." Then I walk as normal. If anyone saw one and then the other, I would be termed a fraud. I did wonder whether there could be a hairline fracture but I was assuming that would make it hard to walk all the time. Yes, I had x-rays of both ankles and nothing showed up...

Me seeing a vascular surgeon who said there was nothing they could do, only to wear support knee-highs (in special thicker fabric) and cut back on (table) salt. I said I already have these knee-highs and I wear them - only in winter and maybe in Autumn/Fall as they are so warm I cannot handle them at any other time of the year. The salt doesn't apply because we stopped using ordinary supermarket-bought rubbish salt a long time ago. Completely devoid of any minerals that were once within and that do a good job - if they're left in place. We used to only use Himalayan (pink) crystal salts (a lovely subtle pink) with kelp added. It even says it's completely unrefined and uncontaminated AND it retains all the minerals, so health-giving! What could be better? We're now onto Herbamare and that's pretty good too, I think!

It was last night's revising where we had lived in the last 18 months that made me realise how I had been physically, and that had been a lot better as we had had Holly. I had taken her out three times a day, even when we were staying up at the Travelodge Hotel out near Pearson Airport (2015). Wow. Time does move on!

Anyhow, taking Holly out when we were also at Pembroke, the bachelor apartment we had, and my walk was much better. I was taking Holly out but not very far as by then she was almost blind from cataracts, very deaf and with a heart murmur, but otherwise adorable. I'm so glad we had her for the best part of 20 years!

To that end I was seeking out either a miniature male dachshund OR Irish Wolfhound! I like the idea of protection late at night and would get it with either, but probably more with the latter, size-wise alone. But the sausage dogs are sooooo cute. I do realise which one needs more "outs" compared to short legs on the other...Either way will be second-hand cos I am not spending a fortune. And have to look at their feed bills too, and vets.

Now the situation has changed. Michael needs more help than he used to. I can't cope with another dog, especially a big one, so it's not happening. At least a miniature dachshund would have found our small garden huge with its cute little legs!

Today's meeting with Dr J and she's been trying to tell me not only how both Herceptin and Letrozole are used with the aim of stopping the cancer returning (by up to 50% and she says there have been studies...) but that the surgery alone has a 70% effect against the cancer returning.

She pointed out that 30% meant one in every three people contracting cancer would be the result. She wanted my percentage raised. Of course, I do too, but not with drugs. She's also pointed out that if I didn't continue on with the Herceptin (and she hopes I'll also start the Letrozole) and if the/any cancer DID return that I would NOT have the option of surgery second time around!

She explained that if it had metastasised to another part of the body, it would have left scattered cancerous cells in its wake (my paraphrasing: not her words but I think I'm fairly apt here.) BTW the last two times I was in Odette (Friday August 4th and 11th) I met three or four women who are on their second, third and fourth chemo! Perish the thought! Dr J's comments are bearing more weight since meeting these three women and on reflection I'm hating where these thoughts are taking me, but I still have a very great need to LIVE and at the moment the choices are still mine - to an extent.

I'M NOT READY FOR
ANY CEMETERY YET!

SHIT! More bloody drugs into my system and side effects too, possibly. Although the idea of more chemo is, I suppose, a better option than a box six foot under! Sorry, I think THAT joke has been "done to death." Oy!

There used to be a programme here in Canada - an American one - called "Inside The Actors' Studio." Lots of different actors and even directors interviewed and what advice they'd give to budding actors. The audience was made up of uni students who were all taking classes relating to film in one form or another. The interview would end by asking what their favourite swear word was. Most only had one and inevitably it was the F word. A long time ago, probably back in England (it hadn't been realised in Oz when I was there) I coined MY preference. Some had a couple. I had, correction, I *have*, four! And with these drugs lining up to be coursing through my veins (and wherever else they get into!) my answer to that question is "Fuck, Shit, Piss, Wank" in *that* order! Very satisfying!

As I have felt for a while, it could well be the Letrozole and/or the Herceptin preceding it, although part of me thinks the Herceptin MUST have left my system by now - or by earlier than now? That could cause this tightness of the feet. Or it could be neither as this appointment today threw up other possibilities. I DO love the auto corrector! I can actually type faster, who knew! We (well, Michael) DID go with me, but almost fell asleep on the examination table. No, I was not on it at the time, just as well! I don't enjoy those. They're far too firm and on my back, with fibromyalgia - not a good mix. Luckily it was for less than a minute. Wanted to check my thyroid and my neck at the same time.

No, I have no idea why and I didn't think to ask as he went on with the next question. The specialist was very good at questioning me and turned out to be from the Philippines. One just doesn't guess the Philippines! I was asked many questions and he was very good at getting what he wanted to find out. Then the prodding began and a pin test with me as the guinea-pig. Then he went off to find an associate, two actually, and talked to them for several minutes and eventually came back and one of them questioned me too. At the moment my big toes are numb on the tip, because last night I discovered I had cut it and it had bled but I hadn't felt it...suddenly everything is ominous. Well, perplexing. He did the pin test by pricking me, and I had my face screwed up with eyes tightly shut expecting the worst but it wasn't that bad. Expectations are often worse than the actual thing and this was one of those.

The other possibility is that I might be diabetic, but Michael said he'd like to think that, if I was, the symptoms would have shown themselves earlier. They're also going to check the thyroid. I'd be delighted if that was found to be "underachieving" because if it is, and then one goes on those meds, one loses weight! This coming from the person who *bought* the Atkins book...and guess who lost the bloody weight - well it wasn't me, it was - MICHAEL bloody Mouse! Yes, slight repetition here, sorry, tough!

We finally think we're leaving the hospital except they first want another blood sample taken. I do hate that. Nine out of ten times they can't get it out of my veins so they look for a morsel on the back of the hands and that's more painful.

It should be the case the way they treat cars. They put cars over a pit in order to look at its insides. Not a bad idea. Bums on show with everything else exposed. A bit like when I went to a specialist urologist, going back several years but very vivid in the memory, talk about having your "tackle" hanging out ! know that word is usually reserved for men.

I had a rash appear on the skin of my upper front. Saw our GP. He's very good but takes getting used to. He "usually" appreciates dry humour. He obviously doesn't get enough of it I don't think.

Hair continues to grow, and very curly which is nice and when it's much longer it will be fully appreciated. I had another nose bleed tonight. Unexpected as it has been weeks. As I have no concept of time it's only a guess, but it has been long since. And bright red. It made me think of, wait for it...getting a bright red lipstick in same! You didn't see that coming, did you? No, I never did and I'm definitely not going to now. Too "harlot-ee" for me.

Friday also saw me get an echocardiogram. And by a Ukrainian male! They don't get dry humour! Shame, they miss a lot. I love it.

Yes, I was tired from Herceptin on Friday, and for the next three weeks it will be so, but I see "my" oncologist on May 10th and it could be that I've had my last Herceptin, but I still continue with the Letrozole for the next four years and probably for life.

Chapter 24

KEEPING TORONTO'S
HOSPITALS IN BUSINESS

It was suggested, as of October 25, 2017, and it already had been suggested weeks earlier, that I wear those very strong knee highs that help the venous (that word again!) vein valves as they do a job of helping the flow of blood back up the legs because the valves are not doing their job well. Well, I will wear them when I've found the one pair and when the weather is colder. I *cannot* handle them in the mild (as in now) weather and in the summer: no way Jose (the J is an H sound.) I had them on maybe three winters ago and they are very good. They bloody well should be at C$100 a pair! For that they should be gold-plated! Initially I had to put them on with rubber gloves! We're actually advised to use rubber washing up gloves! Unbelievable but true. Later, when one is good at doing it, as in getting them on, it's easier, then they're not needed. In the beginning it's not unlike the fun of trying to shoe a horse. Not that I've ever done that.

The tablets are working, not before time. The venous specialist mentions a word meaning to scrape the inside of these very porous veins. He immediately reminds me of my late Mother who had this operation (varicose.) Yes, it would mean another operation and my Mother was very happy with her result. We have a picture of Mother sitting up in bed, both legs exposed and bandaged from knees to toes and whereas her very dark hair was usually in a bun, was down fully, in two pretty braids with a pale pink bow. I cannot imagine having a decent pair of pins, as they (legs) used to be called.

We were all in our little respective rooms sitting on an examination table - legs open and all ready for the specialist to come and have a poke, a prod and whatever they needed to peer at. It reminds me of that movie The Chicken Shed with the male voice being taken by Mel Gibson. That is SUCH a good movie. Animation, not usually something I rush towards but there's an exception in every case, and all these chickens sitting on their nests. The only difference here is they don't have their legs open. When I had arrived I had seen the little rooms from a distance and it was exactly like a row of beach huts on Brighton Beach UK (without the soothing colours!) You feel a prized prat sitting there with all exposed and her bedside manner left a lot to be desired. No, Stuart, again, I know they're there to help, but I don't think you've ever been in a row of cubicles with your "tackle" hanging out...or maybe you have. One never really gets used to it. One does know it's for one's own good. There, I've said that cliche.

As they had seen Michael moving very slowly (BTW last week we found out Michael's left big toe has GOUT!) Hence his limp. I always thought gout only came from drinking. Apparently not as he is a very rare drinker. He has the occasional cider. They offered to get him down to where they take blood as they decided they wanted to check my blood for diabetes and something else. They *offered a wheelchair* which I really didn't want him having, but by the same token I didn't want to spend the night at the hospital, ie, taking so long when walking anywhere in that hospital. We waited an eternity and finally *gave up on the wheelchair* and walked it. Another prick and three minutes and we were actually leaving, near...5pm! I was very tired. It is tiring being at a hospital, especially if you're not doing much, amazing. Although walking miles of corridor is at least a form of exercise. And a good place to collapse if one is going to!

We did actually leave at 5pm. Two-and-a-half hours after we'd arrived, but the specialist and his associates had been very thorough with me and I have to say Sunnybrook on the whole has been like that consistently. Now if we can find out why my feet feel like they're so tightly bandaged I'll be doing very well! (NB - I never have.)

We are finally back on the train and I get chatting to a lovely young woman who shows me how to delete texts! Another tiny thing taught and as it comes isolated I remember it better. Where technology is concerned I learn better in small increments. I should expand here slightly. We have upgraded our cell phones. We are both on Androids! Sounds like sex with an alien!

Actually, like its predecessor, I found my way without the booklet because it's actually easier that way. I still manage to press the next letter rather than the one I want, and if I don't look up at what I'm texting I THEN find out I've just written gibberish. Yes, I know, time will improve that... and it has. Learning how to delete texts today was a goodie.

Three times this month I've put my arm up over my shoulder to adjust the bra strap that doesn't exist anymore!

And three times this month I've gone to pull out the scrunchie that is holding my imaginary hair up! I also used to put the cinema ticket in my cleavage so as not to lose it. Can't do that either. I don't "miss them" per se, but I also DO know that I did absolutely the right thing in my own case. I have not had a single regret for what I finally decided to do. I am so glad I didn't go the lumpectomy route either. That would have merely delayed the final route and would have meant another anaesthetic and another recovery, and every anaesthetic is a risk. My hair has grown minutely but now I can grab it with my thumb and forefinger. That is good, I know, but to me it looks like a chosen style and it is anything but.

It has been a huge learning curve, but one I'm glad I went through. That said, I didn't like losing my hair but in the great scheme of things it could have been so much worse. I've also found out just how wonderful Toronto train commuters are. They are a wonderful mixed bag of every colour, creed and religion and many are such lovely people. Many take one look at Michael and me as soon as we get on and *immediately* offer their own seats to vacate them. So lovely and so appreciated. Many revere the elderly. I had more offered when I was imitating a hardboiled egg but Michael and I frequently got offered. I think when I'm offered a seat now it's more reverence to my age, and the fact that there's quite a bit of silvery white.

Throughout all this Michael has been wonderful. I don't really expect less. He said something yesterday about being there for each other, which is very true. It's actually lovely that he said it, because it's not often that he makes remarks like that. It's a nod to our alliance. We're very comfortable with each other but we're also still romantic with each other and it's not an effort to be so, which is as it should be. It's a very calm atmosphere to live in. It doesn't matter what we do, whether it's in or when we're going out, if the plans change, the other just falls in usually.

DECEMBER 29, 2017

Well, do I start with all the side effects? Why not? Such fun! Well, it is said that He only gives us what we can cope with and that does seem to be true. I'm now regularly having irregular nose bleeds (work that out if you can!) Just when I think I'm not going to get one, another one does start. And the tiredness comes and goes. When I'm out it lasts, till I get back here, and then I realise I'm rather tired. Another side effect is dizziness that only started relatively recently...but in an odd way, and only at one time of the day, luckily. Late at bedtime. I lay down to go to sleep and suddenly my head is spinning! Very odd. I've never heard of dizziness when one lays down, only if one gets up too quickly. It's actually an OK feeling. Maybe because I'm not in any danger. That is, until I do a trip to the midnight bog! (now I've really come down to Michael's level! Sorry Michael! It IS years since you used that word and I should not be encouraging you here) but I have walked into our en suite (apparently the French do NOT use this en suite expression, so Brits must have made it up!) I've been into our washroom and swayed! Luckily not fallen because I really don't want to and I don't want to waken "him indoors" ie, Michael.

Michael gave me his cold two weeks ago, and it is still with me! Coupled with a sore throat that is also a side effect of the Letrozole! So does that mean it's staying with me indefinitely? It certainly feels this way. The sore throat is on and off. That's odd in itself, and I have become hoarse (hurray, I hear Michael say.) He's also warned me not to speak too much. Brilliant coming from the ONLY man in my life who makes me say EVERYTHING twice! (I know I do the same to you, I hear Stuart say!). Grrrrrrr. I TRY and do tit for tat, but when one hears a question it's a *natural reaction* to reply, not to suddenly show him what it's like by making HIM say it twice. If I got a dollar for every time he made me repeat I'd be very comfy!

Last Saturday, I was at the Odette Cancer Centre for the Herceptin intravenously. They had too many patients for Friday so asked a few of us to come in Saturday. The good thing there was I was told not to wait in the waiting area on arrival but to go straight into the wards, where the recliners are. It was all done and dusted fairly quickly. They do make us as comfy as possible. There are real armchair recliners and we're all offered a large fleecy WARMED sheet to go over us if we wish. And we're offered the choice of juice. Also, Druxie's (a well-known sandwich joint that is American.) This one covers lovely foods but the other regular ones are even better with hot pastrami sandwiches and all manner of Montreal's smoked meats heaven. Jesse, my would/could-be son-in-law adores Montreal's Delis. He's American.

(The other place that does exactly the same, but I think has very recently closed, is/was Carnegie's Deli in NY. The BEST of the BEST! Hot dogs 12" long! A pickled cucumber that is 8" long. Homemade coleslaw which I can still taste now, and hot corned beef sandwich with approximately 30 thin slices of brisket in-between sliced rye bread with caraway seeds, and fresh homemade coleslaw. I've really mentally gone back there. Pity it's only in the mind. One would eat one half and take the rest home or back to the hotel for dinner. It was Food Heaven!) OMG the memories – and that was B4 Mr Mouse.

The one thing I'm not happy about (I am grateful my hair is growing back as I was told it would) is my hair is now a good 1" long and grows "every which way." I cannot change its very odd way of going in every direction at the same time. It also goes to a slight peak in the middle. It's made up of very curled hairs. Very hedgehog-like. Not unlike Ena Sharples from Coronation Street tv minus the hair net!!! I really do not like the look. I will be relieved when it has grown 7" more. At least. Even Michael agrees I look like one of the "purple rinse brigade" and - I'm not offered so many instant seats on the subway anymore. At least when I was bald they knew instinctively it was the chemo.

I'd like to get a pair of earrings made in the shape of RAC…A talking point which will be people assuming it's my initials. In fact, it's now been changed - not Royal Automobile Club but Regrowth After Chemo! The hat is a lovely cosy one with two pom-poms on the ends, beige knitted, courtesy of my daughter Lisa!

We are surviving in our cosy condo without the heating on as it is on the blink! Yes, and today was minus 22 which did include the wind chill factor. That's how they describe it in this city. Well, it's slightly working. I think it's taken the chill off and we are very lucky to be on a cosier east, west and south corner. The masses of sun we get makes a huge difference. Otherwise we'd be freezing our tits off, if I still had any!!

A FEW MONTHS LATER

Well, our 21st wedding anniversary (16th February 2018) is looming, 16 days away! The last one had me being diagnosed with the malignant breast cancer. Quite a lot has happened to both of us. This time last year Michael was in rehab after stumbling at our last rented place. Then he was in surgery and at this time at the convalescing hospital out the back of beyond. And worse, a very long two-stage subway journey and then I had to wait for a rare bus as well, and waiting in a literal wind tunnel because that's where the bus stop was. Whoever designed that place had a car! Most miserable spot to have a hospital and the corridors were so empty and quiet it could be used as a film set. I kid you not. Empty corridors in a hospital with no immediate staff anywhere...is very creepy. I will not forget that place - except the name escapes me for now!

My hair is now 1 1/2" long and very slow and rather curly. How it was when I was three or four? Then I was a natural Swedish blonde! Yes, I appreciate my hair regrowing and curly makes a change, when it's…longer. Being told previously in the hospital that I look like the Queen was not appreciated. I do appreciate the hair but I know it doesn't sound like it. Being compared to a 91-year-old female monarch doesn't help!

We have our 21st wedding anniversary and are in a slightly better shape than we were 12 months ago. THAT said, Michael is still suffering with his feet and is limping. I'm so tired of seeing him limp. If anyone has any good ideas to improve a diabetic's walking we are both all ears. EVERYTHING takes SO long to heal and I'm talking *months* for everything. He cancelled an appointment today with the podiatrist because it had been snowing since early and the podiatrist is "about" 1,000 YARDS away and via traffic lights, but being snowy and icy IS risky for him. I kid you not - if Michael was in a race with a snail the snail would win! I want to "attempt" to heal him from within. I have many nutritional books but I'd still like to "put it out there." Anyone with any ideas? Foods, super foods, special plants with healing qualities. Maybe a Chinese herbalist. Everything, short of voodoo!

FEBRUARY 16, 2018

One year on exactly since my malignant breast cancer diagnosis, and Michael's recuperation from the fractured spine.

I seriously thought today, for the first time, that hair extensions might be the answer but found out they are horrendously expensive. Mummy would have loved it, hers was always straight hair and she lamented that. I lit a yahrzeit light (memorial candle that burns itself out 24-36 hours after being lit - it does not get blown out) for my Father on February 11th. He died in 1962. Such a long time ago.

I'm still on the same two drugs, one finishing in April all being well. The other is indefinite and it's weakened my nails.

Not bad you might think, and you'd be right, but every single nail has split on my hands at one time or another and it's at its peak now. Forever filing them. It does put the whole business of cancer into perspective. Rather pathetic on my part, I can hear murmurings. The whole idea of these drugs is supposedly stopping cancer returning to my body. I just hope it does. It's bad enough that I'm on meds that are pretty much perpetual now. And they tire me, but I AM lucky. I can go about most normal things on a daily basis.

The "portal" gadget that was inserted under my skin on the right side of my chest high up near the breast clavicle will be...wait for it...actually removed when I stop receiving the intravenous Herceptin and I will not miss that!

Last February 2017 introduced me to a whole new world: the world that suddenly became very different to be in when one has had a diagnosis of malignant cancer proclaimed and it changes one's perspective on many things. If another person has a cough and doesn't cover their mouth, I come close to being very vocal! Several times I have wanted to shout out – "please cover your mouth so you *don't* spread disease!" One woman sitting opposite leant over to tell me she only had hay fever. She'd seen my expression of horror. Good sometimes that I can be read so easily. She did make me breathe easier.

This whole past year has been a HUGE learning curve. Something I'm glad I've learnt from. Well, I hope I have, though I wouldn't have chosen this way to learn it. I suppose He chooses this way because He knows we'd never choose it ourselves. He's so right there!

Michael goes to most places with me. He is very much slower these days and I am trying my best to improve on that for him. Between his stoop (that I cannot fix) and his limp and pain in either knee/foot, that I CAN try and do something, we are progressing too slowly. What he really needs is another fall and a cracked spine in the "right" place that would bring his head to the "upright" position, but one cannot book that in!!!

If I could relieve his limp and have him walking properly and slightly "faster" I would be delighted. In a dictionary there is the word "snail" and next to it is "Michael!" Maybe not original but very apt.

Our apartment's inhabitants have grown. My daughter Lisa has finally joined us. I'm glad because she has not been well in the past two years at least and needed to come back to the fold to regain her strength. She has long baths and lights incense so there are wonderful aromas wafting through. She's also helped out, as many daughters do, and without being asked, and has done wonders with meals that she has produced from the times she has worked in hospitality/restaurants and picked up ways of making things, and...they are delicious. She does have a built-in knack for instinctive cooking (even before these places and can throw biscuits together *without* any recipe and - again - they are...delicious. She "creates" beautifully. She has also done the laundry to the point of finding it on our bed, washed, dried and folded, and ALL has been very appreciated. My two drugs (hopefully down to one soonish) have another side effect, which is to tire me out, so when things are magically done it's twice as nice.

Lisa has odd hours, so she can be awake when we've gone to sleep. Not all night obviously, but she can be watching even later than us. She very quietly closes our bedroom door and has the TV on numbers four or five for volume! If I had it on that I'd give up trying to hear, but she succeeds and we stay asleep!

Today is our 21st wedding anniversary. It wasn't very original but we decided to have lunch in Greektown. Michael couldn't remember which subway station it was but knew it was between Chester and Pape.

We walked and walked in that wind tunnel laughingly known as The Danforth. Gave up looking for this restaurant which we should have googled before leaving home...and finally had a shared appetiser for two in this place. Very nice too, but it wasn't cosy and I had stupidly come out without a hat or scarf. Idiot comes to mind. We decided to leave after that and continued walking...20 steps maximum to suddenly find the restaurant we had been searching for!!! Grrr!

So we decided to have the same appetiser as we'd just had, and compare. Nicer, slight difference. The place was warmer and lovely white tablecloths and...500 yards from the subway we should have got off at. Wasn't it, Michael!!!!! Next time it's Chester subway and then spitting distance! Exactly where it would have been if we'd got off at the right subway in the first place! Michael Mouse mumbling under his breath, "I'm not going to hear the end of this, am I?" "No, you're not," but I said it nicely. I can never be mad at him for long. I've said it before and I'll say it again, we laugh AT and WITH each other. One has to be strong enough to take that, and he is. It has to work both ways.

We are very good for each other. He tells me he loves me nearly every other day (and I tell him too). We're doing something right.

MUSINGS, APRIL 16, 2018

The creative juices are flowing again. And this City of Toronto apartment is my version of the garret (attic) in a poor man's Paris. That is perhaps a slightly unfair description of

Toronto as it's hardly a "poor man's anything!" Although it is genuinely cold as we have intermittent heating on: our heating system is not working properly, and...believe it or not...we have snow outside! Very beautiful but hardly mid-April! And I'm sitting here with a scarf on and I've put the oven on, too, and left its door open! So the whole "set up" is very Parisian but I'm also missing the parquet herringbone wooden floor. Oh, what I would do to have that down instead of this vinyl mock mid-oak wood look.

My hair is longer. I told Stuart the other day it's different for Michael, Lisa and him, as they have got used to it as they look at it all the time. I get a surprise every time I look in the mirror and I still don't like what I see. Yes, I can appreciate it is growing. I just don't "sound" appreciative! And I do look in the mirror as little as possible!

My visits to the Odette Cancer Centre are still ongoing but I've written to my oncologist (funny how one refers, like everyone else afflicted with this, as "my".)

Stuart has temporarily moved in with us and brought his stuff too. He's actually managing (off his own bat) to keep his stuff tidy and I applaud that. He cannot stand many of the pieces we have had around here and it had already made him lean towards minimalism in a bigger way through growing up with me than it might have.

On a positive note, he's made me view things, literally, through his eyes and I have "said goodbye" to pieces he wouldn't actually notice they've gone. Yes, that DOES mean I have had a lot of pieces but to be fair they've travelled with me from Sydney to Manchester to St Albans to Buxton, Derbyshire - and on to Toronto and Macclesfield! One such lovely piece was a two-tiered glass-topped hall table possibly from the 1960s in cream metal and scroll work. I have adored that piece but it was taking up space on our new (and more spacious SQUARE balcony!) …and could not be used because the removal company lost the glass shelving! In the year we've been here I had hoped it would turn up but it hasn't and I've had that piece 16 years but have now said goodbye to it. It gave me much pleasure but it's gone. And that's OK too.

Stuart called me a hoarder! If he saw the tv programme Hoarders he would realise just how much I'm *not* one! When I compare myself to those who have really hoarded, I think it's mightily unfair but I am still decluttering and will get there, although what Stuart deems "there" might be different to my "there!" The funny thing is that my Mother was VERY modern for her time and wanted clean lines and no curly dated, Victorian "bits" or anything remotely "vintage." That made ME go old and in turn has made Stuart go modern. Lisa likes my stuff as it's homely. Interesting watching all this play out.

Stuart asked if he could commandeer the dining table as his desk and I said yes. We have dinner together in the lounge and it's fine.

It's how many older Chinese are with their attitudes that I applaud: just "bend with the wind or you'll break." A good philosophy. It's easy to see how decisions are made as one gets older. Many things are "just not a big deal anymore." And Stuart's stuff *neatly* around the apartment is a case in point. He's going through his own private relationship challenges and where belongings are is really not a big deal in the great scheme of things. I try and help him through. Not necessarily saying anything. Many words, sayings, come out just smacking of platitudes and that can often be worse.

Lisa is also back with us, and has been here longer than Stuart. Much of the time I'm actually enjoying both "adult" children here, together. It's good to see them interact. I've become stronger through the whole chemo cancer shenanigans and it is just that, shenanigans, because no one expects it and we all fight it in our own ways.

Michael continues to print off my chapters while he continues to write articles for magazines covering a very large area from Chile and Cambodia to Western Australia and South Africa and northern Canada, all the while waiting for the second opinion from an ophthalmic medical specialist as to how soon he should have his cataracts removed. It's apparently going to be quite soon.

This came about after he had a very recent eye test for the first time in six years and the new specs recently picked up are not helping him! I think that is because he does his viewing from the top of the specs but the optometrist has put the "viewing" part of the specs in the "normal" place, ie, further down the lens so the result is that he still looks through a blurred part. Not smart on the part of the optometrist but his cataract does have to take some of the blame. We're both nervous for the operation. He's very stoic though and copes admirably with his limitations.

I'm not far away from getting the "portal" implant removed that had been affixed to the upper right part of my chest allowing all the chemo drugs, and later the Herceptin, to be administered intravenously. That is very visible and a nuisance and will need a mini "operation" to remove it. Local anaesthetic so I am awake. I prefer that.

I had another nose bleed tonight. Unexpected as it has been weeks that I was back at Odette on Friday. I'm using quotation marks instead of capitals. Stuart (No 1 son!) said that capitals come across as shouting. Perish the thought!

Sometime very soon the "portal" gets taken out of my chest and I won't have to get Herceptin every three weeks which has been the norm. That will be a good special day! Stuart has already informed me it looks very Alien just in my chest top right side as I look down to it, under the skin with its lumpy nodule surface looking creepy. Friday also saw me get an echocardiogram, and by a Ukrainian male! They don't get dry humour! Shame, they miss a lot. I love it.

Michael has been unwell. He's had tummy-aches and has been retching. And throwing up. Yesterday, Saturday, after seeing our GP's associate he came home and lay down on the bed. I went in to see how he was and something was not quite right. He wasn't slurring his words but he wasn't clear either. I thought initially he was having a stroke, so I asked him who I was. He said his Mother! (No, I didn't say "charming", but it was a temptation!) I asked him where we were and he said Cheyneys! Neither answers are good, and for those who aren't aware, Cheyneys is the street that he lived on in London!

I went back into the lounge and told this to Lisa. We both knew it was serious. Then Michael is calling out to me and wanting to use the washroom, but Lisa and I found it hard to get him upright, although we did, with difficulty. Lisa was wonderful with everything. At this point I knew to call 911 (as opposed to 999) and requested an ambulance.

To cut to the chase (ok, NOT my natural style but it shows I CAN do it! Stuart, take NOTE!) Lisa and I went in the ambulance with Michael to hospital - he'd already shown up a very high temperature. Six vials of blood were taken from his arm sometime in the course of the evening and after I'd left they took him down for a scan.

Gallstones and quite a few...and to REALLY cut to the chase (yes, she CAN do it!) he's having keyhole surgery tomorrow morning at 8 am to remove his gall bladder! Between last January (2017) when he fractured his spine up high at the back of the head and down the spine about 8-10" and then my cancer diagnosis on our wedding anniversary of February 16th and the subsequent surgery, we're both actively keeping different hospital staff in six jobs!!! Where are gallstones and slurred-speech related?! We never did find out.

It was depressing going in the ambulance with Lisa and Michael. Oh, we weren't like that, I'm just reflecting on it. It did bring home how Michael is very special. It also brought home just how much of him is not right. How he simply copes with his unyielding body, which would drive me or anyone somewhat nuts to have so many restrictions. Yet he just accepts it and plods on.

Btw and all take note please, for all your own sakes - stretch yourselves when you get up off your computer/ laptops and anything else you might regularly bend over. Hood of a car comes to mind, ie, don't get too hunched over as you'll start getting to the point of no return…as Michael Mouse has found out.

Now I'm knackered! Between my Fridays intravenous, and Michael having a weekend at the hospital we're really living it up!

Try and do better than us!

Chapter 25

I WISH I'D THUMPED HIM JUST ONCE!
OR
THEO, MY STEPFATHER, THE
CATHARTIC CHAPTER

What a lovely birthday surprise - not! I was eleven. We still lived at 36 Framingham Road, Sale, Cheshire and Mother had done those gorgeous tiles around the lounge fireplace in cornflower blues, oranges and turquoise. I wonder if they are even still there! Anyone with any design and colour awareness would surely not have ripped them out...?! With long full-length burnished orange curtains to the floor. So Ruth Ward and so Mummy!

Theo was my stepfather. It's funny - not really - how at school the other kids used to say, and I quote, "why don't you call him Dad?" I'd reply, "because *he isn't*" and, adding mentally, "And he never will be!" Children at school never really understand until their own Mothers might say, "well, Milly, if your Daddy died would you want to call another man Daddy?" Likely not! Yes, you could tell they had never lost a parent!

He had moved in with Mother after they married. Like a lot of men they want their own place and usually the woman complies and they both house-hunt for a new first place to share. Mother and Theo were no different.

Before they moved though, I had *that* birthday. Memorable for all the wrong reasons. There I was with several friends in the morning room and Theo came through. He said something to me and I have NO recollection of it, but I didn't agree with it, and wanting to "try" and be nice about it but I called him a liar, which was too strong but I said it softly, cheekily and with a smile on my face (a forced smile but trying to be light about it.) Theo was having none of that and naturally he couldn't leave it AND felt he had to make a point, so he told me to BEND over, and as I have ALWAYS complied, and *felt rooted to the spot* - every time - I complied this time too and with my face as red as a beet, and **IN FRONT OF MY FRIENDS** HE SPANKED ME. I'm sure he never told Mother, and Neil was brand new in a bassinet upstairs. Mortifying. I remember it like yesterday.

Fairly regularly he would ask me certain things and, because I was nervous of him and could never relax around him, it was always a case of and I quote, "I forgot" which he used to repeat back to me...*whilst tapping my forehead*, "oh, I forgot," mocking me and tapping hard, knowing I was rooted to the spot. I only realised about fifteen years ago that this was/is a form of abuse. Abuse is a strong word but it doesn't have to have a sexual connotation, and this tapping happened many, many times. I've worked out it was "only" a decade in time but feels so much longer. That said, when at home, which never felt like home when HE was around, there was this "atmosphere" - Mother's appearance in the room helped slightly, but the air didn't change unless the boys were there. Russell and Cedric (in order of seniority) both wrote to me airmail letters much later covering the fact that they were more aware than I realised (Internet had yet to be invented!) but by this time I had flown the so - called nest.

My G-d - it sounds like the dark ages before TV! I came across those two references, one from each older brother, both noting that life had been horrible and hard for me when they weren't around. Russell even penned the thoughts that he realised something was amiss and that, "calls from me every two days would have helped you." It came in a couple of letters he wrote whilst a patient in Hammersmith Hospital London, while he was fighting leukaemia. Cedric said something similar earlier. This was 1989 and the same year the Berlin Wall came down. That year Russell died. Now two darling brothers have gone.

Theo would have dental meetings at the house. One such time there were several dentists at this meeting in the lounge and discussing the concept of a male dental assistant over a female one. I decided to add my tuppence worth.

Boy, was *that NOT worth it*! I had had instantly the image of a lovely young man back in Australia who was then involved in some of our car rallies. He's still involved in the racing on a particular TV channel, and I remember him with much fondness. He had the nickname of Rusty...

This was a sweet, GENTLE man who would never harm ANY female, and I had HIM in mind when I made the mistake of piping up.

Theo immediately "crouched down like a Sumo wrestler(!)" on his chair which was already lowish, and said, "DO YOU KNOW...?" in his inimitable way, and never finished the sentence, because my sweet darling brother Neil jumped up and said "I can't stand this!" He knew *exactly* what Theo was launching into, and why the sudden change in posture, and only because it had been ME starting to speak forth in the first place!

Neil strode out of the room and down the corridor with me trying to keep up with him. "I don't know why he does that," said Neil. I was half crying because it was sobering to see this "played out" in front of Neil, although it saddened me at the same time that these "shenanigans" had even ensued. I *knew* it had never been my imagination and Neil's always known, but here was Theo finally showing his true colours in public.

I also told my stepfather 25-odd years ago that dairy products can cause mucus (and can also play havoc with younger people's skin if they're having break-outs.)

Theo's reply? "Don't be so bloody daft" in his northern Manchester accent. THIS is only because *I* had stated such.

Then, 12 or so years ago I heard him say to someone in their kitchen, "Dairy causes mucus!" Holy shit! No, I didn't say anything but I was dying to. I would have been accused of "stirring." It would have blown up out of all proportion.

I got the pleasure of knowing he'd FINALLY learnt, and told myself something would resonate that I had said it initially? I can dream.

Give dairy a complete break and get the calcium from green vegetables which are a better source anyway and that the body can utilise better than any dairy board claims, because they're not about to say otherwise. A very good book to read is WHITEWASH... there's a reason for that title.

HOW TO THOROUGHLY EMBARRASS YOUR STEPDAUGHTER - AND NOT GIVE A SHIT!

Michael and I got engaged at the end of 1996. We were duly summoned to afternoon tea at my Mother's and Theo's house, where there were also three other guests and Neil. One of those guests was Barry Spillane, bookbinder (who works too hard, but such a lovely man. Was a guest at our Mouse wedding!)

Naturally, the subject of our wedding came up.

Then, clasping his hands together, above his head, and shaking them together, Theo shouted out his tactless and barbed comment: "Hooray, I'm getting rid of her for the second time!"

Now, isn't *that* charming!

You could have heard a pin drop. Utter silence. Even my Mother was stumped for a comment.

Michael heard this of course and wryly observed, "It is a shame that the now-defunct lead mines of Derbyshire are no longer producing, otherwise I would have bought some shares in lead balloons".

OUT OF THE MOUTHS OF BABES

Now I'm going forward to a Saturday in November 2009. It's 5.45 pm and Theo (stepfather for those who might have forgotten!) has come to pick me up from Neil's. It's gone dark. I follow Theo out of the house and close the front door. And I went to the car. Felix, my nephew, follows and promptly opens the front door again. I mention this to Theo who says, "he's just saying goodbye." To which I said, "no, he's coming down the path" and then Felix is there and says, "why are you two together(!)" And continues with, "Dad says you always fight!" Out of the mouths of babes!

Theo and I looked at each other and Theo just said, "Goodbye Felix." There really wasn't anything to say at that point. And nothing was needed anyway. He'd only stated the bleeding obvious.

When Theo brought me back at around 10.15 he stayed and talked to Neil and I went upstairs. I later came down and waited till Theo had gone before telling Neil what Felix had said only to find Theo had told him already and Theo had been amused as was Neil…as was I!

Theo barely ever gave me eye contact. I've counted the times. Maybe 50 times in as many years and that's being generous (again)!

From a certain point in time, and I have no idea when it started, but I regularly forgot things and, usually in the hallway, near the under stairs where we were never viewed or overheard it would begin.

"Oh, I forgot." Theo would mock my words. And then get his very strong forefinger - all his fingers were strong through being a dentist - and tap me on the forehead several times. Yes, it hurt, but no, I couldn't move. I was rooted to the spot. I had no idea how to leave and didn't even know how to fight it. Much later on, I became stronger. Neil wasn't blinkered either and was actually privy to some things that came later but the tapping he never knew of. Although he doesn't know about the birthday humiliation. That's now changed…

Mother was never privy to it. When I finally confronted her one day, in the garden, whilst she was sunbathing, I did the same tap on her forehead and she came out with a textbook reply: "Well, you must have done something to deserve it." I left it at that. It wasn't satisfactory but I'd brought it up and knew I wasn't going to improve on that. I'd finally raised it with her, and it was over. Fini.

Several times over the years I've had a "daydream" where I've "punched his lights out." I just wish I'd had the guts to carry that out, just once! A regret gone unfulfilled! I'm not advocating it for everyone – just me – and to him.

I should feel sorry for him. He needed something to make him feel all powerful. He got it in the form of little old me. Who'd have thought it!

I have also to give credit where credit's due. He used to go into the lounge and put on the record player and I'd go in and sit in some armchair. I didn't want to be in the same room - but he was listening to classical music, and inadvertently introduced me to it, and for that I'm very appreciative. I even penned an email to him and included this. I thought he might as well realise I'd benefitted from *something* he'd done.

Didn't make me undo the wish of punching his lights out, though. Nothing would have undone that.

I have a wonderful relationship with Neil, and I also have his permission to go ahead with this. (Well, he did read three early chapters and pointed out my repetitions!) "Permission" to write about his Dad. He's said that without reading any of it! That takes guts, but he does know a fair bit of it. There should be few surprises for him.

How I wish the boys had been around. Life would have been very different, and a lot happier. These things are supposed to shape us…but I would have adored having them here, growing older with me.

Family is everything. Hold on tight to yours.

Chapter 26

YONGE STREET, THE WORLD'S LONGEST STREET
OR
MICHAEL MOUSE'S MEDICAL MALADIES

Mr Mouse takes over for a short while!
The years 2017-2021 on average threw up one medical problem for me each year. I was not able to take part in the move into 5940 Yonge Street as I had a fall in the hallway of the apartment we were renting. Actually, I walloped my head against the hallway wall and collapsed. Hazel had to call 911 and they sent two strong paramedics. That's where the real problems started, at North York Hospital.

I was immediately admitted to a ward and the next morning two physiotherapists came to walk me along the corridor. I couldn't speak properly and I needed to lie down on my hospital bed as I was feeling faint. These two physiotherapists thought I was taking the mickey as my speech had changed, becoming more hoarse and metallic.

I was told that intensive care staff would come to see me. They did – six hours later. Hazel and Stuart came to see me and noticed that my voice had changed and asked why.

Hazel was fuming and asked for a doctor to visit the ward, who duly came. She expressed horror at what was basically dereliction of their duty in that discovering that *no CT scan had been done in the first instance!* One expects the medical profession to do the right thing in every department. Basic medical procedures shout out SCAN! Therefore, to have Michael walking the next morning after NO scan was - no pun intended - SCAN-dalous! She added that these two physiotherapists could have turned Michael into a paraplegic, or worse, a quadraplegic! The doctor *agreed*! He couldn't have not.

Hazel wanted me moved to St Michael's Hospital. Being Downtown Toronto, it made access much easier and she felt the treatment couldn't be worse than North York! MRI at St Michael's confirmed the problem – half-a-dozen cracked bones on my upper spine. Surgery was the key! I was taken by trolley to meet Dr Jefferson Wilson, the surgeon in question (I thought that maybe Jefferson was after Jefferson Davis of the US Confederacy and the Civil War; it turned out to be after Jefferson Airplane, the pop group of the sixties!) I was told to lie on my front – something I had not done for many years as I sleep on my back. Mercifully, no problems. Surgery got underway. For SIX hours and it needed TWO anaesthetists to brought in to rescue me!

Hazel got a phone call around midnight. "We nearly lost him," commented Jefferson Wilson. I was "one sick puppy" and was taken to intensive care which did take place this time. I recovered well. Hazel's just glad and relieved she insisted on having me transferred.

Two weeks in rehab followed – in some obscure suburb of eastern Toronto. A Doctor Ledger brought round some of his students. "Normally, we have to break bones in our patients to enable surgery. Michael very considerately broke his own bones in advance…"

In this respect, everything went well and I moved into the North York condo. Which brings us on to my other conditions…

In 2018, my gall bladder and I decided to part company. I had arranged things so sneakily that it took the surgeon and his team an hour to find my gall bladder. The offending item and I have lived separate lives ever since.

Then in 2019 there was the cataract surgery. I can now see clearly! I thank Dr Rootman every time I sit down in front of the television without glasses or walk along the street looking at the autumnal vistas.

In the same year, I tripped over a rug. I was taking some rubbish to the garbage chute. I tripped over the rug and launched my own airline, Air Mouse, but the landing procedure did not go well. The bridge of my nose caught the edge of the dining table, with consequent bruising and a hairline fracture of the nose. Lisa helped me sit up so that the crew of an ambulance could lift me up more easily.

I had to wait a long time as I was not an emergency as I was still breathing! A few days later, the lady in the convenience store saw my bruises and wondered if Mrs Mouse had been thumping me.

Taking refuse to the garbage became an occupational hazard for me. It was Friday night early 2021. I bent over to pick up the plastic bag with the garbage. Two candles had been lit on Friday night. My hair caught fire!!!! In fact, I did my own version of Johnny Cash's song Ring of Fire.

I shouted out for Hazel to help. She was stunned but forced me under cold water at the sink. The smell of burnt hair was over-powering. The sharp pain lasted for over three hours. I even felt unable to watch the repeat of Heartbeat…

MRS MOUSE RESUMES

Back to condo hunting briefly. In the condo block I really hoped for, the sellers didn't take their realtor's advice and leave the property, so we had three pairs of eyes watching us looking at their place; a young woman sitting on her bed watching tv and two in the lounge. *Very off-putting.* Rather distracting and one *cannot speak freely.* Not clever. Might explain why their place was not snapped up in three weeks. We didn't go for it either.

When our current place came up four months later in the same block, we went in with a view to buying it if it came remotely close to what I knew we'd both like; and it did. I'd have preferred to find the light grey but that wasn't to be till we got to *Macclesfield.* This condo was warm, light and inviting - and south-, east- *and* west-facing. A remarkable combination. An angle the whole building was at and a huge bonus. One just doesn't get that usually. The afternoon sun bathes our whole condo in wonderful light.

We've been in about two weeks now and the place still looks like a messy warehouse, partly because Lisa had emptied all the dry foods into all the upper cupboards and left me with nowhere for all pots and pans! She thought she was helping! Stuart and Lisa had also both painted the condo before we moved in, from a mid-curry-yellow to white. Huge improvement!

I am very tired. I didn't realise how much of a toll this has had on me.

I'm worried about Michael. There are several things wrong with him and several are there within him as permanent tenants: psoriatic arthritis, hiatus hernia, progressive deafness, two new hips, ankylosing spondylitis, and type 2 diabetes, separated from his gall bladder.

He's very precious (which can mean different things – Michael Mouse.)

I'm very glad we have our balcony. It's good to be able to sit out there whatever the weather, and we get good cross breezes being on a corner.

SETTLING IN

I do count my blessings, regularly. As I survey our apartment it is looking very cluttered. It's the only word for it although Robert, my handyman, can see it slowly coming along as he does things in it for me. I can too, but I see what hasn't been done too, and I'm a little impatient there too. The dining table behind me has framed pictures that will be found a home on the walls. Two are pictures of soft pink peonies with a delicate green background and my Mother's signature on both.

That precious item which unfortunately is not a priority in Toronto where we are concerned, namely a car. I have adored driving ever since my ex, Gerry, introduced me to rally driving in the Australian Outback. I get a natural high from driving, especially if it's on rough roads. Boy, the memories I've got of that! But here in Toronto we decided a car was not a high priority and living Downtown certainly didn't warrant it.

We ARE actually getting to the point where we might even have a dining table for use as - a dining table! I was told to be careful with no heavy lifting otherwise I'd probably pop my stitches!

The stuff one accumulates over 40 years is incredible! I'm coming across things that I bought in Sydney and am so glad to see again. Some I'm just ready to say goodbye to and luckily it's only up to me, in that they're things bought in Sydney and Michael has no claim on. TG!

Michael has stuff all around him in this apartment and NEVER complains about it to me. He also NEVER complains about any meal. IF it's lovely he will say so. If it's crap he will say something like, "It doesn't matter, better next time" or "well, I liked it" or, if I just don't feel up to it (and this also applied before chemo started) he'll just say it doesn't matter and he'll go and make himself a cheese sandwich OR whatever he can rustle up. He is SO easy to please. He NEVER (well, VERY rarely) criticises me. On the other hand, when he does something illogical, which IS getting rarer, I have a go at him. Makes me feel guilty in that respect. I am VERY lucky, but I do tell him so. He needs help physically, but was still able to cook for me in the early days immediately following the operation.

He's a very sweet Mouse.

THAT said, on my birthday (June 4th) I didn't feel like going out. I think I had the start of a cold. Stuart rang up to find out what Michael had made me for dinner and said, before I replied, *"He didn't just make you scrambled eggs again, did he?!"* I'm afraid I had to say YES! Also washed up which is always appreciated. He's getting (*slightly*) better at that, too! Nothing worse than "double handling!" And he (still) tells me he loves me (it's not a given so I'm very lucky) and I tell him, too. It's keeping the romance alive, and we do.

Again, Michael was/is easy to live with. That said, we do have a lot in common, more than we initially realised.

We both love reading and as we have different kinds of literature we're as happy as clams. We still have at least six boxes of books to go through and I pray they aren't mostly Michael's. It's much easier to put them down in recycling if they are not his and if I'm ready to give up one or two! We already have the master bedroom that is also doubling as a "library" that we sleep in! Three book-cases and a tallboy with other stuff stored in it are in our bedroom and not going anywhere. As they're painted white with a white wall they are less intrusive. We'd only need an armchair or two and it really would be a library albeit with a bed!

The didgeridoo has finally got a permanent home as I had Robert display it high on the wall and it really makes a statement. I've "only" had that for 22 years, and it's now finally on view! Well, Mr Ex and I had it for much longer, but I'm counting from when I took possession. Michael has an "office" in the bay window of the bedroom and is often found there. He's also getting better, much better, at sitting down on the subway train, and this is happening only very recently! I have praised him hugely and will continue to do so. Yesterday I was very impressed. We went down to St Lawrence Market and he was sitting in his seat within seconds. He's actually fractionally speeding up and I'm very proud of him! We also complement each other with our ailments! They may not be identical, but each of us has things that slow us down, so we don't try and rush each other off our feet. Very clever on "someone's part…"

G-d doesn't give us more than we can handle (well, there are exceptions): the loss of my two brothers was devastating and I remember the moments of both in minute detail. This cancer diagnosis and subsequent major surgery were "easier" if I may use that word, than, for example, if it had been cancer of the left or right leg. I've not become an amputee. I think I would have found that much harder altogether physically.

I don't feel "less of a woman" even though I've lost the two main components that make up a woman - hair and boobies! My hair will grow back eventually but my boobs won't but they've never defined me. *I just hope nothing else is going to be taken off*! I've already mentioned that last week my eyelashes decided to grow wings and flew off, without my initially even realising it. I've seen other women who have drawn eyebrows on; luckily I have those - somewhat. I've seen drawn on eyebrows and for some reason the women have not followed the contours of their original eyebrow, very odd!

When I see Michael in the distance, maybe in the supermarket or across a street if we're meeting up, I get a warm fuzzy feeling that is still there. "It's mutual," says Mr Mouse (he also says, whilst I'm proof reading this, "It's all part of being a Mouse!") There's still romance and long may it continue. Though it does take two and it works. In fact if I lost him I'd feel as though I lost a part of myself. There was some very real worry when he almost collapsed near the supermarket (as above) but we hope we're getting that "sorted" (an in-house joke) through nutrition.

SNOW - NOVEMBER 30, 2017

It's arrived! S N O W! It'll be SO cold but oh SO beautiful!

Five months since my bilateral mastectomy. I was still looking a little like Ena Sharples! (google is very handy!)

We have a small round marble table on the balcony here that only yesterday I managed to finally cover with a blanket and to tie underneath with a long "ribbon." (I bought it at a large secondhand warehouse on the outskirts of Toronto when I first arrived ahead of Michael Mouse, and they later delivered. I was on Shank's Pony). Perfect for shielding it from the elements, as it has wood underneath and I didn't fancy that wood's chances. And my timing couldn't be better. The wind is howling again and is very atmospheric. It reminded me of the wind that surrounded the funeral of Yuri Zhivago's Mother at the very beginning of Dr Zhivago, my favourite movie of all time. I've "only" seen that 33 times (and the rest!) The layers that that movie has...like an onion. Winter has so much going for it, and makes for wonderful movies.

The Holiday was on just now (set in Winter!) and the movie could well have been Eli Wallach's last. I haven't checked that, but his early ones were in Clint Eastwood's "spaghetti westerns," as in The Good, The Bad, and the Ugly. If you want something wonderful to give you a break at your laptop, click onto the UK's Own Ukelele Band playing The Good, The Bad, and The Ugly. SO clever and wonderful hearing it all come to life and a visual too. Absolute Magical.

Just wanted to share some of life's little pleasures.

I've now got two meds to take every morning and two meds to take every night, doh! First I looked like a hard-boiled egg (or Kojak - Telly Savalas to those that remember him!) Now I look like a hedgehog on a bad day! I've even taken my hairbrush out of my bag a week or three ago as it's totally unneeded at present. It's now 12.50 am and the wind has started to howl again.

A HANDBAG WITHOUT THE REQUISITE HAIRBRUSH.

Totally redundant at present!

My hairbrush has stayed out of my handbag for two years now since the diagnosis! And for the foreseeable future it's staying that way. Any of you know what a Brillo pad is? Well, if you're going to Google it - that's what happens to my new "regrowth after chemo" hair, if I put a brush to it! Now I just use my hands! One less item for the handbag, for now. Makes for a lighter bag, too! That *is* good!

The creative juices are flowing again. And this city of Toronto apartment is my version of the garret (attic) in a poor man's Paris. That is perhaps a slightly unfair description of Toronto as it's hardly a "poor man's anything!" Although it is genuinely cold as we have intermittent heating on as our heating system is not working properly, and...believe it or not, we have snow outside! Very beautiful but hardly mid-April! And I'm sitting here with a scarf on and I've put the oven on too, and left its door open! So the whole set-up is very Parisian but I'm also missing the parquet herringbone wooden floor. Oh, what I would do to have that down instead of this vinyl mock mid oak wood look. *I'm only in Paris in my head.*

My hair is longer - well, it's now 2" long and curly. I won't mind this at all - when it's grown to shoulder-length. I'll even embrace the curls as long curls are lovely. I just

287

don't like the look that I have now. It's the "blue rinse brigade" of England of the 50s, 60s and 70s, without the colour! I told Stuart the other day it's different for Michael, him, and Lisa as they have got used to it as they look at it all the time. I get a surprise every time I look in the mirror and I still don't like what I see! Yes, I can appreciate it is growing, I just don't "sound" appreciative! And I do look in the mirror as little as possible!

My visits to the Odette Cancer Centre are still ongoing but I've written to my oncologist, (funny how one refers like everyone else afflicted with this as "my" but she was.

LIFE GOES ON

Much of the time I'm really enjoying both adult children here, together. It's good to see them interact, and Lisa is a very innovative cook. I've become stronger through the whole chemo cancer shenanigans and it is just that, shenanigans, because no one expects it and we all fight it in our own ways.

Michael has also written on our travels, specifically on the Moscow Beijing Railway and also Australia and China for the Mastermind Club magazine, appropriately called *PASS!*

APPLIANCE ANNOYANCE!

An exhausting day and month. Trying to organise a replacement new washer/drier stacked combo, ie, separate washing machine and dryer above. THAT has taken the best part of at least a month! And the first I ordered was a stacked washer/drier with its knobs in the centre and at the base of the drier.

So what happens? It arrives and I checked it out downstairs. It has a big dent in the front (I could live with one at the side because it wouldn't be noticed) and guess where the knobs were? After requesting EVERY time I spoke to the company (and there were several times!) "knobs in the middle where we can ALL reach," including Michael who is ergonomically challenged(!) WHERE are the knobs???!!! On the frigging top where NO one can reach! Except all the members of the Chicago Bulls basketball team! I mention them because Stuart has always been a fan and now supports the Toronto Raptors.

And the fridge had become worse. Have not been able to set the fridge and we/I found out why. We shouldn't have been sold it in the first place! I couldn't set the number for it to be at whatever. No number meant whether at the top or in the humid drawers: I regularly found frozen lettuce!

Twice the company has sent fridges that didn't match my criteria. Today we finally got the right one and it's lovely. When we get a plumber to hook up the water-line we'll be able to get chilled iced filtered water with 85% Ibuprophen taken out of it and other medications!!! That which had already got into our collective watering holes; horrifying that that can be the case in the first place!

We set the alarm for six. This way, yours truly can trick herself in to "sleeping in" for another half hour till 6.30am. Then I have my little ritual which I love: making freshly-brewed coffee (I love those three words) and taking it on the balcony. A beautiful sunny morning. Sunnybrook again for 9am after putting on the provided numbing cream that takes an hour to work. Finished by 10.10am. On my way home!

Apart from seeing "my" oncologist in early August I could be finished with Sunnybrook! I'm probably jumping the gun but I'm now "only" on Letrozole and Levothyroxine and my Amitriptyline. A regular chemist! So much for being on my bandwagon of not having drugs through my system!

I have also discovered why I have a very thick left leg and frankly it looks horrible. I "thought" it was the chemo drugs exacerbating things. No, but close. It's the lymphedema that was caused by the chemo that has caused the legs to swell and the tissues have become too porous, letting blood and G-d knows what else into the tissues and once they go through, they don't return…BUT on the net I found some very interesting facts and for once I WAS right. There IS a dietary component of fresh foods, and clean food, ie, not processed. That said, they're not improving things, yet.

Digressing, for a bad - and a good - reason!? Today was hospital day. Later it was new fridge day and emptying the old and filling the new. Lisa helped me with the former. Then the technician came to look at the apartment's faulty air con in the second bedroom. It never rains but it pours. This was an extra $300 that hadn't been budgeted, the only relief here being, as Francesco the Superintendent said, "if that knocking sound continues it will eventually flood your floor and then seep into the apartment below, with hefty bills coming from them." So after that $300 was deemed not so bad!

Dennis was the technician for the air con, and turned out to be a lovely man whose mother has had the same breast cancer. We talked pH factor and other food-related facts and...he put himself on a healthier food regime. Losing 40 lbs - the bastard! I ended up giving him a copy of my WHITEWASH, by Joseph Keon. I'd bought about three on special and it highlighted why we shouldn't have so much dairy.

With a forward by John Robbins...of Baskin Robbins fame, son of the ice cream magnate! Managed to get his father off ice cream! A fascinating book. No, I don't get a percentage!

The lymphedema that was not nearly so bad when we had Holly the Jack Russell. Then I was taking her for walks three times a day. Michael doesn't have quite the same speed!

Friends have mentioned the side effects that you, Stuart, have regularly noticed: the dry mouth and and speech, very hard when it's been a while since a drink, I mean an ordinary drink, not alcohol. The meds are doing that. Also the tightness of both feet, mentioned yet again. I hope this sock thing is not permanent. Now, seven years later, 2024, it's still with me and I scour the news for any new development.

This is where Fibromyalgia rears its head again.

When I saw Dr S he did something I'd completely forgotten he would do. My dreaded BP. And he said it was very high. Not surprising because it squeezed my arm SO bloody tightly. Very hard to "keep calm and carry on!" Hurt like crazy. Actually I've realised now it felt like a boa constrictor!

I actually emailed him last night to tell him that when I was in Humber Hospital several years ago they used a bigger cuff for my arm and could he do the same. It will still hurt but maybe fractionally less. I can hope, and I can try and put it out of my mind.

MUSINGS ON TORONTO PROPERTY PRICES IN 2021

Toronto is VERY expensive and more so than England! In Toronto the three-bed semi that one would get in England – but which would be larger in Toronto - has at least two large bathrooms if not three, plus decking and a basement. In other words, the Toronto three-bed property would be vastly superior to a three-bed semi in the UK...and would be put on the market in Toronto for C$1.3 million, GBP730,000(!)

However, couples who put in joint offers will make offers at C$125.000/GBP70,000, C$150,000/ GBP85,000, C$175,000/GBP100,000 or even C$200,000/ GBP112,000 *over* the asking price! So the average paid worker won't even get a look in!

That kind of pricing/offers just doesn't happen in the UK, and you cannot buy a two-up, two-down in Toronto anyway. They just don't exist. They do, however, in Manchester and the north west and plenty of places all over England and they have other properties which are less expensive. Let's face it, anything would be!

We also have a building site opposite that is the very slow start of five new condos that will one day "start" going up when they have finally built the four underground levels of basement parking! Meanwhile we've lost our supermarket as they demolished all those stores there and we won't see them back until at least 2023, although they reckon 2022. So we now have an expedition for the supermarket on an irregular basis and we have Coronavirus 19 in our midst.

I call this our invisible World War Three because this is exactly what it is.

LETTER TO MICHAEL MOUSE 2019

Your experience before and after having cataract surgery. I cannot imagine being you, with you not being able to see properly. When we lived in Charles Street; fairly early on there, I had an eye test at Eyes On Church. They saw the start of cataracts then and said I would need the eye surgery (whatever kind - laser or other) in about ten years time. We're now in our 12th year here and my eyes are better, not worse, I believe. I used to have "floaters" as they're known. They were very irritating as I couldn't shift them. I now haven't had those for a very long time, in fact, not since we left Charles. I think my eyes are better than they were then. We eat a lot of fruit and vegetables and salads, and I feel sure better foods help. I *know* they do. The raw stuff basically.

For you, Michael, we/I should be making more raw salads to help with your overall health and lack of real movement, and try to improve you internally as much as possible.

Your eye surgery went very well and you were done in the hour that Dr Rootman said you would be done. Your face had the two plastic eye pads over each eye and tape holding them in place. I welled up at that point but it had all gone well and you are seeing better than before. You are now reading the news across the bottom of the screen to me. It may seem not much to some, but you haven't had that ability.

At present, we're in Winter with masses of snow around. You're finding it very bright with the light bouncing off the snow. You'll adjust in time and I can't wait to go to the cinema with you knowing you'll be watching and seeing like most of the others. Seeing a movie through your experience will be something else! It'll be funny, you won't need your specs for this but I will. Just going shopping with you or an eatery will be fun as you marvel over the myriad of colours.

At home you've done things meticulously, because you've had to, and you've been very slow, which won't change unless we/I can find a supplement that "oils your joints." I want to find that very much. I want to see your body loosen up as much as it can. You walk very slowly everywhere and I want to improve that, no end.

How you maintain your composure and sanity I will never know. It wouldn't be the same if I had gone through this, or was still going through this. You do have patience with yourself. You've said to me on more than one occasion that you didn't want to be like your father and give yourself at least one ulcer.

You haven't, and you've achieved being nothing like him which should raise a glass to you from everyone around you.

And, for the most part, you've kept your sense of humour, and that's very attractive in a man, and a mouse, and to your wife, Mrs Mouse.

I love you very much. Oooodles in fact.

Chapter 27

M*A*S*H - NO MORE WAR - ANYWHERE!
A TRIBUTE TO M*A*S*H

I have found a very good stress reliever for my Lymphedema and the two leg ulcers: the anti-war series that should be on *every* school curriculum. Worldwide. M*A*S*H stands for:

Mobile Army Surgical Hospital.

Set during the Korean War of 1950-1953, "M*A*S*H Means Mobile" from its commander Colonel Sherman T Potter.

At the time of writing, it is on weeknights on UK tv, Channel 50 7-9 pm (four complete back-to-back episodes.) The series would suit 15+ year olds and has subtle messages in every single episode. All 256 episodes are very good, many were excellent and some even surpassed that.

There is the "wrong blood" episode where a white soldier protests that he has been given blood from a black donor. How they go about teaching him is simple but brilliant.

So many excellent episodes. This whole series has gone down in tv history and rightly so, but it should be shown worldwide and to every country that pushes for war in one way or another.

Every episode is so clever. There's no other word for it. The army gets lampooned in various ways but it is ironically a good ad for an army medical life.

The main star of M*A*S*H is Alan Alda's Captain Benjamin Franklin Pierce, alias Hawkeye. Hawkeye, like so many personnel in M*A*S*H 4077, has been conscripted into a war which he and they resent. This is reflected in the cynicism and disillusion he and his colleagues feel – and which the script-writers bring out so brilliantly.

Many actors had early appearances: Laurence Fishburne, Ron Howard, Patrick Swayze, John Ritter, Blythe Danner, Ned Beattie, James Cromwell, Stuart Margolin, Susan St James and many others.

The scripts vastly excel themselves! The episode where Major Charles Emerson Winchester III, is proven (only to Orderly Max Klinger) not to be the mean type that everyone thinks he is, in the Christmas episode where he goes alone to the local orphanage to give presents. The later interaction between Klinger and Charles is so moving and gets me every time - and I've seen this "several" times! The episode where Charles has toothache! They always have at least 2 storylines, if not 3, but this one is particularly clever and unexpected.

They even cover circumcision when a Korean woman who married a GI wants their son "done." And it is performed via satellite, from a US navy air craft carrier with a "portable" Rabbi! The actual circumcision is "performed" by Hawkeye who murmurs convincingly like a rabbi whilst Trapper (earlier episode) drops wine onto the baby's lips, part of the ceremony. Hawkeye's eyes are moist at this juncture - I first thought this because in real life his wife is Jewish but he has three daughters and no sons, so I *felt* he was experiencing the closest next best thing!

In addition, for anyone familiar with the series, they'll remember Major Stanley "Stosh" Robbins acting with Hawkeye. Stuart Margolin played plastic surgeon Stosh, from Hawkeye's medical student days. Also a soldier who has a hang up about his nose, given how many tease him about it. I won't spoil the rest, but a cute dog plays a part!

This series NEVER dulls and even when you KNOW what's going to happen, it's funny, sad, poignant, and above all TEACHES, but subtly. It's as fresh as when it was made. It doesn't get better than that.

To quote Hawkeye, "WAR IS UGLY." He's so sick of death. He never wants DEATH to win.

THAT's the message that comes across loud and clear and should be in all schools till the end of time, and then some!

Chapter 28

BACK TO GOOD OLD BLIGHTY

These days, I go up stairs slowly as I now also have my walking stick ever since our GP sent me to see a "phySIATrist" (no, I didn't know such a person existed either - but they do!) And Dr Raphael Chow was very good and said I needed a walking stick to help with my left arthritic ankle - and it has made a huge difference I was simply limping before, not very clever. This was still in Toronto.

People help everywhere, till, in London around September 12th, 2019, we're at Chalk Farm tube. The train comes in and Michael is struggling to step up to the train because it is quite a bit higher than the platform. I'm behind him, also ready to "struggle!" This time it was also five men - *FIVE MEN* - and they *watch* Michael struggle until eventually one says, "do you need any help?" to which Michael says, "yes, please" and thanks him afterwards.

I manage to get in, with difficulty. That said, after discussing it with my Mr Mouse, I've realised there is a difference between the north and south divide. I'm referring to England here, of course. People in the north, for the most part, are much warmer.

This would never happen in Macclesfield, Cheshire, where there is much warmth.

Why Macclesfield? Because that is where we now live and we love being part of it. Yes, we have left Toronto!

What can I say? Toronto is a wonderful city. Mixed with every colour and creed and all the better for it. Yes, Toronto is a very lovely city and, at the time we emigrated, less expensive than England. Or so we thought.

Condos, or apartments, were very decently priced by comparison with England.

We'd chosen Toronto because it did get much sun - contrary to popular opinion - and had TIFF, the Toronto International Film Festival. Something my son, Stuart, was very interested in, being a freelance photographer and a very good one. His photo of Michael in a sand-coloured jacket in this book attests to that.

Torontonians are lovely and also very willing to help where they can. What I realised was that if I wanted to leave my children anything, the only way we could do that was to return home after selling our property and buy a smaller place. Which would have been nigh on impossible for us in Toronto because, Michael, as a freelance journalist originally specialising in mining, wasn't going to earn thousands.

Toronto also doesn't have small houses with the kind of price tags that can be had in England. So, all in all, the right thing to do.

I should add that condos are owned while apartments are rented. Condos attract fees: our monthly fee was $780. Not an amount to be sneezed at. A chunk going on that every month adds up. Money that could be uilised elsewhere.

Maintenance fees in England are much better, especially up north.

Living in Toronto was exciting and "different" to use a favourite word of mine and one that Stuart used to tease me with. It was different from everything being in Canadian dollars to the Moose being a natural part of the love of Canada, and "Poutine" – a national dish! Also, Moose - one of my favourite animals! Down to the accent. While I still can't differentiate between American and Canadian (sorry!) I can easily differentiate between Aussie and Kiwi…it's all down to one's ear I suppose.

The Poutine - a wondrous Canadian invention of chips, cheese curds and gravy! It's OK if you don't mind mixing milk and meat! And the delis in Toronto and Montreal - yum! The food IS good.

The Gay Village, too, is lovely and so are Kensington Market and St Lawrence Market. Both real landmarks. Yes, a lovely city if you can afford it.

My son, Stuart, said: "If you really wanted to stay you'd have found a way." Nothing was that simple and I miss my family like crazy. I'm also missing my granddaughter growing up.

I miss my own children like no one knows.

Emigrating is exciting but boy have I paid for that!

Would I do that again? NO. It wasn't worth the separation. Ever!

Chapter 29

LYMPHEDEMA - THE HURT
TAKES OVER THE HEAT

Lymphedema has 450 000 sufferers in the UK and over 15 million globally, according to what I've just googled. A lot whichever way one looks at it.

I've had it since its development in 2017 when I was diagnosed with breast cancer. Actually, to be accurate, it developed directly *from* the chemo, which started shortly after the diagnosis which in its turn came on February 16th 2017, our 20th wedding anniversary as already stated. That said, my baby brother Neil stated I'd had this Lymphedema prior to 2017, and if he's right, but if it wasn't Lymphedema, what was its precursor...?

"No known cure" is what I see on my little cellphone every time I google in the hope of seeing a different result when I'm sitting up in bed, late at night, having redone my bandages – again, and the resultant changing has flared up the pain, grrr! Not forgetting the pain killers. The "several knives in my shin" feeling puts the pain level on 15 on a scale of 0-10!

I'm bandaged up, both legs, looking very like the Michelin Man - still! I'm so sick of this "look."

Leg ulcers, or whatever the hell they are, are a mess, even though the nurses claim they look alright. Not to my untrained eye! And they hurt! Both when the bandages come off and the cleaning gets underway. Then fresh special covers which have tape that doesn't irritate the skin, and then a special bandage stocking over the top. My legs are already both swollen from lymphatic fluid which is a mixture of blood, water, plasma(?) and anything else that is part of this. Hence Michelin Man impersonation.

I don't mind looking like this SHORT term but for ever...??!!!

The Lymphedema was not nearly so bad when we had Holly the Jack Russell. Then I was taking her for walks three times a day. Michael doesn't have quite the same speed! Actually then, it was a dog taking a Mouse for a walk, and the dog leading! Not a good combo, hence I took over, for safety's sake.

When does it ever improve!?

I was advised to use a cane from March 5th 2019 and have used it ever since. It makes me feel, as I call both Michael Mouse and myself, Mr and Mrs Decrepit but it does help people realise we might need the odd door opening for us and everything is appreciated. I now walk similarly to my late Mother-in-law, Doris and so does Michael! Not dissimilar to how the Penguin walks in the Batman franchise!

What I'd really like to see is some Lymphedema specialist looking for guinea pigs to try out a new valve in both legs so I could one day stop this whole, ongoing cycle that has no end in sight. And we both move SO slowly (or crikhing and crutzing!)

I want to have leg liposuction purely for Lymphatic reasons. I don't care how it makes my legs look afterwards.

I'm not vain, and they look like lumpy sausages at present. They couldn't look worse even if surgeons did stitches all over resulting in train tracks all over. Would I care? Not a jot!

The only trouble is - apparently I'm not a good candidate because I have that dreaded word - Fibromyalgia. Many doctors used to claim it was "all in the mind." There's a word for that - arseholes! When a doctor finds him/herself with this "malady" I will have zero compassion!

The word *my* old doctor used *on me*, back in Buxton, was Fibromyalgia. *He* thought *I* had it, and his brochure explaining the symptoms proved it. I was put on a low dosage of Amitriptyline and stayed on it for several years. *He* thought *I* had it, and was proved correct.

I just want this liposuction, under a local anaesthetic... and then walk and walk and walk, without the use of a cane and get my life back.

Is anyone doing any research out there?

I take it back. It's not just the ankles. My legs between calf and toes are tight. Very tight, feels like how they used to bind Chinese women in the Imperial Chinese Dynasties circa 1911. I remembered about the binding of the feet from my old copy of Daily Life In People's China, a hardback brilliant book. One of my favourites. My legs and feet feel like they have five pairs of socks on, feeling far too tight but - from within, so there's no let -up.

Both legs have lymphatic ulcers in what amounts to a mess. Unsightly I can cope with when I change the dressings, or when the local nurses change the dressing, but it's the length of time that is stretching out into the future with no change in sight and that is very depressing.

I have to try and lessen this Lymphedema and the tightening of the immediate ankle area on both feet that gets tighter as soon as I go to bed, for which this lymphedema is the culprit (?)

Compounding it is that I hate to overheat, and that's exactly what all this bandaging does. I prefer heat over hurt but I'd really just like to get rid of these leg ulcers for good, or whatever they are!

Where does this Lymphedema story end? Is there no specialist who is looking into fixing the valves in one's legs? There are surely enough of us to warrant a huge study on it. A new approach, anything?! Maybe a pacemaker for the valve if that is remotely possible? Hell, I don't even know what to ask for, I'm just desperate!

There's *got* to be another way and I'm willing to be a guinea pig in the Lymphedema fight. Russell did it for Leukemia. I can do it for this...hopefully.

Chapter 30

ON G-D, DIVORCE, NUTRITION, SUICIDE AND HEALTH…

Since I've been home from the hospital (July 4, 2017) I have regularly lost my balance standing in the bath having a shower. I suppose it's all part of losing one's "balancing bits!"

We've just watched a wonderful programme called Genius Of Britain and the host was none other than Richard Dawkins. I have his book The Blind Watchmaker which I started to read: it was fascinating. He started out about bats and how they find their way around. Then life got in the way again, but it did, however, reinvigorate my belief in G-d oddly enough. On this earth we have animals, humans, birds, plants, trees, bugs, flies, flowers and insects, and all have different DNAs that have different molecular structures that surely no alien would have gone to the trouble of "creating" and which no human can. OK, we can take Dolly the sheep and clone her but the scientists have had to use cells from the original sheep to do it. When scientists have tried to make human skin they've still needed some skin, or cells - or whatever they *did* use - to make it. So it "started" (as in a wedding) with "something borrowed!" Which proves my point: there has to be G-d, because everything on this planet had to have been created. That's why the Big Bang Theory in my mind doesn't work. Just puff, and it's all suddenly here!? From how, from where, a black hole/whatever?! Doesn't make any sense.

I thought about this again yesterday when we had one of our hottest Toronto summer days on record even though we are now September 4th. It was something like 31 degrees Centigrade – about 90 degrees Fahrenheit. I can honestly say I do not like extreme heat. I wilt like a flower. I was only in it for five minutes yesterday and that was enough.

The sun is *93 MILLION miles away* and I *cannot* get my head around that. This planet thrives because of air and sun and a sun that is *so* very far away but puts out heat that warms us, and helps grow plants and us. With nothing in between it to stop that flow.

There is only one creator and he's been proving it ever since the dawn of time.

There HAS to be a heaven - otherwise where do we all go? And what is the point of being here if THIS is all that it is? No, we HAVE to meet up with everyone again. It's the only thing that makes any sense, apart from making many people happy and that includes me.

My rationale for this is that G-d DID create us, and I'll tell you why. NO lab can reproduce anything of a human without first having a tissue sample of whichever sort, to work with. We humans cannot be replicated in a lab from scratch. If a chef makes a cake, he HAS to start with flour, eggs and sugar etc. He cannot make it out of a chemical lab – it just won't work. When Dolly the sheep was made, all they made was a clone. They started with something that came from G-d – an actual living thing, that *cannot* be replicated in a test-tube.

GRANDPARENTS DON'T DO
THEMSELVES ANY FAVOURS...

I've read all too often about wives, or I should say ex-wives, who bad-mouth the father to their children and NO ONE benefits. And in this regard my Mother was no exception. Ok, the Grandparent. (Nor was my stepfather.) True, she had her axes to grind, and unfortunately some were valid BUT the children don't want their grandparents bad-mouthing their father/mother and when grandparents do this who do you think ends up looking bad? I'll tell you, it's not the parent. The grandparent might not be the erring one but all the children know is that the parent has been bad-mouthed. *It likely will be proven in time.* Children have a knack of working things out and realising these things themselves. Pointing this out does you no favours and it is *never* appreciated. You will NOT be thanked for it, and you could well be shouted at for it, probably more than once. And, if they don't work it out, leave it be; it wasn't meant to be, and all that.

Just be the parent who doesn't stop your children from seeing the other parent and the more accommodating you can be the more appreciative it will be for both children and the other parent and you will reap rewards if only to show that you helped create harmony. Not a bad thing to be known for. And the children WILL remember later in life and this shouldn't have a backlash. The children have to learn that just because you and he split doesn't mean he loves the children any less. That Daddy doesn't want to be with Mummy is a bitter pill to swallow, but there are SO many learning curves for all those involved. And one thing I learnt - and this applies to losing a loved one as I did twice through the death of my brothers - is that it DOES get easier, but one HAS to go through that pain and you cannot circumvent it. Fact.

BEREAVEMENT

The pain of losing two brothers, seven years apart, I wouldn't wish on my worst enemy. The pain was so raw you think you'll never get over it. Well, you don't, you learn to live with it and it does get easier over time. As time goes on, usually very slowly initially, you come to cry less and remember happier times more and you do start doing other things. You don't usually fall in a heap. Well, some do. When Mother lost my father she told me she stayed in bed for six weeks with the shock of losing him.

She had three children. She couldn't just wallow in bed but she obviously got them to school and picked them up and just sat on her own during the day or lay in bed is what she told me.

When Cedric died in 1982, the same year my son Stuart was born, she told me later that all their female friends dropped by regularly and had just clubbed together to make this seem "random." A "random" drop-in so it was seen as casual. Such a sweet thing to do, and repeated when Russell died seven years later. I'm crying again for two lost darling sweet bothers whom I adored and still do, of course. My vision is blurred through tears. It's now (2024) 35 years since Russell died and 42 years since Cedric died. Stuart was in his highchair when I got the news. We only have the one highchair picture and that is where he was when I got that news.

NUTRITION AND LONGEVITY

Not very often do articles about the Hunzas or people in certain parts of Japan or Georgians come up but when they do it's to point out that they not only live very long and healthy lives but that they do NOT participate in western-style food consumption and there is our biggest, most obvious clue. They also don't even have "cancer" in their vocabulary. Why? Because they don't eat/consume the absolute and utter CRAP that many of us in the West DO and, let's not fool ourselves, it IS crap, which comes in the form of the following among others: cured sausages and meats with nitrates. (Michael: which one, please, nitrites or nitrates? Michael Mouse's reply: I do not know, I'm a writer not a food technician.)

I've discovered it is nitrates. Having that said, he IS a Font of knowledge: history, politics - of so many different countries - and a linguist, teaching Modern Greek at university level, speaks fluent French, business German and wooed Mrs Mouse in Russian! (And I'm his Mouse PR agent!)

Back to food.

Basically, cattle, beef with growth hormones added and antibiotics ALL end up being ingested by us when we buy most foods that come from a farm/factory and are sold in a supermarket. Kevin Trudeau said it best in his book Natural Cures They Don't Want You To Know About when he said to only buy organic. Admittedly easier said than done for many budgets, and by the way last year (2016) I asked at St Lawrence Market, Toronto, at one of the organic meat counters how organic they were. Their beef was allowed to feed on grass exclusively - for the final six or eight weeks leading up to slaughter! I thought "big deal" - no one would normally even think of asking such a question, and will assume it's throughout the animal's complete life…a smidgeon in the animal's life.

Most people when they get sick do not equate cancer with the foods they get. Oh, they know that what they eat is not very good and they turn, in some cases, to a healthier regime but how many really make that change BIG time? I must admit, we eat well, but we also eat "rubbish" too. We're no saints.

In St Lawrence Market was also Harry's Fresh Fish and he and his mother and family were wonderful. They sold all three types. First is ordinary farmed fish. Next is wild fresh fish which is the best - and naturally more expensive. Then there's a middle one which is from the Great Lakes, neither farmed nor wild but somewhere in between. I've bought this in-between one. It's as close to wild as we can sometimes afford and psychologically I feel I'm doing us good. I'm trying my best to keep my Mouse and me healthier so we can get to our dotage in our early nineties. The Hunzas and other long-lived groups don't even HAVE our illnesses. They lead such a different life that they would laugh at us taking all our meds when they barely get a sniffle. The only way one could do that is possibly by moving away, to what some people have done in Ben Fogle's series "Life In The Wild," definitely off grid in many cases and with much healthier foods. A fascinating series my Mouse and I love.

I suppose if these Hunzaz and other such groups ate fresh, wild, organic and not processed food, but also not being subjected to cigarette smoke, and coughs and sneezes that wouldn't even exist around them, they would actually be at extreme risk if they left their native areas, having not built up any immunity.

Case in point is what came up in the news only recently. A tribe in Mozambique that are losing their habitat to loggers. They would have no built-up immunity and thus could easily succumb to even a flu. That said, they have much healthier lives, real fresh air, no pollution and enough sleep. We'd pay for this at some top holiday resort!

NUTRITION AND RELIGION

Through all my books on nutrition runs one common thread that becomes apparent to most – cut out what we shouldn't ingest in the first place. The chemicals (in Kevin Trudeau's book in particular but others too) that have no right to be put in our foods in the first place and are paid for heavily by companies to make foods taste so good we want to keep buying it. The fact is that these cancers and other debilitating diseases are mainly(?) brought on by crap in our system that our bodies weren't designed for!

Sixty years ago we didn't have E numbers; so many additives, colouring which causes hyperactivity in children and I know that from my best friend's child in Sydney, Oz. Jan, who has a son, Michael, now an adult. Jan would come around for coffee with him and my two, Stuart and Lisa, would be there too. Little Michael would tear around the lounge and be very hard to control. Luckily it was not for the whole of their visit. When Jan looked into their food habits and realised they were drinking coloured lolly water with

E numbers that cause hyperactivity she had her solution. Although G-d knows why the manufacturers feel they need to put this chemical garbage into us in the first place.

It doesn't matter what we buy or ingest that totally pollutes our bodies and makes us sick with all sorts of AVOIDABLE diseases; *as long as we buy them companies will keep making them.* They are *not* going to say, "do you realise our products are slowly, very slowly, killing you AND making you unhealthy in the process?"

For the most part IF it tastes good people want it. IF it has nitrates in it, so what? The mental aspect is, "I haven't (yet) been diagnosed with anything too awful and until I get that way I'm going to enjoy ALL foods even if many of them shouldn't even be under the "food" banner! Unfortunately, these ailments take years to manifest and by then much damage has been done.

Earlier today I remembered again about a woman who had been in the Mini Car Club of NSW that I joined with my ex back in 1975. I will call her Charlene. She was much slimmer than I was back then, but she wanted to be even slimmer so she joined Weight Watchers and the next time we had a meeting that happened to be at their place I saw the foods she was buying on a regular basis. Personally, I was horrified. Here was margarine, and she was having sweeteners in her tea and coffee, and a certain brand of everything (bread too) with different additives making everything taste supposedly wonderful but still made in a lab. Result: Years later after I'd returned to the UK I had a phone call to tell me she'd needed a triple by- pass...! Yeh, that food was sooo good for her...! No, she was not a smoker; most of the Mini car Club weren't at that time.

My rationale for this is that G-d DID create us, and I'll tell you why. NO lab can reproduce anything of a human without FIRST having a tissue sample of whichever sort to work with. We humans cannot be replicated in a lab from scratch. If a chef makes a cake he HAS to start with flour, eggs and sugar etc. He cannot make it out of a chemical lab – it just won't work. When Dolly the sheep was made, all they made was a clone. They started with something that came from G-d – an actual living thing, that *cannot* be replicated in a test-tube.

PERMANENT SOLUTION TO A TEMPORARY PROBLEM

I want to devote a few paragraphs to suicide. I have known three people who have committed suicide. Number one came in the form of a boy I was very keen on but he never noticed me so it went as unrequited love on my part. I don't think he ever really realised I even existed. I accepted that a long time ago.

The next one came with a name. Alan. He'd actually given me a New Year's kiss on the lips which I didn't see coming and didn't appreciate at all. I don't like sudden kisses full on the mouth unless I'm vaguely attracted to them, and even then I'd like some say in it!

The latest one to commit suicide is a more recent person. We met him here in Toronto. I wish people who contemplate suicide would realise the impact on their immediate family and possibly friends too. That said, I can also see why some would see only hopelessness all around and indeed that is why they commit suicide. I realise my next point may very well not be original in its thinking and I don't know where I first heard it but, "suicide is a permanent solution to a temporary problem."

My theory here, for what it's worth…

I've also read of many suicides in the newspapers online and many people related to the deceased always say something in the realms of, "I saw him/her the day before, or the night before or even just a week before (whatever the short time-frame is), and they seemed very happy and relaxed or happy within themselves," and I DO think this is actually a key that all is NOT well within them. I think it is BECAUSE they have DECIDED to "leave" that they are more relaxed, as they have MADE UP their minds and it's a great weight off their minds. This would make it much harder to detect, but one way might be to ask why they are so seemingly happy and to be perturbed if they give no real reason. It's the "happy" state that they're in because they've finally decided to do "it." Their thoughts could be overwhelming.

However bad something is, one can get through it - in time. Time IS a great healer. That's why it's a cliché. I briefly did contemplate too, just to be with Cedric again, but common sense said to me, "it's very much a one-way journey." There IS no going back but one does know one WILL meet again. We HAVE to! Where else could we be going? It HAS to be the same place. G-d can't have planned a different place for every human being, otherwise there'd be lots of "places" all over the universe. Somehow, I don't think it works that way. If we're basically good we must surely end up in the same place. What it must be for suicide bombers is something else.

Whatever it is, I think it must be a lovely place full of wonderful tearful reunions. But still a one-way ticket leaving others with a permanent gap that can never be filled. The indescribable pain of losing a child or parent to suicide is beyond contemplation. Those left to pick up the pieces never really get over it. You never get "over it." You "learn to live with it" and you do learn to smile again, but there's an ache that rears its head every so often. I suppose that's what makes us (mostly) good humans. There's always a better way through the pain other than suicide that leaves so many wondering what they did wrong OR what they didn't do. Which is not necessarily the case at all, either.

And the void is never filled.

In our religion we name a child after those who have passed. Not necessarily the first name. Often just the middle name as a memorial. It's amazing which older names are popping up now. It took me a long time to appreciate my name – like only in the last decade. Don't ask me why. I think because the children used to use it when they were annoyed with me. Luckily not lately.

MICROWAVES, MILK AND - MARRIAGE!

Russell cooked everything in his microwave and I had an abiding distrust of those machines from years ago now, when I read a very good and damning article online, "The Hazards of Microwave Cooking." It said it all. It distorts the blood chemistry, apparently, and changes the molecular structure of the foods and how it interacts in the body. There was nothing good to read in that article and from then on our microwave was defunct. Null and void or, as Monty Python says, "it is NO more, it is a dead parrot, it has gone to meet its maker." It said it all. And when we redid the kitchen it went out and wasn't replaced. Same for this new apartment that did have a newish microwave. It went to Habitat for Humanity here in Toronto.

People use microwaves at the drop of a hat and I think it's doing lasting damage but the facts about that will not see the light of day for about another 40 years if companies have their way. And most people just want an easy life and don't think about aspects that harm their very being until diagnosed with a "big C" and THEN they go mainstream and compound it with toxic chemo whereas if they went back to real food, ditched the microwave and had unadulterated and food free from growth hormones - grass-fed instead of grain-fed - milk (if you must) that is raw and thus INCLUDES enzymes that pasteurisation has usually killed off...I could go on. "Dairy causes mucus." Fact.

Now I've done an about-face and finally got a new microwave after baby brother Neil pointing out that Mother and Theo used one every day and lived into their nineties so I suppose it can't be sooooo bad. But I think there's an element or two that is correct about it, but I have gone back to using it... So I'm a hypocrite.

Previously mentioned how I told my stepfather (wonderful Theo) how dairy causes mucus 25 odd years ago, and his reply? "Don't be so bloody daft" in his northern Manchester accent. Eight or so years ago I heard him say to someone in their kitchen, "Dairy causes mucus!" Holy shit. No I didn't say anything but I was dying to. I would have been accused of "stirring." It would have blown up out of all proportion.

I got the pleasure of knowing he'd FINALLY learnt, and told myself something would resonate that I had said it initially. I can dream. Dairy also plays havoc with younger people's skin so if they're having breakouts or just a horrible mottled skin with redness and well, you know what you have. Give dairy a complete break and get the calcium from green vegetables which are a better source anyway that the body can utilise better than the industry claims because they're not about to say otherwise.

HEALTH

Yesterday, I read a wonderful article in Toronto Life about vaccines and the brigade of mothers baulking the norm. I salute them and just hope that when I know I'm going to become a grandmother that this article will resonate with both (adult) children. When my nephew Felix was very new I spoke to Neil imploring him not to have the MMR jab given whilst such a little body. As they all are. He talked it over with his Dad, Theo, and I think some other medical professionals but I did feel that talking to them was rather a case of talking to those who are already for the vaccines. So when he said he felt it was alright and they were going to allow him to be inoculated I felt apprehension. Luckily, for whatever genetic makeup he has – touch wood, he's not fared any the worse. That said, they don't know long-term effects but people will only start changing things when things go awry on a grander scale. OR when a medical person's own child has a reaction OR both.

I have Fibromyalgia. I was luckier than most in that I was diagnosed by my own GP, Dr King, back in Buxton UK. I think he was wonderful. I went to him with late-night leg pains and he prodded me in the different various pressure points which at the time I didn't realise were the key. Plus a couple of questions, followed by something on the lines of, "I think you might have Fibromyalgia." When I later heard about it from other sources I found out that many people get "dissed" by their GPs for imagination or anything else, but not taken seriously.

I was very lucky to have a GP *telling* me. And it seems he was right. He put me on Amitriptyline and it helped. Actually, a lot. It was, he told me, an anti-depressant but the powers that be had discovered that it worked with fibromyalgia sufferers and that I indeed was not depressed or in need of anything like that, for that. I started taking one every evening at 9 pm and by the time I was ready for bed at around near 11 it worked wonderfully.

I was on it for about seven years with no problems until I got cellulitis of the left leg. We'd moved by this time to Toronto. Apparently, many people get a tiny cut on their legs and it lets in a microscopic bug that was lying dormant on our skin. I suddenly had a bad infection which actually started at 2pm one afternoon. I can remember it clear as a bell. I took myself off to bed shivering and stayed there for the next three days. In the process I completely forgot to take my medication and after three days I suddenly remembered it. I realised I had inadvertently gone "cold turkey" in coming off it suddenly but here was my golden opportunity to stay off it. And I have. I don't know whether it's eating an "even" healthier diet than before or what, but

I do know I've become even more health conscious since we left Buxton, UK.

I have stayed off Amitriptyline and both Mr Mouse and I are eating healthier than ever before. He still has arthritis - I think that takes a long time to get rid of, probably time we don't realistically have. He has also had two hip replacements and has ankylosing spondylitis preventing his head being totally upright and also preventing him being able to turn his head fully so he doesn't drive anywhere anymore. That said, that does mean when we go to the UK I am the designated driver which is brilliant because that does at least mean we get to our destination the same day...!

This is a great pity as by all intent and purposes he could pass for 75 when he is in actual fact 70, but I love my Mr Mouse very much regardless and there is still an excellent brain in there, and a lot of love flowing towards me, (and back to him too!) I'm lucky on many levels.

I am deeply against sticking needles into children (ESPECIALLY babies and toddlers.) Yes, my own children got the required jabs when they were little and I didn't give it a second thought and TG they are healthy and normal as can be. Though I DO believe some things show up immediately and some later, and very late *depending on what triggers them.*

I've said this before, but when one gets food, and I use that word very loosely, nowadays the companies that make certain foods are basically putting a chemical factory together. Kevin Trudeau's book from a few years ago said if you can't pronounce the words in the ingredients list you shouldn't be ingesting it. So true. Chemicals, E numbers, colouring, et al combine to wreak havoc on ALL our bodies.

I believe that is part of the reason for cancers occurring. SO many people do not have much of what has been supplied for on this planet, ie, not enough "real" food.

Disease = DIS-EASE No, I'm not the first to coin that one.

We do eat a lot of vegetables. That said, too, we don't eat nearly as many vegetables in their raw state as we should. It's VERY hard for me not to get on my bandwagon when I walk into any coffee shop and see so many "rubbish" carbs.

Many commercial places used to wash their lettuces and leave them soaking for however long. That just loses valuable nutrients. One thing I learnt from Delia Smith, that wonderful British cook with her own show in the past, was that she did not wash her lettuces and I stopped washing mine from that day onwards. Except for the odd outer leaves that have the odd grub. And I'm staying that way. She was so right in that. And I haven't caught anything from that method either!

We, Mr Mouse and I, eat much healthier than we ever had. That said, we still eat what I term as rubbish, but not nearly as often as many Americans who are sporting wide girths. That said, too, if anyone saw me they'd say, "you can't talk" and they'd be right. With my lymphedema legs, I look like the Michelin Man!

We had a tenant, Kassie. A lovely Korean woman who has a boyfriend. And it's his mother whom Kassie spoke to me about the other week. She said to me, "you have Fibromyalgia, don't you?" I said yes. Apparently, the boyfriend's mother also has Fibromyalgia but is in a much worse state than me, and is on very strong pain medication – daily – that she is hooked on from the sounds of it. So I must be doing something right and I would say she must be doing something very wrong, and one of those things could well be the so-called "ordinary" food that Michael and I term as rubbish. He is just as familiar now with all the rubbish stuff that masquerades as food (E numbers, colouring, added growth hormones etc.) One reads the ingredients and after the first three (usually the ubiquitous wheat – and that's another food that causes immense problems!) the rest are things that have no place outside a lab.

I'm a very good ad for someone with Fibromyalgia. Yes, my nerve endings are all sensitive so if I catch my foot on a corner of a chair, or something similar, it canes! That said, if people come over to visit and have a coffee, for example, they'd usually have no idea…so I must be doing right to some extent.

My Michael Mouse is a similar kettle of fish, which reminds me that we eat much more fresh fish now, and either wild or raised in an almost organic environment. We very rarely eat beef, partly because I hate the idea of mad cow disease and partly because unless it's a steak I just *cannot* cook it. Lamb however is different…

To balance things out we have just naturally progressed to a lot more fish. My baby brother Neil discovered fish long before I did. Don't misunderstand me. I've always adored plaice but he eats fish often and pointed out just how many different kinds there were over meat, and so much healthier…

I have amassed about 53 wonderful books, each leading me to the next. This is not in any preferred order: The China Study, WHITEWASH, and Wheat Belly – which had six luscious bagels on the front cover beckoning Michael in before he found that these and many others were exactly what was causing so many problems!

IF they did teach it they would STILL be promoting the dogma teachings of 40 years ago because I still read about nutritionists spouting forth about "whole grains" and "everything in moderation" and they themselves will still promote meat and dairy. Yes, we still eat both, BUT from what I have read we have learnt to eat much less cheese, to try and buy organic meat when we can afford it, to eat much more fruit, salad and most of all vegetables and preferably many of these in *their raw state* so their ENZYMES are not lost. When did you last read an article about someone in hospital being advised on such a route? They WEREN'T because it's in no one's interest, except an up-to-date naturopath/and or nutritionist to GO down a food route.

People in India and China and other countries away from western countries do not eat the huge amounts of protein that we do here. People here get diagnosed with cancers all the time, and they continue to eat in the normal western way, mostly, but they accept the doctor's only solution as "he knows best, so I trust him." So they don't look into it from a nutritional point of view; they continue their burgers, BBQs, cured meats with nitrates, whatever, and cooked vegetables if we're lucky, and salads that are often over-rinsed losing much of the enzymes that are SO precious to life and that most people have no inkling that they're not even getting. It's really sad because unless you look and see the whole picture, one doesn't see that one is blindly going about their day, eating acidic foods all the way and when does cancer occur…when the body is too acidic.

Actually, now many people are looking at their food regime and changing it. And when is the body too acidic? When we're eating a mostly western diet. Don't get me wrong, I love a bbq; I just don't eat it nightly and don't eat it the way Americans and Canadian and Australians do.

We, Michael and I, do still eat the wrong things. It's just not daily, although it is still too often. The message is very plain to see if you read enough.

And I must admit, I like these "rubbish" foods too, unfortunately.

It made me realise that there HAS to be a G-d because HE has provided for anyone to have a healthy body. He didn't know companies were going to set up and make crap packaged foods with everything in it designed in a food "lab"; now there's a word that shouldn't even BE associated with food…

Today happens to be Wednesday August 13th 2014 here in Toronto and I have just been "talking" about that so-called old wonderful food pyramid. Only it's not so wonderful any more by any stretch of the imagination and I've just been vindicated by a Dr David Brownstein's newsletter that I get in the mail from the States. He's a physician AND a holistic medical doctor. Not bad getting the two combined in one person.

Well, I'm here spouting forth about the crap food triangle that was developed and totally "bought into" mentally about 50 odd years ago. Actually, it was indeed in 1974 – Michael Mouse.

Today I get the post and it's Dr Brownstein's newsletter and how is it headed up? It was music to my eyes, if that makes any sense. The title said it all: The Famous Flawed

Food Pyramid. If you want to read more and be highly enlightened, google him and while you're at it another doctor that I have several of his books and that makes an awful lot of sense is a Dr Cass Ingram. He was at the Toronto Green Show at the Exhibition Centre. I bought five of his books. They'll knock your socks off as they're doing to me.

This IS the way you learn not to rely on mainstream medical know how. Yes, antibiotics have their place and I was on them recently, but I also have learnt in the last decade or more just how much "let medicine be thy food and let food be thy medicine," resonates. There is a lot of information out there both on the internet and in good books that should be read.

Whitewash was written by John Robbins. When I ask people if they've ever heard of John Robbins they naturally say no. Then I say but you've heard of Baskin Robbins and if they're American or Canadian they naturally say yes. Sometimes Brits say so too; it depends if they've visited across the pond.

John Robbins rejected his father's business – a multi-million-dollar empire after he realised he *didn't* want to promote dairy. Don't get me wrong, we still love dairy but we have it in little spurts and Michael still tells people his ultimate death wish…he wants to have to eat his way out of a huge pile of stinky blue cheese, then have his body enveloped with dark molten chocolate and then he "expires" having devoured his favourite foods. All nonsense of course but we all have our little fantasies. That's just Michael Mouse's most bizarre one!

Chapter 31

MOUSE PHRASES

Distinctly out of place: **mouse-fit**
Alexander the Great's dad: **Philip of Mousadonia**
Great mouse in motor racing: **Sir Stirling Mouse**
Chickpea special: **Hu-mouse**
What do lonely mice get up to? **Mousturbation**
A real cute fast car: **Mouserati**
Epic of modern fiction: **Zorba the Squeak**
Imprisonment: **under mouse-arrest**
Papers, TV, radio: **the Mouse Media**
A great cheese: **mouscarpone**
I got it wrong: **mouse-understanding**
I got it wrong 2.0: **mouse-guided**
EU agreement: **the Mousetricht treaty**
Lack of compassion: **mouse-treatment**
Chinese dictator: **Mouse Tse-Tung**
Delicious fruit: **mousachino cherries**
Hairy mouse: **mousetache**
Fictional character: **Count of Mouse-te Cristo**
Domestic bliss: **a Mouse-boat on the Thames**
Very varied: **Mousecellaneous**
Clever person: **Mouster of Arts**
Posh part of North London: **Mousewell Hill**

Greatest composer of them all: **Wolfgang Amadeus Mouse-art**

Personal hygiene: **mouse-wash**

Dangerous German plane: **Mouse-rschmidt**

In outer space: **mouse-tronauts**

Cattle plague: **foot-and-mouse disease**

Italian actor: **Mouse-ello Mouse-troianni**

The Mouse of Lords: **All those in favour say "squeak"**

The Elite Guard: **The Mouse-Hold Cavalry**

For the property seeker: **Mouse Hunters International**

A lovely chewy meal: **Mouse-tication**

Chapter 32

EPILOGUE - OR - TYING UP LOOSE ENDS

My mother Ruth Ward (later Ruth Roland) was a painter all her life – and a very successful one. Daddy (Leslie Joseph Ward) was a scientist who worked behind the scenes in an effort to bring the war to a shuddering halt, hence not called up. A pacifist and a gentleman and gentle man. He would have got on very well with Michael, as would Russell and Cedric.

I became a Mother and have gone through a lot but want to share much of it and give people pleasure and laughs from reading it. And try to pass on to all that War is NOT glorious and that it only brings pain and suffering. The more people who learn that from a young age, maybe we can "phase out wars?!"

There have been so many lessons both in life (and on tv, the medical series M*A*S*H just for starters!) that should be on every school curriculum (!) and that I want to share.

And I want to leave a legacy for my children that *they* will be proud of something I wrote that hopefully touches many. I want my family to be proud of this book but also hope that it resonates with many people over different issues.

My Michael Mouse has many limitations and I've been his carer for a while now. That's a learning curve in itself!

I'm always thinking ahead whether out and about with him or at home in our Mousehole.

I also try and do a PR job on him whenever we meet new people. They likely see an old man (not forgetting the Korean woman in a newsagents in Toronto who thought he was 85!) whereas I like to promote his still sharp brain, and his linguistic abilities which I'm always in awe of.

Michael Mouse is still romantic and tells me he loves me (as I do him) and we both make Mouse faces, at home and at all sorts of odd times and places. Like at a restaurant table when no one is looking!

If Michael leaves me first…

Many months ago Michael told me that he wanted to leave his body to medicine science. Whether they'll actually find a use for it, or just use it as a door stop...who knows! Anyway, he'd said this over the last several months and I kept saying to him "if you don't do something about it, I will not be able to enforce it. You have to do this yourself and contact whomever."

So he did - to MRI in Manchester and…he got a reply, and apparently it's now official! So, whenever he departs, there won't be a burial as such. Just a service for being a good and loving MOUSE!

And very recently (this year 2024) I read (online Daily Mail) about a man who owned a builder's yard(!) and his son, who wanted to carry out his late father's wishes and did so all the way through. He made the coffin out of scaffolding planks and took his late father to his own funeral in the Works truck! The cost? GBP150 altogether and I want to ask him to do mine when the time comes! Hopefully he'll be around and maybe I won't be the only one! It's ridiculous paying thousands for what ends up being buried!

I suppose it also has to be "consecrated grounds," therefore maybe slightly more than the GBP150 that the article mentioned...Or just find a pretty field where I can become fertilizer, oy!

This way my family won't get clobbered by funeral home costs. The $ can go on the living. Far better spent on those who can still enjoy earthly pleasures! At present, my walk is like a cross between a penguin and Douglas Bader and Michael's is only marginally better!

As for my immediate family, I hope I see my adult children Stuart and Lisa again before too long. I miss my son and daughter very much. I ache to hug! I have one granddaughter, Aurora, also too long since seeing her and her Daddy, Jesse. An American born with a real American name!

And a good man. I miss them all so very much.

IF I include where I've lived from the get-go:

Letchworth (Herts), Sale (Cheshire), Sydney (Oz), Cheadle (Cheshire), Redhill (Surrey), St Albans (Hertfordshire), Buxton (Derbyshire), Toronto, and finally Macclesfield (back in Cheshire.) We've now moved, my Mouse and I, (and incorporating my own moves) a total of nine times! Maybe I've also put Letchworth on the map even more than the person who attempted to by putting *that* question to the Mastermind team!

We have a sweet ex council house that had almost no kerb appeal although the two trees in the front garden help, a large Hazel (!) tree and a smaller Honeysuckle and something else which I have no idea what! And masses of wild flowers commonly known as weeds! We now also have a very needed reconditioned Stannah in the hall, too.

But Mrs Mouse also got her little garden and although it's very hard to get around and about with lymphatic ankles and legs, it's great to get outside on our own little domain. If it's been really wet it makes weeding very easy!

No, Michael doesn't do anything in the garden. He wouldn't know where to start! He has arthritic hands and no logic, and absolutely NO idea what needs doing, ever! He will come out, if we get some sun this year, and sit and read. There are still a large number of books in our study.

And the garden has a birdbath that Lisa bought me years ago in Toronto when we didn't even have a garden! I love it though - made from resin and two carved squirrels chasing each other and it's now finally IN our garden after many years. And I think of Lisa when I look at it, and I love it, and her.

I've had cream and white gravel put down all over. My attempt to make a courtyard garden reminiscent of Greek or Italian gardens and I'm succeeding! A Bay tree in the middle and pots of I don't know what yet, to add colour, and some roses, and a small Eucalyptus tree starting! It's not all as lovely as I've described but it's a "work in progress" and evolving. It has the makings of a lovely garden.

We've now been married 27 years as of this past February 16th. And earlier this month was my seventh anniversary since my operation.

Several anniversaries for all Michael's ops!

I'm Michael's designated driver! I drive better than I walk (wouldn't be difficult!). I still adore driving. I take Michael Mouse to most of his medical appointments and sometimes have to fit mine in too!

He should be written up in a medical journal one day and could well be since he has now finally arranged to leave his body to science.

When I weep for him it will not be over a grave, assuming he goes first (!) but with friends and family, ALL of whom will have known him well, and with a repast that will have all his favourites - many cheeses and molten chocolate - separate of course!

I do hope you have got some pleasure, quite a few laughs and maybe a good amount of knowledge, too, from this book.

Indeed, I hope this book has given many people much to take them away from maybe the humdrum, made them laugh, made them slightly cry, imparted some knowledge but above all gave them a bloody good read!

This is Mrs Mouse signing off.

Mrs Hazel Mouse. cedrussstulis@gmail.com

www.ingramcontent.com/pod-product-compliance
Lightning Source LLC
Chambersburg PA
CBHW030818090426
42737CB00009B/774